Women's Ways of Knowing

TENTH ANNIVERSARY EDITION

WOMEN'S WAYS OF KNOWING

The Development of Self, Voice, and Mind

Mary Field Belenky

Blythe McVicker Clinchy

Nancy Rule Goldberger

Jill Mattuck Tarule

BASIC BOOKS

A Member of the Perseus Books Group

Excerpts from "Unlearning to Not Speak" copyright © 1969, 1971, 1973 by Marge Piercy. Reprinted from *Circles on the Water*, by Marge Piercy, by permission of Alfred A. Knopf, Inc.

First BasicBooks edition published 1986, reissued 1997.

Designed by Vincent Torre

Library of Congress Cataloging-in-Publication Data

Women's ways of knowing.
    Bibliographical references: p. 239
    Includes index.
    ISBN-13: 978-0-465-09099-0   ISBN-10: 0-465-09099-0
    1. Women—United States—Psychology. 2. Women—United States—Education.
    3. Self-actualization (Psychology). 4. Feminism—United States. 5. Knowledge, Theory of. I. Belenky, Mary Field.
    HQ1206.W88   1986
    305.4   85-73881

DHSB 07 08 09   30 29 28 27 26 25 24 23 22

To our mothers . . .

Julia, Daphne, Virginia, and Corinne

And our daughters . . .

Alice, Vanessa, Estelle, Uli, Elayne, Jessica, and Shara

And our granddaughters . . .

Sofia, Ella, and Sarah

Contents

Preface to the
Tenth Anniversary Edition:
Telling Tales

LOOKING BACK OVER the decade since the publication of *Women's Ways of Knowing* (WWK), it seems to us that the book's most important effect is the work that it has spawned. The essays contained in our new book, *Knowledge, Difference, and Power: Essays Inspired by "Women's Ways of Knowing"* (Goldberger, Tarule, Clinchy, & Belenky, 1996) give an account of that work. Here, we tell a more personal tale, beginning in the period before there was a *WWK*, even in imagination. This is the story—four stories—of how it was for us: how we came together and worked together in what began as a project and turned into a book, and how conversations among the four of us grew into increasingly public discourse with an expanding community of colleagues. Finally, we reflect upon how it is for us now, no longer part of a collective "we," but forever affected by that experience.

How It All Began

Jill tells it this way: The Women's Ways of Knowing Project was conceived in a Jacuzzi in French Lick, Indiana, where each evening, after a day spent evaluating projects supported by the Fund for the Improvement of Post-Secondary Education (FIPSE), an informal meeting would materialize in which she and Nancy, along with others, began to talk about the experiences of women in higher education. The project was born, Jill says, in a Jacuzzi in White River Junction, Vermont, where the four of us had gathered to discuss the possibility of making a proposal to FIPSE on this topic.

All four of us, individually, had been studying student development and all of us were perplexed by and concerned about certain complaints female students had about their educational experiences. Nancy and Blythe were both in the midst of longitudinal research tracing the development of students at their own institutions (Simon's Rock Early College and Wellesley College, respectively) and had become especially interested in William Perry's (1970) "scheme" of intellectual and ethical development. Mary and Jill had recently completed their dissertations at Harvard (where they had studied with Perry, among others). Jill was involved in setting up programs for adult students at Goddard College. Mary was continuing research on women's development with Carol Gilligan.

It was Nancy who organized us, partly because it was she who could claim to know everyone—Jill from the FIPSE meetings, Blythe from the fledgling meetings of what came to be called the Perry Network, Mary from the Harvard School of Education crowd working with Kohlberg or Gilligan. Blythe, on the other hand, hardly knew anyone, and she recalls feeling anxious as she chugged up Route 89 toward that first meeting at the motel in White River Junction. She was pretty sure she was the last to be asked to join the group, and wasn't sure why she had been chosen. Perhaps, she thought, it was that in order to get a government grant they needed the ballast of a colleague from a more traditional (stuffier?) institution than the ones the others represented. Maybe they didn't really want *her*—just her credentials.

Blythe reports that her qualms receded almost as soon as she arrived at the motel:

> Almost immediately, we were passionately engaged in what the women we were to interview would call "real talk." Clearly, all three of these women cared deeply and had thought hard about research, my kind of research. And clearly, too, we shared a sense of missionary zeal—an uncommon commodity in the academic milieus where I plied my trade.

Mary, too, approached the meeting with qualms. She recalls,

> I had been certain these three women would have little interest in the questions I wanted to pursue. They were immersed in studies looking at the impact of college experiences on women's development; I wanted to study poor mothers raising small children—one of the most marginal and demeaned groups in the society. I also wanted to look at several social agencies that seemed to be making a real

difference in the lives of poor mothers. These were organizations largely founded and run by women for women. I thought such a study would provide a rare opportunity to see how women shape organizations when they have a real say in the way things should be run.

How would these women deal with me and my interests? I knew from personal experience that eyes glaze over and conversations stop when you try to talk about mothers and mothering with most social scientists and educators. It reminded me of the way I had been treated when I was a "stay at home" mother with no other well defined social role that people could relate to.

Like Blythe, Mary soon learned that her fears were unfounded.

The eyes of these three women did not glaze over. Instead, they listened to me with great care. They asked good questions. I can't remember who said, "Okay. Fine. We will call these programs for mothers 'the invisible college.'" The words still ring in my ears. The moment those words were uttered I realized that I was being included, as were my questions and concerns.

Still, we faced a formidable task. Each of us wondered, How could we ever fashion a single project out of such diverse pursuits? It would be a jumble. No one would ever fund such a hodgepodge. Nancy recalls "lolling about someone's room—talking, talking— trying to figure out what exactly we wanted to do (or could do) together:"

What kind of umbrella rationale and structure could encompass all the questions we had? One breakthrough insight: Women don't just learn in classrooms; they learn in relationships, by juggling life demands, by dealing with crises in families and communities. We realized together, at a particular moment, that "education" need not be narrowly defined. I remember feeling as exhilarated by the collaborative discovery—the group "ah-ha"—as I was by naming what we wanted to do: Education for Women's Development.

Although all four of us had been deeply affected by the women's movement and, in our "private" lives, active in it, feminism had not yet profoundly shaped our work, except perhaps in Mary's case. Nancy had observed gender differences in her studies of adolescents' development and experience of college, but she had not yet made gender central in her research. Blythe studied women not because she had any particular interest in gender but because they were all that was easily available in the women's college where she taught. And gender played no part at all in Jill's dissertation. In those early conversations at French Lick, Jill and Nancy had begun to dream of creating a project that would link their public work on student development with their private work on women's issues. All of us now shared this dream, and the proposal that began to swim into view at White River Junction gave promise of fulfilling it.

How We Worked

When one of us referred to that very first meeting as "the best pajama party I've attended since the sixth grade," we made an unwritten agreement to work "in the women's way" all the while we were trying to name what that way might be. We resolved, for instance, that if FIPSE funded the project we would insist on having four coequal investigators instead of the traditional single "principal investigator." To our surprise, FIPSE agreed to this and other unorthodox features of our proposal.

Thanks to FIPSE's generous moral and financial support, the pajama-party model of research became a reality. We were able to get together for three- to four-day meetings at least once every two months, usually at one of our homes, to discuss the design of the project, the piloting of the interviews, and, ultimately, the interview data we collected. We sat around living rooms and kitchen tables as we worked. Dogs barked in the background; children wandered through. We took long walks, talking, always talking. Sometimes our husbands cooked for us.

At first, and for quite some time, we were nearly overwhelmed by the task of organizing the data. Our interviews were long and wide-ranging, exploring among other things the women's self-concepts, their educational experiences, their relationships, their approaches to moral issues, and their ideas about gender. How were we to sort out such a jumble? Our friend and colleague, the writer and educator Mildred Henry, came to the rescue. We all remember the moment: We have gathered together for several days to begin the work of analyzing the data. We are seated in a huge, barnlike room, its four long walls completely papered with seemingly hundreds of interview excerpts. The walls appear to be closing in upon us. Endeavoring to be utterly open to the women's words, to hear them without bias, we have tried to empty our minds of all preconceptions, but we are sinking under the weight of these words; we hear only a cacophony.

Milly Henry rises and strides to the front of the room. Metaphorically, at least, she shakes her finger at us. She challenges us to use our minds, instead of emptying them. You are smart women, she says; your heads are full of knowledge. Use it. She proceeds to lead us in a discussion that yields a list of categories which will serve as preliminary ordering devices. Mary remembers the room being diffused with light at this moment, although she knows that, in fact, it was nearly windowless. In time, these categories evolved and were reconstructed as the "Educational Dialectics" that appear in the back of the book. Privately, we called them "Millihenrys," and we spoke of "Millihenrying" the data, rather than "analyzing" it.

At some point in the course of this work we made the key decision to sort the interviews in terms of responses to questions in the section of the interview now labeled "Ways of Knowing" but referred to at the time as "the Perry part." We greeted the decision with relief, certain at once that it was right, but it took us a long time to reach it. At first, the questions themselves had seemed problematic to Mary who was about to launch into interviewing mothers of young children in one of the poorest rural counties in the country. She protested: "You can't knock on the door of a trailer in the woods and ask a woman with three little kids hanging on her to tell you about her theory of knowledge!" Not having to undertake such a task ourselves, we assured her that of course she could; she'd find a way. At our next meeting Mary appeared, radiant: "You can!," she said. "I did! And it's so important! So many of these women don't think they can think." Gradually, as we read and reread the interview transcripts, we came to feel, as we say in the first paragraph of this book, that the women's epistemological assumptions were central to their perceptions of themselves and their worlds. Epistemology became the organizing principle for our data analysis and for the book that we were beginning to imagine. To hasten the book's gestation, we rented a house at the shore for a month and settled down to frame a proposal aimed at achieving a book contract. Families came on weekends; dogs got to stay all the time.

By then it was clear that many of the answers the women gave to the "Perry questions" could not be wedged into the "Perry scheme." In this instance, as in others, when the data the women provided diverged from the theories we had brought to the project, we forced ourselves to believe the women and let go of the theories. It was surprisingly painful to discard theories that had served as scaffolding for the project and that we had come to cherish as parts of ourselves. We referred to the process, privately, in brutal terms: "shrinking Perry," "killing off the fathers." Jill remembers a day during our month at the shore when we had sat outside discussing our work and Gilligan's, poring over her book.

> That night it rained, and the next morning we awoke to find her book still outside, soaking, unreadable, falling apart. It scared me. It was the first time I realized that in forging a new statement, we might leave other theorists behind, we might alter irrevocably our relationships with them. I was particularly concerned about Perry, who had been a major advisor to me at Harvard. I began to seek a metaphor for what we were doing: separating individual raindrops in a storm. Shucking my mainstream training as a developmentalist was painful.

We forged ahead, however. Having coded the transcripts in terms of our reconstructions of the Perry positions, each of us then took responsibility for intensive rereading and analysis of a batch of transcripts representing a particular position. By the end of the month at the shore we had a book proposal. Book contract in hand, we began to write. Nancy reminisces:

> Each of us took on a writing assignment and prepared a first draft of a section. We then passed this on to all the others for commentary; if the group wasn't satisfied with the project, someone else would take over the section and do a rewrite. (We only became computerized midway through our project; our four word processors were incompatible so disk transfer was impossible; we had to do a lot of retyping.)

As we moved the conversation onto paper our ideas continued to proliferate and became even more interconnected—as did we. Nancy:

> Of all the many memories of our collaboration, one particular experience always comes to mind when I am asked to describe what it was like. I am sitting before my new computer. I have Blythe's or Jill's or Mary's words before me and the marginal commentary on the text from the other two by my side as well. My task is to rewrite, but first I must type the words from my colleague into my word proces-

sor. I decide to edit as I type. What astonishes me is the process that evolves; I take someone else's words (someone I respect and trust and who trusts me), slowly read her text, try to understand her intention behind her choice of words, try to place myself in her place so that I feel inside her mind and heart, search for her meaning before I impose new words or meaning of my own, imagine what might be so important to her to say that I must take care not to lose her meaning. Only then do I allow new words to flow from my fingers—the words are mine, yet hers as well. It was this slowed-down process of reading—attending—typing that led me to an understanding of a friend and colleague in a way that I had not attained in conversation or in the initial reading of the text. I felt so close to her, inside her, that I could almost feel her generate ideas, make jokes, become digressive. I knew her in a new way. Later, as I thought back on this experience, I began to think this kind of process might work in classrooms. Give students the task of editing Plato, for instance. Tell them to rewrite Plato in their own words.

Mary remembers a similar experience of connecting to the women we interviewed as she typed their words: "I felt myself opening to these women as their words flowed through my body out onto the paper."

As the writing of the book continued, conversations that had been so expansive and freeing became more nuanced, focused, and selective. Mary:

I would send out a draft and several days later the piece would come back with the margins filled with such remarks as: "?," "not clear," "evidence?," and even "awk." Also: "Say more; this is *very* interesting," and "Reread interview #42; she articulates this idea well."

I wrote surrounded by piles of interview transcripts, salient quotes and notes from the literature we had read, and photocopies of my previous draft. Each copy would be covered with the distinctive hand writing of one colleague or another. Blythe's comments were always penciled in with a very light hand. There would be the tiniest question marks wherever she had found my thinking fuzzy. The other two women used bold, clear inks. Jill's, as I remember, was often purple. I felt as if I was in a dialogue with a great array of voices—the many women we had interviewed, the thinkers whose books we had read, and my dear colleagues. It was my job to speak to as many of them as I could.

Our first drafts, Blythe remembers, looked a lot like the first paper she wrote for English 1 in college, for which she received a "D" and the comment, "At least you've joined your quotations with conjunctions, which is more than I can say for some of your classmates." Our editor at Basic Books, Jo Ann Miller, made the same point: "There's nothing but description here: You keep saying, 'And then another woman said, . . . And then another woman said . . . '" We were reminded of words we sometimes write in the margins of our students' papers ("Where are *you* in this paper?") and of Milly Henry's earlier admonitions ("*Use* your minds").

But wasn't it the women's voices that mattered? After all, we had decided to write a book because we found their words so moving, their thoughts so important that we felt the world had to hear them. We came to see, however, that in serving merely as conduits for the women's voices, we were behaving with the double-edged "selflessness" common among women, exhibiting an appropriately humble respect for the wisdom of others, but also a cowardly reluctance to construct and communicate our own knowledge. At Jo Ann's behest, and, gradually, at our own internal behests, we pushed one another to create "better and better concepts." Mary:

> Whenever one of us had a hunch about something that seemed important, the other three would help marshall quotes that might substantiate and expand the idea. We were like detectives tracking down clues, building a case, solving a great mystery. Sometimes someone would say something like, "That idea of yours seemed just right. I am simply amazed it is not substantiated by the interviews. It ought to be, but it isn't."

We were ruthless in pruning one another's words. We had no choice but to toss out arguments that remained obscure or could not be backed up sufficiently by the interview data. These were our ways of holding ourselves accountable to the women we had interviewed. We wanted to represent their words fairly; we also wanted to write the book in a way they would enjoy reading. When things went well, it was exhilarating. When things went poorly, it was excruciating.

We do not wish to idealize our collaboration. Jill, in particular, recalls:

> We had wonderful insights, and agonizing disagreements, some still unresolved. As the theory began to emerge from the mist, we each held a different relationship to it, and struggled over issues of ownership, the individual versus the group identity, all the while

surrounded, I felt, by our interviewees and our other collaborators.

We were hard on each other in the writing of this book. We felt we had
to be, because the book had taken on a life of its own; it came first. We had
made a decision early on that everyone's name would be listed alphabetical-
ly as an author of the whole book—not of the particular pieces they had
worked on the most. That agreement, we believe, was crucial to achieving the
"one voice" quality that so impressed our readers (and us). Because we were
each listed as an author of the whole we felt we had a right (and an obligation) to keep pushing until we really liked what was being said and the way
it was being said.

But the "we" did not always predominate in the writing of the book.
While, as Nancy says, we truly welcomed one another's comments and
even revisions of our thinking and our writing, each of us also became
somewhat possessive of our "own" chapters. For instance, Blythe remember engaging in some pretty sharp trading with Mary over "good quotes"
from the interviews. When Mary argued that she needed for the family
chapter a quote from "Patti" that Blythe was saving to illustrate "connected teaching" ("My mother . . . is the type that can draw stuff out of a person"), Blythe said, "NO! It's *mine!*" Shrewdly, however, Mary offered in
return a quote she had planned to use in the chapter on received knowledge
in which a poor rural mother we call "Lillian" describes a patronizing pediatrician who made her feel stupid when she asked for information about
her child's projectile vomiting ("Don't worry about it," he said). This quo-
tation, Blythe saw, would fit perfectly in the education chapter. They had
themselves a deal.

Paradoxically, these negotiations over individual turf demonstrated
the fact that we shared a common ground. As Nancy reports, as early as
White River Junction we had suspected that "'education' need not be narrowly defined," and the ease with which quotes could travel from chapter
to chapter reinforced the suspicion: clearly, education (and miseducation)
happened at home and in the clinic, as well as in the classroom. And the
quote-swapping among us "I-s" contributed, ultimately, to the seamlessness,
the "we-ness" of the book.

After finishing a first draft of the book, we knew we needed a "hard
read" by someone not so immersed in the process, someone who could tell us
whether we had achieved a "single voice" and coherent story across the
chapters. We turned to Sara Ruddick whose own work so resonated with
ours and whose clear thinking we trusted. Nancy says:

I remember sitting with Sally at her big round dining room table after she had read our first draft, pages spread around us, feeling both grateful for and overwhelmed by the extensive commentary she was providing to "improve" the book. I wondered: How am I going to tell the others that Sally thinks we are far from finished with this thing?

In essence, what Sally noted were the disjunctions from chapter to chapter as voice and content shifted; themes developed in one chapter were too often left hanging in the following chapter. Nancy worried about getting killed as the messenger when she reported back to the others:

> Was a single voice impossible? Maybe we were going to have to choose one of us to write the last draft, smoothing out the bumps and filling in the gaps for the sake of the book. But I hoped not. We had worked too hard to join our voices and pool our thoughts to give that up. And anyway, if collaborative writing is possible at all, we wanted to prove we could carry it through to the end.

And so the collaboration continued—for another entire year—as we reworked the text yet again. We finally found the voice we were striving for.

Blythe's most vivid memory of the writing collaboration concerns a time when, physically at least, she was all by herself, alone with the manuscript.

> On a glorious summer day in Vermont, I was toiling, as I had been for days, over what I hoped would be the final draft of the final chapter in the book. At last, it seemed, I had reached the end, earning the right to turn off the computer and transplant the lupines, but as I started to hit control-S (or whatever it was in those days), the last sentence of the chapter caught my eye: "These are the lessons we think we have learned in listening to women's voices." I stared at the sentence for a full minute, and then, with the stroke of a key, deleted "we think": the sentence then read, as it reads now, "These are the lessons we have learned in listening to women's voices." We didn't *think* we had learned these lessons; we *had* learned them, and if anybody out there in the world wanted to fight about it, we were ready for them.
>
>   If I had been the sole author, could I have made this correction? I doubt it. Although *we* knew it, did *I*, perhaps, only think it? No, I knew I knew it, but I was glad that I didn't have to say so. Some years later, in notes hastily scribbled for a talk describing our col-

laboration, I wrote, by mistake, "speaking up *four* ourselves." The mistake told the truth.

Engaging With Others: Creating Conversations

In fact, of course, our group often included more than four. Both before and after the book was published, we were engaged in richly varied theory-making conversations with a host of collaborators. In the course of the project, our working group expanded and contracted depending on the task. Sometimes only the four of us met; other times we included liaison members from the nine different sites where we had interviewed the 135 women. Occasionally some of the women we interviewed joined us, lending their voices and perspectives as we tried to make sense out of what we were learning about women and education.

We also met with faculty groups in the colleges and agencies where we were interviewing to present what we were learning and to discuss implications for their institutions. Jill remembers those first attempts to take our work into the public arena:

> For a number of years, I had been doing faculty workshops on adult learning, so it seemed as if these new meetings were simply experiences of the old with a new topic. But quickly it became apparent that what I was reporting out from our project was far from benign. Some faculty got mad at us for suggesting their women students might be suffering, or that the faculty should consider doing something different from what they were doing. Others allied themselves with us and welcomed us for naming what they had been thinking. Focusing on and emphasizing women's experience unleashed passionate responses—positive and negative

Those early interactions with faculties and staff challenged us. We were beginning to grapple with how this work should inform or transform not only theory, but also pedagogical and other practices in learning environments.

In the third year of the grant, we had planned to "disseminate" our "findings". The process of research was presumably over; it was time to distribute the product. It was suggested that we hold a national conference and invite important people to make speeches about higher education for women. Instead, we decided—and FIPSE, bless them, agreed—to invite people who were doing some sort of work involving women, epistemology, and education to submit proposals for projects that they were working on, or wanted to work on, and would like to discuss.

We held the first meeting with a group of about thirty women (and one man) in 1982, launching the network we called "National Conference on Education for Women's Development" (NCEWD). Over the next decade, the network continued to meet annually. NCEWD became a test site where we could begin to experiment with ways of working in groups that extended the pajama-party model. The group would spend two to three intensive days together, if possible in a lovely but inexpensive place where we could take walks as we continued to talk.

In this group, individuals found their own work developing in ways they had not imagined. Each year we would gather to learn about new babies, reappointments and promotions, tenure, new and lost lovers, dissertations and degrees, our latest writing and thinking, and, of course, familiar struggles that each of us had dealt with during the year. For many of the participants, the NCEWD group provided critical support as they moved more fully into their profession. It was a spawning ground for many articles and a few books.

To this day, many of us are still in contact, still sharing work with each other, although eventually NCEWD began to disintegrate and ultimately stopped meeting as a large group. But for that decade the conversations, when we met together annually as a large group and more frequently in regional sub-groups, were some of the richest and fullest we had ever experienced. In NCEWD, we had a chance to transform the pajama-party scholarship model into a learning environment. We began to feel hopeful that it might be possible, as Jill puts it, to "put your practice where your theory is."

Going Public

After the book was published, we had many opportunities to give talks. Each of us was invited, often, to address groups of college faculty or national conferences of various sorts; it was a new experience. Sometimes we could go "on the road" together, and this rapidly became our preference. Whether doing a keynote address or running a workshop or consulting with staff or faculty about the use of the scheme in different settings, it always felt more natural to have one or two or three of the others along side. The collaborative dialogue had not only become natural for us, it was central to our theory. As Nancy puts it:

> You can only *talk* about collaboration when you're on your on own; with the group, you can *demonstrate* it. Our style of interacting—bouncing ideas off one another as we talked, being playful with ideas and each other, sharing the job of moving the audience (or group) along, eliciting comments and ideas from those who sometimes thought they were just there to listen—tended to set the audience at ease.

Drawing on both NCEWD and our collaboration, we began to work our way from the lecture to new formats. The assumption of many who invited us to speak was that we, as Experts, would deliver tablets of Truth. Postbook, Jill remembers that she slipped briefly into believing that she should deliver what people were asking for, a lecture on *Women's Ways of Knowing*, but she soon began to realize that she didn't want to lecture; she wanted to run workshops and recreate the collaboration. All four of us had come to hate the traditional model of academic conferences in which an individual takes the podium, speaks at an audience who can only listen or at most ask a few short questions at the end of the talk, then sits down so that the next speaker can also talk at the audience.

We were also learning that, if called on to lecture, we could do it differently. Instead of speaking at an "audience," we began to construe it as conversing with colleagues, working on questions that matter to all of us. Instead of disseminating knowledge and protecting our turf (our theory), we tried to involve others in questioning and expanding our ideas. We were not delivering a product; we were engaged in a process. Blythe:

> I now feel genuinely at home talking about ways of knowing even in a large lecture hall filled with strangers, while, when the project began, I felt uneasy discussing such matters with a single stranger. I recall, for instance, an image from those early days. Seated behind my own desk in my office, I am interviewing a sophomore. There is a pile of books on the desk. The student leans forward to shove the pile of books aside, saying, "just so I can see your face."
>
> Gradually, first when we four were together, then within the

network, and finally "on the road", my private voice went public. Classrooms and lecture halls have become for me, to borrow Mary's phrase "public homeplaces" (see below). I might as well be in my own living room.

We were beginning to feel authentically "voiced" when we spoke about our work, finding ways to inhabit the expert role and to speak authoritatively while encouraging collaboration. (Jill remembers asking five hundred people in a large lecture hall to do a guided imagery and discuss it with the person next to them.) It became important to "use" our expert status as a tool to insure that there was a dialogue about the work.

We worked hard to devise formats that could convey the spirit of our collaboration, creating workshop designs that replicated our process of collecting and analyzing data. For instance, we would begin by clustering people into very small groups to analyze interview data. Each group worked with excerpts from several interviews representing different ways of knowing. Participants would read the transcripts out loud and discuss the underlying assumptions each of these women held about the nature of knowledge and her approach to learning. The groups would be asked to consider the same sorts of questions we had used to "hear" what the women were saying: How does this person think knowledge and ideas originate? Does she imagine sharpening her wits and ideas through argumentation? Does she use empathic role-taking processes to expand her understanding of things? Finally, we would ask the groups to think of environments, interventions, or pedagogical strategies that might support the women to claim the power of their minds.

We loved watching these conversations unfold. At first the auditorium would be rather quiet. A sense of awkwardness would pervade the place. When the conversations finally took off, the room would begin to vibrate with the kind of excitement that comes with discovery. Participants were actively engaged in constructing a theory of knowledge, using the same methodology we had found so useful. By the time the whole group reconvened, everyone had had a good chance to develop and articulate their ideas in a small group. Even people who seldom speak in public places would find themselves contributing to a discussion in a large auditorium.

At day's end, participants talked with pleasure about the process of collaboration and discovery. Invariably we shared that pleasure. Even though we had worked on old interviews that we had read many times over many years, the discussions always deepened our understanding. It seems that one can go on thinking about thinking forever.

How It Is Now

Although to a large extent we have gone our separate ways since the publication of the book, the WWK project spawned for each of us a set of questions that we have been pursuing ever since with various colleagues in the "collaborative, egalitarian spirit" which we said in the preface to the first edition of WWK we hoped to find in all our future work. Each of us has written a chapter in *Knowledge, Difference, and Power* to present this more recent work.

Nancy has been involved with her students in a five-year study of diversity in ways of knowing, exploring how culture, social power differentials, and the bicultural experience in the U.S. affect individual strategies for knowing. Jill's research has focused on collaborative learning classrooms and on how dialogue and collaboration affect thinking. Blythe has been engaged in the systematic study of "connected knowing," a concept that we stumbled upon serendipitously in the course of the project, and she has managed to infect a series of colleagues with her obsession. Mary emerged from our collaboration, she says, with a clearly etched prototype of what Maxine Greene (1988) calls "an authentic public space . . . where people can appear before each other the best they know how to be." Mary calls these spaces "public homeplaces, places where people work at the very edges of their abilities, constantly pushing each other's thinking into new territory, giving names to things that have gone unnamed, dreaming of better ways, discovering common ground, and finding ways to realize shared dreams." In a forthcoming book (Belenky, Bond, & Weinstock, 1997), Mary describes several such public homeplaces that she has studied over the past few years. Members of these groups are continually expanding, testing, and refining their ideas through hands-on action projects or experiments and impassioned conversations. As the ideas develop coherence and clarity, the people find ways of making bold statements to the world.

Women's Ways of Knowing was our bold statement to the world. It launched the four of us into research and conversations that would never have happened without our experience of the WWK collaboration. Recently, we have had a chance to revisit the experience. When we gathered to devel-

op ideas for our new book, it was gratifying beyond words to find the collective older yet wiser, somewhat changed but intact. Like a really good family, we could laugh, argue, listen, talk, eat, play, think, and feel together with
the kind of comfort that only a common history and love produces.

—The authors
April, 1996

Belenky, M., Bond, L., & Weinstock, J. (1997, forthcoming). *A tradition that has no name: Public
    homeplaces and the development of women, families, and communities.*
Goldberger, N., Tarule, J., Clinchy, B., & Belenky, M. (Eds.) (1996). *Knowledge, difference, and
    power: Essays inspired by "Women's Ways of Knowing."* New York: Basic Books.
Greene, M. (1988). *The dialectic of freedom.* New York: Teachers College Press.
Perry, W. G. (1970). *Forms of intellectual and ethical development in the college years.* New York:
    Holt, Rinehart & Winston.

Preface to the First Edition

IN THIS BOOK we describe the ways of knowing that women have cultivated and learned to value, ways we have come to believe are powerful but have been neglected and denigrated by the dominant intellectual ethos of our time. We also describe the multitude of obstacles women must overcome in developing the power of their minds. These descriptions are based on intensive interviews with many women whose words we have tried to honor and give voice to by presenting them as we heard them—at times faltering, at times eloquent. Although we have changed the names and identifying characteristics of the women, and occasionally edited their words for the sake of clarity, the women speak for themselves.

As we steeped ourselves in the women's recorded and transcribed words we found ourselves drawing ever closer to their frames of mind. We emerged from this long process with an extraordinary sense of intimacy and collaboration with all the women, even though each of us had met face to face with only a few.

So, too, during our work together, the four of us developed among ourselves an intimacy and collaboration which we have come to prize. We believe that the collaborative, egalitarian spirit so often shared by women should be more carefully nurtured in the work lives of all men and women. We hope to find it in all of our future work.

In collaborating on writing this book we searched for a single voice— a way of submerging our individual perspectives for the sake of the collective "we." Not that we denied our individual convictions or squelched our objections to one another's points of view—we argued, tried to persuade, even cried at times when we reached an impasse of understanding— but we learned to listen to each other, to build on each other's insights, and eventually to arrive at a way of communicating as a collective what we believe. Hence, this book is not separated into parts that we wish to attribute to one or the other of us, even though each of us took the primary responsibility for different parts. There may be stylistic differences from one section to the next, but the book as a whole is the product of our joint efforts and interchange of ideas.

—The authors
April 1986

Acknowledgments

THE LIST OF PEOPLE we wish to thank is long. From the first days of our planning to the final editing of the book, we have felt enormously supported by our families, institutions, colleagues, and friends.

From the beginning, the work of Carol Gilligan and William Perry inspired and informed us. Our work could never have been accomplished without their bold new constructions of human development.

The Fund for Improvement for Post Secondary Education (FIPSE) is an agency that has played a major role in our professional lives. For over a decade, it has led the way in funding programs to improve understanding of the needs of minority and women learners. It supported the early work of three of us and provided both financial and professional support for The Education for Women's Development Project, which became the basis for this book. Carol Stoel, FIPSE's acting director and our program officer, gave us her enthusiastic backing as well as useful suggestions and counsel. Anita Landa, the project evaluator, provided insight and helpful criticism throughout.

Many educational institutions and social service agencies participated in the study and/or provided the authors with ongoing support during the data-analysis and writing phases. Since the institutions are not mentioned by name in the text, we would like to take this opportunity to thank the participating colleges and agencies for opening their doors to us. The study sites included Bard College, Goddard College, LaGuardia Community College, The Middle School of LaGuardia Community College, Simon's Rock of Bard College, Wellesley College, The Children's Health Program of Great Barrington, Massachusetts, Parents Anonymous of Vermont, and the Vermont Parent-to-Parent Program. Over the years Simon's Rock of Bard College and The Stone Center at Wellesley College shared the responsibilities of administering the project. The Austin Riggs Center supported Nancy Goldberger's participation during the final phase of data analysis and writing and Wellesley College supported Blythe Clinchy's sabbatical year.

Leadership and support at the various sites came from Janet Lieberman, Linda Small, Teresa Vilardi, Ellen Cole, Jean Lathrop, Jean Baker Miller, Laura Latham Smith, Char Marrow, and many others. We received extensive help in administrative tasks, interviewing, data analysis, transcribing, and preparing manuscripts from Barbara Allison, Kathleen Galotti, Joanne Hardy, Betty Homich, Christine Miller Massey, Bonnie Nordoff, Patricia O'Brien, Jo Ann Reilly, Lisa Strayer, and Rona Weiss.

Two groups connected with the FIPSE Education for Women's Development Project helped us extend the work into a larger context than we had originally envisioned. One was the Project's National Board of Advisors which included Alison Bernstein, William Birenbaum, Zelda Gamson, Mildred Henry, Robert LeVine, and Sara LeVine. The second is an ongoing organization that was spawned by the Project, The National Conference on Education for Women's Development, which supports collaboration among researchers and practitioners from around the country in working toward new understandings and programs that promote women's development. All of the women who participate in this network have supported us and our work.

There are a number of people we especially want to thank for the part they played as we brought our ideas into book form: Jo Ann Miller, our editor at Basic Books, has been a friend and adviser—responsive, thoughtful, and positive throughout. Claire Zimmerman and Mildred Henry participated in the generation and articulation of the ideas before this book was conceived and have continued to be among our most important colleagues. Leo Goldberger and Evans Clinchy read and criticized draft after draft, contributing their good sense, caring concern, and necessary morale boosting during the periods of frustration and tedium. Sally Ruddick and Joe Katz did the first careful reading of the book in its entirety and provided us with new visions of what the book could be with a little more work. Many others read parts of the book and gave valuable feedback to one or more of us: our deep appreciation to Robert Belenky, Pat DeCaro, Will Hamlin, Tom Lickona, Jack Lindquist, Nona Lyons, Lanie Melamed, Nancy Nager, Jeanne Paradise, Lisa Peattie, Abby Pratt, and Rob Tarule.

In searching for an image of women with an evolved life of the mind to adorn the cover of our book, we looked for pictures created by women. We were surprised to find how seldom the works of women artists are represented in our museums and libraries. We thank Greta Berman and Joan Marter for assisting us in that search. We thank Bessie Boris for making her portrait of her daughter available to us.

And finally, we want to thank the women whom we interviewed. Their willingness to open up to strangers and to talk about the painful as well as the happy parts of their lives has humbled as well as educated us.

Women's Ways of Knowing

Introduction:
To the Other Side
of Silence

If we had a keen vision and feeling of all
ordinary human life, it would be like hearing the grass grow and the squirrel's heart
beat, and we should die of that roar which
lies on the other side of silence.
—GEORGE ELIOT
Middlemarch

WE DO NOT THINK of the ordinary person as preoccupied with such
difficult and profound questions as: What is truth? What is authority? To
whom do I listen? What counts for me as evidence? How do I know what
I know? Yet to ask ourselves these questions and to reflect on our answers
is more than an intellectual exercise, for our basic assumptions about the
nature of truth and reality and the origins of knowledge shape the way
we see the world and ourselves as participants in it. They affect our definitions of ourselves, the way we interact with others, our public and private
personae, our sense of control over life events, our views of teaching and
learning, and our conceptions of morality.

In this book we examine women's ways of knowing and describe five
different perspectives from which women view reality and draw conclusions
about truth, knowledge, and authority. We show how women's self-
concepts and ways of knowing are intertwined. We describe how women
struggle to claim the power of their own minds. We then examine how the

two institutions primarily devoted to human development—the family and the schools—both promote and hinder women's development.

Most of what we say is based on extensive interviews with ordinary women living ordinary lives. Our informants were rural and urban American women of different ages, class and ethnic backgrounds, and educational histories. At the time of the interview, many of the women were in the midst of dramatic personal and intellectual changes, and they told us about recent, as well as distant, transitions in the way they perceived themselves and the world around them.

We listened as women told us their life stories and described the people and events that were catalytic in shaping the way they viewed themselves and their minds. Not all of the women's stories were happy ones. This is as much a book about pain and anger and static lives as it is about hope and lives in blossom. It is also a book about the "roar which lies on the other side of silence" when ordinary women find their voice and use it to gain control over their lives.

Background of the Study

The project began in the late 1970s. As psychologists interested in human development, we had spent a large part of our professional lives studying the intellectual, ethical, and psychological development of adolescents and adults in educational and clinical settings. We became concerned about why women students speak so frequently of problems and gaps in their learning and so often doubt their intellectual competence. We had also become aware of the fact that, for many women, the "real" and valued lessons learned did not necessarily grow out of their academic work but in relationships with friends and teachers, life crises, and community involvements. Indeed we observed that women often feel alienated in academic settings and experience "formal" education as either peripheral or irrelevant to their central interests and development.

Looking back on our experience and talking with other women inside and outside the classroom reinforced our feeling that education and clinical services, as traditionally defined and practiced, do not adequately serve the needs of women. Anecdotal reports as well as research on sex differences indicate that girls and women have more difficulty than boys and men in asserting their authority or considering themselves as authorities (Clance and Imes 1978; Cross 1968; Maccoby and Jacklin 1974; Piliavin 1976; West and Zimmerman 1983); in expressing themselves in public so that others will listen (Aries 1976; Eakins and Eakins 1976; Piliavin 1976; Sadker and Sadker 1982, 1985; Swacker 1976; Thorne 1979), in gaining respect of others for their minds and their ideas (Hagen and Kahn 1975; Hall and Sandler 1982; Serbin, O'Leary, Kent, and Tonick 1973); and in fully utilizing their capabilities and training in the world of work (Gallese 1985; Kanter 1977; Ruddick and Daniels 1977; Sassen 1980; Treichler and Kramarae 1983). In everyday and professional life, as well as in the classroom, women often feel unheard even when they believe that they have something important to say. Most women can recall incidents in which either they or female friends were discouraged from pursuing some line of intellectual work on the grounds that it was "unfeminine" or incompatible with female capabilities. Many female students and working women are painfully aware that men succeed better than they in getting and holding the attention of others for their ideas and opinions. All women grow up having to deal with historically and culturally engrained definitions of femininity and womanhood—one common theme being that women, like children, should be seen and not heard.

In spite of the increase in the number of women students in higher education and professional schools, faculties, usually predominantly male, argue against a special focus on women students and resist open debate on whether women's educational needs are different from men's. Although women's studies programs began to proliferate in the 1970s and to attract female students and faculty, they were typically assigned a marginal status in the academy and have had relatively little impact on the mainstream curriculum and academic programming (Howe and Lauter 1980). Even when the content of coursework includes issues of concern to women, strategies of teaching and methods of evaluation are rarely examined by faculty to see if they are compatible with women's preferred styles of learning. Usually faculty assume that pedagogical techniques appropriate for men are suitable for women.

Along with other academic feminists, we believe that conceptions of knowledge and truth that are accepted and articulated today have been shaped throughout history by the male-dominated majority culture. Drawing on their own perspectives and visions, men have constructed the prevailing theories, written history, and set values that have become the guiding principles for men and women alike. Our major educational institutions—particularly our secondary and postsecondary schools—were originally founded by men for the education of men. Even girls' schools and women's colleges have been modeled after male institutions to give women an education "equivalent" to men's. Relatively little attention has been given to modes of learning, knowing, and valuing that may be specific to, or at least common in, women. It is likely that the commonly accepted stereotype of women's thinking as emotional, intuitive, and personalized has contributed to the devaluation of women's minds and contributions, particularly in Western technologically oriented cultures, which value rationalism and objectivity (Sampson 1978). It is generally assumed that intuitive knowledge is more primitive, therefore less valuable, than so-called objective modes of knowing. Thus, it appeared likely to us that traditional educational curricula and pedagogical standards have probably not escaped this bias. Indeed, recent feminist writers have convincingly argued that there is a masculine bias at the very heart of most academic disciplines, methodologies, and theories (Bernard 1973; Gilligan 1979, 1982; Harding and Hintikka 1983; Keller 1978, 1985; Janssen-Jurreit 1980; Langland and Gove 1981; Sherman and Beck 1979). Feminists are beginning to articulate the values of the female world and to reshape the disciplines to include the woman's voice, while continuing to press for the right of women to participate as equals in the male world.

THE ABSENCE OF WOMEN IN PSYCHOLOGY

Until recently women have played only a minor role as theorists in the social sciences. The authors of the major theories of human development have been men. As Carol Gilligan (1979) has pointed out, women have been missing even as research subjects at the formative stages of our psychological theories. The potential for bias on the part of male investigators is heightened by the recurring tendency to select exclusively or predominantly male samples for research. This omission of women from scientific studies is almost universally ignored when scientists draw conclusions from their findings and generalize what they have learned from the study of men to lives of women. If and when scientists turn to the study of women, they typically look for ways in which women conform to or diverge from patterns found in the study of men. With the Western tradition of dividing human nature into dual but parallel streams, attributes traditionally associated with the masculine are valued, studied, and articulated, while those associated with the feminine tend to be ignored. Thus, we have learned a great deal about the development of autonomy and independence, abstract critical thought, and the unfolding of a morality of rights and justice in both men and women. We have learned less about the development of interdependence, intimacy, nurturance, and contextual thought (Bakan 1966; Chodorow 1978; Gilligan 1977, 1979, 1982; McMillan 1982). Developmental theory has established men's experience and competence as a baseline against which both men's and women's development is then judged, often to the detriment or misreading of women.

Nowhere is the pattern of using male experience to define the human experience seen more clearly than in models of intellectual development. The mental processes that are involved in considering the abstract and the impersonal have been labeled "thinking" and are attributed primarily to men, while those that deal with the personal and interpersonal fall under the rubric of "emotions" and are largely relegated to women. As dichotomous "either/or thinking" is so common in our culture and as we tend to view human beings as closed systems, the expenditure of energy in one part of the system has been seen inevitably to lead to depletion elsewhere. Historically, it has been assumed that the development of women's intellectual potential would inhibit the development of their emotional capacities and that the development of men's emotional range would impair intellectual functioning. Although it seems ludicrous to us now, just a century ago the belief that women who engaged in intellectual pursuits would find their reproductive organs atrophying was widely held and used to justify the continued exclusion of women from the academic community (Rosenberg 1982).

From the moment women gained a foot in the academic world, they sought to examine and dispel beliefs suggesting sexual polarities in intelligence and personality characteristics. However, research studies and critical essays on the topic have focused on the demonstration of women's intellectual competence, minimizing any differences that were found between the sexes (Maccoby and Jacklin 1974; Rosenberg 1982). The focus has been on studying the intellectual capacities most often cultivated by men rather than on identifying aspects of intelligence and modes of thought that might be more common and highly developed in women.

WOMAN'S VOICE IN DEVELOPMENTAL THEORY:
THE WORK OF CAROL GILLIGAN

When the woman's voice is included in the study of human development, women's lives and qualities are revealed and we can observe the unfolding of these qualities in the lives of men as well. The power of the woman's voice in expanding our conceptions of human development is amply illustrated in the work of Carol Gilligan (1982).

By listening to girls and women resolve serious moral dilemmas in their lives, Gilligan has traced the development of a morality organized around notions of responsibility and care. This conception of morality contrasts sharply with the morality of rights described by Piaget (1965) and Kohlberg (1981, 1984), which is based on the study of the evolution of moral reasoning in boys and men. People operating within a rights morality—more commonly men—evoke the metaphor of "blind justice" and rely on abstract laws and universal principles to adjudicate disputes and conflicts between conflicting claims impersonally, impartially, and fairly. Those operating within a morality of responsibility and care—primarily women—reject the strategy of blindness and impartiality. Instead, they argue for an understanding of the context for moral choice, claiming that the needs of individuals cannot always be deduced from general rules and principles and that moral choice must also be determined inductively from the particular experiences each participant brings to the situation. They believe that dialogue and exchange of views allow each individual to be understood in his or her own terms. They believe that mutual understanding is most likely to lead to a creative consensus about how everyone's needs may be met in resolving disputes. It is the rejection of blind impartiality in the application of universal abstract rules and principles that has, in the eyes of many, marked women as deficient in moral reasoning.

In recent work Gilligan and her colleague, Nona Lyons (1983), have extended their study of gender-related differences in moral perspectives to the area of identity development. They have shown how the responsibility orientation is more central to those whose conceptions of self are rooted in a sense of connection and relatedness to others, whereas the rights orientation is more common to those who define themselves in terms of separation and autonomy. Although these differences in self-definition do not necessarily divide along gender lines, it is clear that many more women than men define themselves in terms of their relationships and connections to others, a point which has also been made by Nancy Chodorow (1978) and Jean Baker Miller (1976). When men define themselves in terms of connection, they also frame their moral judgments in terms of responsibility rather than rights (Lyons 1983).

Such insights are transforming our understanding and study of psychology and human development, paralleling transformations that are occurring in all of the intellectual disciplines that have begun to include the woman's voice. When scientific findings, scientific theory, and even the basic assumptions of academic disciplines are reexamined through the lens of women's perspectives and values, new conclusions can be drawn and new directions forged that have implications for the lives of both men and women.

EPISTEMOLOGICAL DEVELOPMENT: THE WORK OF WILLIAM PERRY

In our study we chose to listen only to women. The male experience has been so powerfully articulated that we believed we would hear the patterns in women's voices more clearly if we held at bay the powerful templates men have etched in the literature and in our minds. However, we did attend to men's experience by turning to the excellent map charting epistemological development of students, drawn by William Perry and his colleagues from interviews gathered each spring from students as they moved through their undergraduate years at Harvard. In his influential book *Forms of Intellectual and Ethical Development in the College Years* (1970), Perry describes how students' conceptions of the nature and origins of knowledge evolve and how their understanding of themselves as knowers changes over time.

While a few women were included in Perry's original study as subjects, only the interviews with men were used in illustrating and validating his scheme on intellectual and ethical development. Later, when Perry assessed the women's development with the aid of his map, the women were found to conform with the patterns that had been observed in the male data. While this strategy enabled the researchers to see what women might have in common with men, it was poorly designed to uncover those themes that might be more prominent among women. Our work focuses on what else women might have to say about the development of their minds and on alternative routes that are sketchy or missing in Perry's version.

In his book Perry depicts a passage through a sequence of epistemological perspectives that he calls *positions.* It is through these coherent interpretative frameworks that students give meaning to their educational experience. Perry traces a progression from an initial position that he calls *basic dualism,* where the student views the world in polarities of right/wrong, black/white, we/they, and good/bad. Here passive learners are dependent on authorities to hand down the truth, teaching them "right from wrong." Gradually the student becomes increasingly aware of the diversity of opinion and the multiple perspectives that others hold, and the dualistic faith in absolute authority and truth is shaken. Dualism gives way to *multiplicity* as the student comes to understand that authorities may not have the right answers, at least in some areas, such as the humanities, which seem to be more a matter of opinion and taste than fact. The student begins to grow beyond a dependency and trust in external authorities and carves out his own territory of personal freedom: "Everyone has a right to his own opinion and mine is as good as any other." As the student's personal opinion is challenged by a teacher's insistence on evidence and support for opinion, multiplicity yields to *relativism subordinate*, where an analytical, evaluative approach to knowledge is consciously and actively cultivated at least in the academic disciplines one is being tutored in, if not in the rest of one's life. It is only with the shift into full *relativism* that the student completely comprehends that truth is relative, that the meaning of an event depends on the context in which that event occurs and on the framework that the knower uses to understand that event, and that relativism pervades all aspects of life, not just the academic world. Only then is the student able to understand that knowledge is constructed, not given; contextual, not absolute; mutable, not fixed. It is within relativism that Perry believes the affirmation of personal identity and commitment evolves.

Since the introduction of the Perry scheme in the early 1970s, educators and researchers have used it as a way of understanding intellectual development in young adults in academic settings and as a developmental framework to guide educational practice. The Perry scheme was very important in our work as it stimulated our interest in modes of knowing and provided us with our first images of the paths women might take as they developed an understanding of their intellectual potential, as well as providing a description of the routes most often taken by men.

There are no agreed-upon techniques for assessing the Perry positions, although a spectrum of techniques has been developed from paper-and-pencil tests (Knefelkamp 1978) to self-report questionnaires (Griffith and Chapman 1982) to extensive interviews (Clinchy and Zimmerman 1975; Goldberger 1978, 1981). Perry himself preferred an approach that is built around an open and leisurely interview that establishes rapport and allows presuppositions and frames of reference of the interviewee to emerge. We share Perry's commitment to this phenomenological approach.

The Women and the Interview

Our wish to explore with the women their experience and problems as learners and knowers as well as to review their past histories for changing concepts of the self and relationships with others limited the number of women we could interview in depth to a total of 135.

The initial interviews and any subsequent interviews were tape recorded and transcribed and were from two to five hours in length, resulting in over five thousand pages of text. We adopted an intensive interview/case study approach because we wanted to hear what the women had to say in their own terms rather than test our own preconceived hypotheses, particularly since we included a number of disadvantaged and forgotten women whose ways of knowing and learning, identity transformations, and moral outlook have seldom been examined by academic researchers. We proceeded inductively, opening our ears to the voices and perspectives of women so that we might begin to hear the unheard and unimagined.

Before asking a woman to participate, we told her that we were interested in her experience—and in women's experience—because it had so often been excluded as people sought to understand human development. We told her that we wanted to hear what was important about life and learning *from her point of view*. When possible, we let the woman choose where the interview was to take place—at her home, office, dorm, or in our office or home. Each interview began with the question, "Looking back, what stands out for you over the past few years?" and proceeded gradually at the woman's own pace to questions concerning self-image, relationships of importance, education and learning, real-life decision-making and moral dilemmas, accounts of personal changes and growth, perceived catalysts for change and impediments to growth, and visions of the future. We tried to pose questions that were broad but understandable on many levels, hoping that all—even the less articulate and reflective women—would respond in their own terms without feeling inadequate to the task. Embedded in the interview were questions we devised for assigning Perry's (1970) epistemological positions and also standard questions developed by Gilligan (1982; also see Lyons 1983) and Kohlberg (1984) for coding moral orientation or stage. We included their questions so that we might place our women on their maps of intellectual and ethical development and assess the adequacy of the maps themselves. (See appendix A for the interview guide.)

We interviewed women who were recent alumnae of or currently students in formal educational settings as well as in what we came to call the "invisible colleges"—human service agencies supporting women in parenting their children. We chose to focus on families and schools rather than women in the workplace because we had to limit the size of our sample. We realize, however, that the contributions and perspectives of working women, even those with well-established careers, are often overlooked or dismissed. A number of recent books have addressed this problem (Gornick 1983; Kanter 1977; Keller 1983; Ruddick and Daniels 1977; Wallace 1982).

The women included in this study were drawn from nine different academic institutions and "invisible colleges." Of the 135 women we interviewed, 90 were students enrolled in one of six academic institutions. These colleges and schools differ markedly among themselves in educational philosophy and in the composition of their student bodies. They include a prestigious women's college with a curriculum fashioned after the male Ivy League college; a long-established progressive college with a coeducational adult-education program serving a rural population widely diversified in terms of social class; a private, coeducational, liberal arts college known for its arts program; an inner-city community college serving a mixed ethnic and less advantaged student body; an innovative "early college" that provides a baccalaureate program to girls and boys who have completed two years of high school; and an alternative urban public high school that serves minority students who are the same age as the "early college" students but are considered at risk for dropping out of school.

In each of these formal educational institutions we chose, in consultation with the administration and faculty, students who were likely to be representative informants—that is, representative of a diversity of ages, major interests, degree of engagement or alienation from the institution, and level of academic performance. At some of the sites we were able to include students and alumnae who had been interviewed one or more times during their undergraduate years as participants in previous studies that one of us had conducted. Of the ninety women from these six sites, we had earlier interviews with twenty-five women, gathered over a period of one to five years.

In addition to the women interviewed in formal academic settings, we interviewed forty-five women from the family agencies that deal with clients seeking information about or assistance with parenting (the "invisible colleges"). Formal educational programs take relatively little interest in preparing students for parenting and other social roles traditionally occupied by women. By exploring how women learn and think about learning in the invisible college, we hoped to cast light on less well known strategies for promoting women's education and development that are practiced in out-of-school settings.

Although most institutions in our society are shaped and directed by men and masculine perspectives, the agencies and programs for very young children and programs to support mothers in caring for children are likely to be among the few exceptions; these are usually organized and staffed by women. We wanted to know what kinds of institutions for promoting growth and development women would create for themselves if they were not so dominated by masculine images, theories, founders, or administrators. We thought this venture especially worthwhile since many of the "students" in the "invisible colleges" found formal education, at best, problematic.

We had yet another motive for including women from the programs for parents. Since mothering—the traditional role for women—has at its center the teaching of the next generation, we were particularly interested in how maternal practice might shape women's thinking about human development and the teaching relationship. We expected that by listening to women talk about mothers and mothering, we might hear themes that were especially distinctive in the woman's voice. We also anticipated that the wisdom women gained through maternal practice and "maternal thinking," as philosopher Sara Ruddick calls it (1980), might be particularly illuminating to those educators and human service providers interested in promoting human development.

We located these women in three different family agencies. One agency, in one of the nation's most isolated, impoverished rural areas, works with needy teenage mothers by providing mentors who are close to their own age and are also mothers. The second is a network of self-help groups for parents who are working to overcome a history of child abuse and family violence. The third is a children's health program with a preventive emphasis that serves rural families by keeping the mothers' needs and perspectives in mind while delivering medical and other services to their infants and small children. We were able to obtain second interviews with fifteen of the original forty-five women a year after the first interview was completed.

Bringing together people of such diverse ages, circumstances, and outlooks departs from common practice in psychological research. Researchers usually study highly homogeneous samples, typically white, middle- and upper-class, male undergraduates who are easy targets for university-based studies. The diversity of the population we studied provided us with an unusual opportunity to see the common ground that women share, regardless of background. Including women from different ethnic backgrounds and a broad range of social classes enabled us to begin to examine and see beyond our own prejudices. It also allowed us to examine the injustices of the society by comparing women who were challenged and stimulated by the most elaborate of educations with women who were essentially uneducated, having attended schools that only confirmed their fears that they had no intelligence to cultivate. We heard something of the powerlessness and voicelessness experienced by women struggling to grow up at the edges of the society where families are buffeted by such uncontrollable forces as irregular, stultifying, and demeaning work; chronic violence; widespread addiction to drugs and alcohol; and inadequate and unsupportive institutions of all varieties. We talked with many women who endeavored to gain a sense of voice and the power of their own minds against great odds.

ANALYSIS OF THE INTERVIEWS

Blind Coding. We separated out the sections of the interview that were designed to yield specific scores based on the theoretical and empirical work of Perry, Kohlberg, and Gilligan. These sections were scored independently by coders who were "blind" to (unaware of) the women's age, ethnicity, social class, institutional base, and other factors.

Particularly important to us in this first phase of the analysis was the scoring of the section of the interview that we designed to elicit information on the woman's assumptions about the nature of truth, knowledge, and authority. When we began our analysis by classifying the women's data using Perry's scheme, we found that the women's thinking did not fit so neatly into his categories. There were digressions of thought ("Do you want me to talk about what society says or what I think?"), twists and turns in perspectives, themes (for instance, the importance of firsthand experience and of gut reaction), and elaborations of points of view that we simply had not anticipated. It was our continued, and often heated, discussion of the disagreements first over our classifications and then over the classification system itself that led to some of the insights from which this book emerged.

Our work and classification system differs from Perry's in yet another way. In Perry's scheme, there is a clear sequential ordering of positions and, although he does not claim they represent an invariant developmental sequence since individuals can retreat or temporize, he does believe that each position is an advance over the last and that the ultimate end point in the move out of dualistic thought is what he calls "commitment within relativism." Harvard is clearly a pluralistic institution that promotes the development of relativistic thought. What we believe Perry heard in his interviews with men and captured so well in his developmental scheme is the way in which a relatively homogeneous group of people are socialized into and make sense of a system of values, standards, and objectives. The linear sequence in development stands out clearly when the context in which development occurs is held constant.

When the context is allowed to vary, as it did in our study, because we included women of widely different ages, life circumstances, and backgrounds, universal developmental pathways are far less obvious. We describe in this book epistemological *perspectives* from which women know and view the world. We leave it to future work to determine whether these perspectives have any stagelike qualities. The question of why and when women shift from one mode of knowing to another, as many of our women evidently did at points in their lives, is an important, though difficult, one—and is not well addressed by our data, which, for the most part, are limited to single interviews with individuals. However, we draw on the retrospective accounts of the women about their life changes, as well as on some repeated interviews with the same woman over the course of several years, to speculate about different developmental sequences or trajectories.

Building on Perry's scheme, we grouped women's perspectives on knowing into five major epistemological categories: *silence,* a position in which women experience themselves as mindless and voiceless and subject to the whims of external authority; *received knowledge,* a perspective from which women conceive of themselves as capable of receiving, even reproducing, knowledge from the all-knowing external authorities but not capable of creating knowledge on their own; *subjective knowledge,* a perspective from which truth and knowledge are conceived of as personal, private, and subjectively known or intuited; *procedural knowledge,* a position in which women are invested in learning and applying objective procedures for obtaining and communicating knowledge; and *constructed knowledge,* a position in which women view all knowledge as contextual, experience themselves as creators of knowledge, and value both subjective and objective strategies for knowing.

We recognize (1) that these five ways of knowing are not necessarily fixed, exhaustive, or universal categories, (2) that they are abstract or "pure" categories that cannot adequately capture the complexities and uniqueness of an individual woman's thought and life, (3) that similar categories can be found in men's thinking, and (4) that other people might organize their observations differently. Furthermore, the small number of women in our sample who fell into the position of silence makes these observations particularly tentative and underscores the need for continued efforts to understand the developmental consequences of severe violence and social isolation. Our intention is to share not prove our observations.

Removing the Blinders. After all the "blind" Perry, Gilligan, and Kohlberg coding was completed and the positions recorded, we conducted what we called a *contextual analysis.* We reassembled the interviews and reread them many times, paying particular attention to the life story. We developed a number of coding categories designed to capture the ways in which women construe their experience of themselves as developing beings and experience their learning environments. Among the coding categories were ten bimodal dimensions we called *Educational Dialectics* (see appendix B)—including, for example, "Rational vs. Intuitive" (What methods are used for analysis? What methods are valued?), "Personal vs. Impersonal" (What is the relationship between self and the content of one's learning?), and "Being with Others vs. Being Alone or on Own" (What arrangements for learning are preferred and have been experienced? Collaborative or solitary? Cooperative or competitive?). We designed these dimensions, keeping in mind that both modes could be valuable and adaptive and, under ideal circumstances, both would be promoted in educational practice. We suspected that in women one mode often predominates whereas conventional educational practice favors the other mode. We suspected that when the women's mode is treated as deficit, women come to believe that they cannot think and learn as well as men. The deprecation of these modes of thought must also discourage men from cultivating their capacities for such strategies for knowing.

In our contextual analysis we adopted a stance of trying to honor each woman's point of view, method of explanation, and standard of evaluation even as we grouped their responses. We asked ourselves: "What are the problems this woman is trying to solve? What is adaptive about the way she is trying to accommodate to the world as she sees it? What are the forces—psychological or social—that expand or limit her horizons? What are the metaphors that she uses to depict her experience of growth and change?" One growth metaphor in particular reverberated throughout the women's stories of their intellectual development. Again and again women spoke of "gaining a voice." "Voice" was added to the Educational Dialectics as another major coding category.

We then devised a labor-intensive method for a contextual analysis of the data collected within each coding category so that the woman's own meaning and experiences could emerge. When we found an idea that might be encompassed by one of the dialectical categories or an idea that suggested gaining a voice, we would underline the text in the interview. We then copied verbatim the most salient quotes and grouped them by epistemo-logical position. The very process of recopying the women's words, reading them with our eyes, typing them with our fingers, remembering the sounds of the voices when the words were first spoken helped us hear meanings in the words that had previously gone unattended. We moved back and forth between these excerpts and the unabridged interviews. This enabled us to maintain a dual perspective, hearing the statements as exemplars of a particular epistemological position but hearing them also in the context of the woman's whole story. Slowly we were able to record how differently each theme was construed by women with different ways of knowing.

Our manner of proceeding was remarkably similar to the process Hay-akawa (1964) describes dictionary editors using to define new words as they enter the language. Editors read extensively in the popular and professional literature. Whenever they come upon a rare word or a word with an unusual meaning, that word and the sentence in which it is used are recorded on a separate card. Then the editors take all the cards that have accumulated for a word, reading them with care, discarding some, dividing the rest according to the several senses of the word. Discerning the meaning of each word from its context, the editors write a definition for that word at that point in history. Just as editors are able to hear new meanings of words emerging, by following a similar procedure we heard in the women's voices meanings neither we nor others had imagined.

The Metaphor of Voice and Silence

In her 1978 book *Silences,* Tillie Olsen documents the history of women writers and points out the relative silence of women as literary voices. In the twentieth century, only one out of twelve published and acclaimed writers is a woman. The burgeoning field of sociolinguistics focuses on male and female patterns of discourse, sex-linked language, and sex dif-ferences in conversational patterns (Bernard 1972; Dubois and Crouch 1976; Lakoff 1975; McConnell-Ginet, Borker, and Furman 1980; Thorne and Henley 1975; Thorne, Kramarae, and Henley 1983). "Women's talk," in both *style* (hesitant, qualified, question-posing) and *content* (concern for the everyday, the practical, and the interpersonal) is typically devalued by men and women alike. Women talk less in mixed groups and are interrupted more often. By the late 1970s feminist sociologists and historians had begun to describe and contrast the private domestic voice of women with the public voice of men and to tie such differences in voice to sex-role socialization. And Carol Gilligan had begun to write about hearing "a different voice" as women talked about personal moral crises and decisions.

What we had not anticipated was that "voice" was more than an academic shorthand for a person's point of view. Well after we were into our interviews with women, we became aware that it is a metaphor that can apply to many aspects of women's experience and development. In describing their lives, women commonly talked about voice and silence: "speaking up," "speaking out," "being silenced," "not being heard," "really listening," "really talking," "words as weapons," "feeling deaf and dumb," "having no words," "saying what you mean," "listening to be heard," and so on in an endless variety of connotations all having to do with sense of mind, self-worth, and feelings of isolation from or connection to others. We found that women repeatedly used the metaphor of voice to depict their intellectual and ethical development; and that the development of a sense of voice, mind, and self were intricately intertwined.

The tendency for women to ground their epistemological premises in metaphors suggesting speaking and listening is at odds with the visual metaphors (such as equating knowledge with illumination, knowing with seeing, and truth with light) that scientists and philosophers most often use to express their sense of mind. Physicist Evelyn Fox Keller (Keller and Grontkowski 1983), tracing the metaphorical uses of vision in the history of Western intellectual thought, argues that such analogies lead to a favored model for truth and the quest for mind. Visual metaphors, such as "the mind's eye," suggest a camera passively recording a static reality and promote the illusion that disengagement and objectification are central to the construction of knowledge. Visual metaphors encourage standing at a distance to get a proper view, removing—it is believed—subject and object from a sphere of possible intercourse. Unlike the eye, the ear operates by registering nearby subtle change. Unlike the eye, the ear requires closeness between subject and object. Unlike seeing, speaking and listening suggest dialogue and interaction.

We note in passing one early manifestation of the feminine predisposition toward connection and conversation. Three- and four-year-old girls are much more likely than their masculine peers to choose the telephone as a preferred toy (Bowlds 1985; Connor and Serbin 1977).

We also note that philosophers and scientists who use visual metaphors to connote "mind" value the impairment of that sense. Thus moral philosophers argue for "blind justice" and donning the "veil of ignorance" so that "she" (justice) may choose impartially without either considering the intimate and the particular or anticipating the consequences. Similarly, the scientist tries to approach his studies "blind" or "double blind" so that he, too, may be removed from the influence of the particular. Attempts to blind the seeing knower have made it difficult for the scientist and the philosopher to acknowledge the role the knower plays in the construction of knowledge. Indeed, it is only now that there is widespread recognition among scientists and philosophers of the importance of "putting the knower back into the known" as they come to understand how intentional blindness limits what one can "see" with the mind's eye.

By holding close to the women's experience of voice, we have come to understand conceptions of mind that are different from those held by individuals who find "the mind's eye" a more appropriate metaphor for expressing their experience with the intellect. By telling us about their voice and silences, by revealing to us how much they could hear and learn from the ordinary and everyday ("hearing the grass grow and the squirrel's heart beat"), women told us about their views of the world and their place in it. We adopted the metaphor of voice and silence as our own. It has become the unifying theme that links the chapters in our story of women's ways of knowing and of the long journey they must make if they are to put the knower back into the known and claim the power of their own minds and voices.

In the chapters that follow, we will return many times to Perry, Gilligan, Ruddick, Keller, and other theorists and researchers whose work touches and informs ours. We discuss their views and findings as they intersect with ours. Our conversation with the theorists is an important part of the story we tell.

During the five-year life of our project, we encountered many other people who were exploring questions of gender and value perspectives and others who were beginning to demonstrate a masculine bias in theory, research methodology, and criteria for the nature of truth. We acknowledge that we are part of a Zeitgeist. Our work is also embedded in a larger context of feminist theory about voice and silence. What perhaps distinguishes our work is that we put flesh and bones on theory by tracking in individual lives the ideological perspectives laid out by others.

Ideally, we would wish the reader the satisfaction of discovery and the pleasure of insight that we experienced during the months of collecting, reading, and discussing our interviews with women. Much of what we now know and want to communicate in this book came to us as *fresh* knowledge, even though, upon reflection and a retrospective look at our own and others' prior writings, we realized that this knowledge was not new but had been, for us, underground, unarticulated, intuited, or ignored. It was as if the voices of the women, their words on paper, and our own process of reading together and culling the interviews for meaning gradually and profoundly modified the lens we brought to the project. As we worked, we were aware of the gradual shifts in our perspectives on the nature of scientific inquiry, on feminist theory, on developmental stages and sequences, and on the nature of human adaptation and potential. The stories of the women drew us back into a kind of knowing that had too often been silenced by the institutions in which we grew up and of which we were a part. In the end we found that, in our attempt to bring forward the ordinary voice, that voice had educated us.

PART I

THE WAYS OF

KNOWING

1

Silence

Where language and naming are power,
silence is oppression, is violence.
—ADRIENNE RICH, 1977

A WOMAN WE CALL Ann described being locked into a world of silence throughout her childhood and early adult years: "I could never understand what they were talking about. My schooling was very limited. I didn't learn anything. I would just sit there and let people ramble on about something I didn't understand and would say, Yup, yup. I would be too embarrassed to ask, What do you really mean?" Trying to find meaning in the words that others spoke was painfully difficult for Ann, but talking with others was even more terrifying. Feeling dumb, Ann was certain that no one could understand her, or that if someone did, it would be only to tell her she "had it wrong." "I had trouble talking. If I tried to explain something and someone told me that it was wrong, I'd burst into tears over it. I'd just fall apart."

Responding to the demands and status conferred by motherhood and to the support of a children's health program, Ann had just begun to acknowledge and cultivate her intellectual capacities. Ann's story of herself as a knower—the notions that she had adopted, questioned, and replaced—weaves in and out of the first chapters of this book. She is a particularly articulate spokesperson for adolescents and adults who have only begun to think about thinking.

In this chapter we begin our description of women's ways of knowing with the simplest way we could discern. While only two or three women viewed the world from this perspective at the time of the interview, others, like Ann, described the outlook in retrospect. These silent women were among the youngest and the most socially, economically, and educationally deprived of all those we interviewed. We met them in the social agencies for parents, not on the college campuses. We recognize that the designation of *silence* is not parallel to the terms we have chosen for the other epistemological positions; nevertheless, we selected it because the absence of voice in these women is so salient. This position, though rare, at least in our sample, is an important anchoring point for our epistemological scheme, representing an extreme in denial of self and in dependence on external authority for direction.

Feeling "Deaf and Dumb"

Figures of speech suggesting gaining a voice were used repeatedly by many of the women we interviewed to describe how they experienced their own growth and development—particularly the growth of mind. Such images, however, were conspicuously absent from the descriptions given by the women of silence.

Even though each of the women had the gifts of intelligence and of all their senses, they were unaware of the potential of such gifts. While no one was actually "deaf and dumb," this metaphor suggests their experience more accurately than does "gaining a voice." They felt "deaf" because they assumed they could not learn from the words of others, "dumb" because they felt so voiceless. As one person said, "Someone has to show me—not tell me—or I can't get it."

In trying to understand the experience of voice for the silent women, we searched their stories for all references that had, by the broadest stretch of the imagination, any association with the idea of voice and found that one theme stood out in bold relief: Words were perceived as weapons. Words were used to separate and diminish people, not to connect and empower them. The silent women worried that they would be punished just for using words—any words. The following examples give the flavor of their experience:

I deserved to be hit, because I was always mouthing off.

I don't like talking to my husband. If I were to say no, he might hit me.

I had to get drunk so I could tell people off.

The baby listens to him. Men have deep voices. But me, I can't do anything with him.

At home people talk about you. People know your business and everything else. . . . Lots of rumors are always going around.

The silent women lived cut off from others in a world full of rumor and innuendo. Words arise out of wrath, and they provoke wrath. One young woman described the war of words that was waged in the aftermath of her father's being sent to jail for their incestuous relationship. "Nobody liked me. Everybody used to make fun of me. This girl came over and beat me up and she said, 'I wouldn't spit on you if your guts were on fire!' Then the landlord yelled at me—not my mother—because the house was such a mess. It was all too much for me to handle, so I ran away." The young woman had only one way to think of herself: "I was a loudmouth. I didn't think nothing of telling someone where to go." She conceived of her voice as aggressive and incriminating.

While we found in these interviews a few descriptions suggesting the barest experience of dialogue with others, there were no indications of dialogue with "the self." There were no words that suggested an awareness of mental acts, consciousness, or introspection. When asked to finish the sentence "My conscience bothers me if . . . ," Cindy, a pregnant fifteen-year-old, wrote "someone picks on me." She did not comprehend words that suggest an interior voice that could give herself mental directions and exhortations.*

Experiencing Disconnection

Although the silent women develop language, they do not cultivate their capacities for representational thought. They do not explore the power that words have for either expressing or developing thought. Language is a tool for representing experience, and tools contribute to creative endeavors only when used. Language—even literacy—alone does not lead automatically

---

* See Jaynes (1977) for a historical account of the development of consciousness and the experience of voice in humankind.

to reflective, abstract thought (Scribner and Cole 1981; Sigel and Cocking 1977). In order for reflection to occur, the oral and written forms of language must pass back and forth between persons who both speak and listen or read and write—sharing, expanding, and reflecting on each other's experiences. Such interchanges lead to ways of knowing that enable individuals to enter into the social and intellectual life of their community. Without them, individuals remain isolated from others; and without tools for representing their experiences, people also remain isolated from the self.

The seminal work of Russian psychologist A. R. Luria (1979, 1981) was one of the first attempts to describe structures of thought held by those who had not developed their capacities for representational thinking. He interviewed illiterate peasants still living a medieval way of life at the time of the Russian Revolution. To distinguish practical from conceptual forms of thought, Luria (1979, pp. 77–80) asked the peasants to solve problems whose content was presented in the form of words divorced from the peasants' practical experience, such as: "In the far north, where there is snow, all bears are white. Novaya Zemlya is in the far north. What color are the bears there?" By following their answers, Luria determined if they were able to draw conclusions based on logical deductions from linguistic propositions as well as from their actual experience. Unable to work from words for making inferences, the peasants would say such things as, "If you want an answer to that question, you should ask people who have been there and seen them," "We don't talk about what we haven't seen. What I know, I say, and nothing beyond that," "Your words can be answered only by someone who was there, and if a person wasn't there, he can't say anything on the basis of your words."

While Luria's peasants had considerable difficulties working and learning from the verbal accounts of others, these interview fragments suggest that they speak with a high degree of confidence in the knowledge they have gained through their own observations, experiences, and actions. The repeated use of the pronoun *we* in the interviews also intimates collaborative efforts and shared learning. Although the peasants' world may exclude meaningful learning and communication with those beyond their immediate experience, one may assume that they live in the midst of a richly populated community where common experiences are readily shared and understood.

Unlike Luria's peasants, the silent women have no more confidence in their ability to learn from their own experience than they have in learning from the words that others use. Because the women have relatively underdeveloped representational thought, the ways of knowing available to them are limited to the present (not the past or the future); to the actual (not the imaginary and the metaphorical); to the concrete (not the deduced or the induced); to the specific (not the generalized or the contextualized); and to behaviors actually enacted (not values and motives entertained).

Unlike Luria's peasants they have no sense of "we-ness" with others. Their difficulties with establishing the most basic connections with others are dramatically illustrated by Bonnie's inability to find meaning in the cries of her baby, an inability that seems similar to the difficulties she experienced in trying to find meaning in the words used by others. When her baby was first born, Bonnie thought all her daughter's cries sounded alike. Later Bonnie realized that her daughter's cries could be differentiated.

> There are certain cries to a baby. If they want to be held, or if they want a bottle—things like that. I never used to listen to her cries. I used to pick her up and put a bottle in her mouth. I thought that's all babies wanted. You put a bottle in the baby's mouth and she'll be quiet. That was before I kind of realized that there's more than just a bottle. For some reason, I never thought about changing her diapers. I don't know why. I couldn't. It never clicked in my head to change her diaper. There are some things that just wouldn't click in my head that I should have done. Now I think of all those nights that I could have just changed her diaper.

Bonnie's retrospective account leads us to believe that assuming the responsibilities of parenthood had encouraged her to move out of silence, and that with this move she had become more able to find meaning in her daughter's utterances.*

Obeying the Wordless Authorities

The inability of the silent women to find meaning in the words of others is reflected also in their relations with authorities. While they feel passive, reactive, and dependent, they see authorities as being all-powerful, if not overpowering. These women are aware of power that is accrued to au-

* Several studies suggest that it is not uncommon for immature adolescent mothers to have difficulty communicating with their infants and conceptualizing their infant's psychological states and needs (Epstein 1982; McLaughlin et al. 1979; Osofsky and Osofsky 1971).

thorities through might but not through expertise. They do not envision authorities communicating their thoughts through words imbued with shared meanings. In their experience authorities seldom tell you what they want you to do; they apparently expect you to know in advance. If authorities do tell you *what* is right, they never tell you *why* it is right. Authorities bellow but do not explain. They are unpredictable.

The women see blind obedience to authorities as being of utmost importance for keeping out of trouble and insuring their own survival, because trying to know "why" is not thought to be either particularly possible or important.

Cindy depended almost completely on authorities for direction. She could not consider abortion because her mother doesn't approve of abortions. When asked why her mother doesn't approve, she said it's because her grandmother doesn't approve. When asked why her grandmother doesn't approve, she said, "I don't really know. She just says she doesn't believe in them."

Cindy then went on to say that she, her mother, and her grandmother belonged to a very strict religion and "we, in our religion, don't believe in abortion." Asked why their religion opposes abortion, she said that no one had ever explained the reasons to her. "They didn't say; they just said we didn't believe in them." The wordless/mindless authorities carry great weight.

Even if the authorities explained their reasoning, there is little evidence that the silent women could imagine themselves actively listening to the authorities' ideas, understanding what they were saying, and then choosing to obey. The commands and the actions are undifferentiated—like puppets moving with the jiggle of a thread. To hear is to obey.

The actions of these women are in the form of unquestioned submission to the immediate commands of authorities, not to the directives of their own inner voices. Because their own inner representations or thoughts do not control their behavior, the women are given such labels as immature, impulsive, having a short attention span, acting-out, hyperactive, delinquent, psychotic, and so on.

Feeling cut off from all internal and external sources of intelligence, the women fail to develop their minds and see themselves as remarkably powerless and dependent on others for survival. Since they cannot trust their ability to understand and to remember what was said, they rely on the continual presence of authorities to guide their actions, if they do not act on impulse. Those adolescents with no confidence in themselves as knowers, when faced with the responsibility of motherhood, cling desperately to their own mothers and other authorities for guidance. Cindy, anticipating the birth of her first child, would not let her mother out of her sight. "I go wherever she goes. She has a hard time getting away from me now. I told her I didn't know that much about babies. If it started to choke or something, I wouldn't know what to do." Another very young mother recalled similar anxieties. "After I had the baby, I had a fear of being by myself. I just felt scared that there would be something that I did not know about. I didn't know what was going on. Right now I know most of it, but—you know, before you thought that you were dumb. Being nervous . . . lost. I thought I was the dumbest one of all." She, like Cindy, was flooded with panic at the thought of losing contact with her mother.

Maintaining the Woman's Place

The extreme sex-role stereotypes that the silent women accept reflect the powerlessness they have experienced. Men are active and get things done, while women are passive and incompetent. This view undoubtedly helps the women make sense of their own dependence and deference to authorities. The culture, needless to say, supplies many experiences that maintain and nourish such notions. As Ann recounted, "I was brought up thinking a woman was supposed to be very feminine and sit back and let the man do all the stuff. . . . You just had to have a man."

Unable to understand what others were talking about and having no sense of her own ability to figure things out, Ann relied on her husband to do everything. She believed that if he were to die, "I would be lost." In actuality, it was she who supported the family financially and raised the children. Given her husband's drinking, violence, and thefts of the family's meager resources, Ann might have seen him as life-threatening to both her and her children, rather than as a source of security.

Another woman explained her dependence on a brutal, violent husband in terms similar to Ann's. "The only reason I did not kick him out a long time ago was 'cause I was afraid I just wouldn't live. I didn't know how to do anything. I couldn't—I was just scared to death." Although the silent are by no means the only women in our sample who have experienced sexual and physical abuse, they are notable for their inability to speak out to protest. Thinking for themselves violates their conceptions of what is proper for a woman. Another woman said, "I didn't think I had a right to think. That probably goes back to my folks. When my father yelled, everybody automatically jumped. Every woman I ever saw, then, the man barked and the woman jumped. I just thought that women were no good and had to be told everything to do."

These women are passive, subdued, and subordinate. However powerless their men may feel, it is agreed that the women will be even more powerless. The men to whom they subjugate themselves, while being very loud, are remarkably inarticulate. A seventeen-year-old described such a husband: "Sometimes he loses control. He gets mad at the baby and then he hauls off and swings at me. So I do whatever makes him happy. As long as he is happy, I am happy. I'm afraid to say no, as he might hit me." This woman even aborted her second pregnancy on her husband's orders: "He told me that I should have it done. I was listening to everyone." Some months later, the husband decided that he wanted another child. Responding to the jiggle of the thread, she submitted, although she wanted no more children and was deeply worried about her ability to care for the child they already had.

The silent women see life in terms of polarities. Everything is either big or little, good or bad, win or lose. "Every now and then, he thinks that he's always right in something and I'm not. Or else, I'm always right in something and he's not. That's what it is with us." They believe that if another were to win, they, of necessity, must lose. Because the women see themselves as slated to lose, they focus their efforts on assuring their own continued existence during a losing battle. They wage their struggle for survival without an awareness of the power inherent in their own minds and voices and without expectation of cooperation from others. It is a stacked game waged against men who seem to be bigger and better, men who think they have a right to be the winner, to be right no matter what the circumstances.

A young mother who has begun to orchestrate her own life looked back on a time when she felt totally dependent on others for the most minute and constant directions, because she could not trust her mind either to know or to remember anything. Trying to explain why she stayed with a man who battered her for ten long years, she said, "You know, I used to only hear his words, and his words kept coming out of my mouth. He had me thinking that I didn't know anything. But now, you know, I realize I'm not so dumb. . . . And my own words are coming out of my mouth now." She now connects the voicelessness, the confusion of tongues, and her blind obedience with her belief that she had been mindless—dumb.

Conceiving the Self

"How would you describe yourself to yourself?" "Is the way you describe yourself now different from the way you would have described yourself in the past?" "How do you see yourself changing in the future?" We borrowed these questions from Carol Gilligan and her colleagues (Belenky 1978; Gilligan 1977, 1982; Lyons 1983) and posed them, not to ascertain what each person's "real self" was actually like but to understand how women with different ways of knowing might conceptualize the self—to see what kind of picture of the self they were able to hold out for their own viewing. The themes we found in the self-descriptions were intricately related to the themes we found in the ways the women thought about thinking.

Describing the self was a difficult task for all of the women we interviewed, but it was almost impossible for the silent ones. One young woman, deeply puzzled by such questions, said, "I don't know. . . . No one has told me yet what they thought of me." As is common with young children (Rosenberg 1979), these women believe that the source of self-knowledge is lodged in others—not in the self. Because the silent women live in a world with so little conversation, those who might have told them about themselves and helped them begin building a sense of self never said a word.

When the women finally attempted to answer the question, they described themselves in terms of their own movements in and around the geographic space that surrounded them. Again, Cindy presented the clearest example:

> I am a person who likes to stay home. Before I got pregnant, I used to go and come as I wanted. [*Is the way you describe yourself now different from the way you used to describe yourself?*] Yah, 'cause I used to describe myself as not being home. And now I am home all the time. So that's about the only thing that is different.

Another young mother spoke in remarkably similar terms. Although she could not describe herself, she could say how she was changing.

> When I was younger I was constantly running the streets. I was never staying home or anything like that. And now that I've got my

kids, I stay at home with my kids more often. As a matter of fact, I very seldom go out. I'm just with my kids more than what I would have been back then.

When these women attempt to describe the self, they remain standing in their own shoes, describing only what they see gazing outward from their own eyes. They find no vantage point outside of the self that enables them to look backward, bringing the whole self into view. They do not even provide a portrait of the physical self. No one says anything like, "I'm tall, fat, blonde." None could describe the changes she anticipates would or should occur in the future. As Cindy said, "I haven't thought about the future."

Seen but Never Heard

Women who live in silence have much in common with each other. While we will explore in chapter 8 the family contexts that give rise to each of the ways of knowing, we will touch on the familial roots of such silence here.

Each of the women grew up in great isolation and, for one reason or another, seldom had friends while growing up. The families themselves were cut off from the broader community. Discussion with family members and anyone else was actively discouraged. "I was never able to ask for help before. I was brought up to think that you kept your troubles to yourself. You didn't talk about them. I never let anyone know what was going on—what was troubling you. You just didn't do it."

In their families at least one parent routinely used violence rather than words for influencing others' behavior. Typically, the other parent remained silent and compliant, often victimized. A woman described the pattern. "My father was a first-class bastard. The only way he believed of doing anything was with a club, a stick, or with the back of his hand. All you had to do was to breathe."

The bleak images that emerge from these stories suggest childhoods with neither much play nor dialogue. Growing up without opportunities for play and for dialogue poses the gravest danger for the growing child. Lev Vygotsky (1962, 1978) and his colleagues suggest that exterior dialogues are a necessary precursor to inner speech and an awareness of one's own thought process. They argue that play itself is a precursor to symbolization and meaning-making. Play provides children with their first experiences in creating metaphors, where an object and the children's actions combine to suggest other objects and events. Thus, when children saddle a stick and ride off on their imaginary horses, the stick becomes a symbol for the horse; and that symbol and the power of their own ideas govern their behavior. The physical stick becomes a tool that helps them dislodge the meaning of horse from its usual embodiment. In play, it is the meaning chosen by children that determines the significance of the stick. Play provides children with their first opportunities for adopting a pretend or a hypothetical stance.

In the ordinary course of development, the use of play metaphors gives way to language—a consensually validated symbol system—allowing for more precise communication of meanings between persons. Outer speech becomes increasingly internalized as it is transformed into inner speech. Impulsive behavior gives way to behavior that is guided by the actor's own symbolic representations of hopes, plans, and meanings. Without playing, conversing, listening to others, and drawing out their own voice, people fail to develop a sense that they can talk and think things through (Vygotsky 1978). (See also Gardner 1982; Luria 1961, 1979, 1981; Piaget 1951.)

A recent review (Belenky 1984) of research on the intellectual and ethical development of the deaf illustrates the importance of face-to-face conversations and the utilization of an effective symbol system. This research suggests that development is greatly facilitated when hearing-impaired children are raised in a sign-rich environment, enabling them to be full participants in any ongoing dialogue. Children with early access to signed language do not have the difficulties with impulsiveness, social immaturity, and academic work that routinely plague hearing-impaired children who have not had such opportunities. When deaf children, adolescents, or adults who have been denied these opportunities move into a stimulating, sign-rich environment, not only do they learn that form of the language very rapidly, they largely overcome the developmental delays that are typical of deaf children (Furth 1973). Such findings lend support to Vygotsky's claims about the importance of outer speech for the development of inner speech and the sense of mind.

The silent women like Ann and Cindy had had little formal schooling or had found school to be a place of chronic failure. Most had been passed along from one grade to the next, as all those words just slipped past. Typically, educators assume that by the time a child enters school he or she will have a well-developed capacity for representational thought (Sigel and Cocking 1977). In most schools, beginning with the earliest grades, the main focus is on the manipulation of symbol systems. However, these symbols and metaphors are likely to be dissociated from the concrete referents, actions, and experiences that the symbols stem from and express (Greenfield 1972; Greenfield and Lave 1982; Scribner and Cole 1973, 1981). Furthermore, most schools continue to provide meager opportunities for the give-and-take of dialogue. Verbal interchanges tend to be unilateral and highly constrained as they are predominantly teacher-initiated and -dominated (Sirotnik 1983). As one adolescent said, "In school you get detention for talking to others."

While the lack of dialogue and the dissociation of language from experience is problematic for all children, concentrating on the written forms of the language before children have developed proficiency in wielding the oral forms is likely to be tragic. The silent women had limited experience and confidence in their ability to find meaning in metaphors were lost in the sea of words and numbers that flooded their schools. For them school was an unlikely place to "gain a voice." For them the experience of school only confirmed their fears of being "deaf and dumb."

We believe that individuals grow up to see themselves as "deaf and dumb" when they are raised in profound isolation under the most demeaning circumstances, not because of their genetic intellectual endowment. That anyone emerges from their childhood years with so little confidence in their meaning-making and their meaning-sharing abilities as did Ann and Cindy signals the failure of the community to receive all of those entrusted into its care.

2

Received Knowledge: Listening to the Voices of Others

She never did and never could put words
together, out of her own head.
—GEORGE ELIOT
Middlemarch

FOR ANN, becoming a mother—rather than having had a mother—
provided the first profound experience of human connection. She said,
"My life was really, really dull. The only thing that really stands out is the
birth of my children. That's the only important thing that has happened
to me ever. So that is about it."

Many women, like Ann, experience giving birth to their children as a
major turning point in their lives. Often, parenthood initiates an epistemological revolution. In response to our question, "What was the most
important learning experience you have ever had?" many mothers selected
childbirth. It is as if this act of creation ushers in a whole new view of
one's creative capacities.

Ann had to reassess herself as a knower when she anxiously assumed
the responsibilities of parenthood. Being responsible for a dependent infant
can easily bring into question a world view that assumes that one is "deaf
and dumb" and dependent on others for care. Although such a view might
have been highly adaptive for surviving a demeaning childhood, it is inadequate as a basis for mothering. Needing help, Ann turned to the experts

at a children's health center and found with relief that they knew everything. They were easily available and highly responsive.

> They were wonderful. It just seems that they know all the answers to
> everything that has to do with children. They have been just ev-
> erything to me. They've been like a security blanket. You know,
> I can call anytime something happens—even at night time. They
> are always friendly and cheerful. You don't have to be afraid.

The authorities were very supportive of Ann. Responding to her in her
own terms, they drew out her questions, concerns, and ideas and refrained
from dictating theirs. Unlike many professionals, they continually emphasized *her* competence, not theirs. "Their confidence in me really spurred
me on. I'd walk in there and they would say, You're wonderful. You're a
great mother, you're great. I'd walk out of there feeling so good. I'd feel
like I could tame the world." The authorities also used language that she
could understand. "When you need them, they take the time to explain
things. You know, they are all very patient; they spell it all out—'cause
I'm not too smart."

Finding that she could hear, understand, and remember the things
they taught her, she began to think of herself as a learner for the first time.
"They teach you everything there is to know about babies. If it has anything
to do with health problems, a nutritional problem—there's nothing I could
learn anywhere that they haven't already taught me." Ann became a store-
house of information. Not only could she receive knowledge from others
but she could also pass that knowledge on to others. "I now feel very
knowledgeable as far as kids go. I advise all my friends with kids, you
know. I say, 'This is what I've learned at the center.' I've learned a lot. I
feel like I could go in there and they could hire me—you know—that's
how much knowledge they have given me."

Listening as a Way of Knowing

Unlike the silent, who think of themselves as "deaf and dumb" and are
unaware of the power of words for transmitting knowledge, women who
rely on received knowledge think of words as *central* to the knowing process.

They learn by listening. As Rachel, a college freshman, said, "I enjoy listening to discussions. I find I am doing okay just through listening."

A young student who had moved from jail to a community college was exhilarated to hear from other students—"those who know."

> The women who are students here know so much and I know nothing. I like to sit back and just listen to what they have to say. A lot of times I feel that way. When I started college I knew nothing and it was for me to get from both the students as well as the professor. Because when I walked into the classroom, I was twenty-one years old and these grown people sitting in the room—they had to know something.

This woman experiences listening as a very active and demanding process. "You get a real taste, putting your mind to work—sitting in class concentrating—listening and really getting something from it. Unless you're taking something *in*, it's not worth it."

The ideas and ideals that these women hear in the words of others are concrete and dualistic. Things are right or wrong, true or false, good or bad, black or white. They assume that there is only one right answer to each question, and that all other answers and all contrary views are automatically wrong. These characteristics were so salient in William Perry's (1970) description of this perspective that he named this outlook *dualism*.

While received knowers can be very open to take in what others have to offer, they have little confidence in their own ability to speak. Believing that truth comes from others, they still their own voices to hear the voices of others. Rachel described the voicelessness she experienced her first year at college: "I don't talk in class very much myself. I am not a participator. Everybody at college is sort of outgoing. Everybody I've met has a vocabulary a mile long. My problem is—is that I have trouble communicating. Even if I have it straight in my head, it's very difficult for me to talk." Another woman recalled a similar experience. "Before I used to talk and the wrong words would come out and people would say, 'What, what?' They would never understand me."

LISTENING TO FRIENDS

The received knowers are frequently surprised and relieved to hear others saying the very same things that they would say. One of the adolescent mothers felt nervous talking with most people, but not with her aunt who had both a baby and a husband exactly like hers.

> My aunt is special. She acts more like my best friend. I could tell her
> what I could tell nobody else. Anything and everything. We don't
> get nervous talking to each other. We think alike. Like you can
> talk to somebody about how you feel and they feel the same way
> you do. The same thing. It's really strange—like, see, her husband
> and my husband are just about the same—they don't talk at all.
> They're alike. We're alike. We think the same things.

Ginny, upon entering an early college and depending on receiving
knowledge from others, was delighted to find that her ideas were identical
to those held by her new friends. "Everyone in my dorm gets along. We
do about the same thing. Usually if one person doesn't like it, everybody
else is not going to like it—because we have the same thoughts about it."

The young received knowers have a literal faith that they and their
friends share exactly the same thoughts and experiences. They relish having
so much in common and are unaware of their tendency to shape their
perceptions and thoughts to match those of others. Looking to others for
knowledge they are likely to be among those who could see the emperor
in full regalia. (See, for example, Asch 1952; Costanzo and Shaw 1966;
Saltzstein, Diamond, and Belenky 1972.) The young women who hold this
perspective celebrate and magnify the experiences of similarities and intimacies with others. To us these relationships have a symbiotic quality
that was not observed among the other women we interviewed when they
described their friendships. But as we will see, it is exactly these kinds of
relationships that provide women with experiences of mutuality, equality,
and reciprocity that are most helpful in eventually enabling them to dis-
entangle their own voice from the voices of others. It is from just such
relationships that women seem to emerge with a powerful sense of their
own capacities for knowing.

Ginny provided an example of how transformative relationships with
peers could be. As she said, during her freshman year she and her friends
had "the same thoughts," but by the time they were sophomores, each
spoke with a distinctive voice. In her second interview she said,

> Before, you know—you do just what everyone else does. You don't
> show what you really feel. You don't just stand out and say some-
> thing. You didn't even know what your friends were thinking
> half the time—they'd just agree with everyone else. Now we tell
> each other just about everything. If you get really mad—you just

go yell at them! They'll sit there and listen to you. They don't get really upset. They usually try to stop [doing whatever it was]. You are really open. It really helps. You know, they'll listen and that's helped a lot, I think.

Ginny and her friends had learned to speak with one another in a way that they could cultivate most easily in relationships imbued with care, trust, and endless discussions.

LISTENING TO AUTHORITIES

Although most women find the powers of their voice and mind most readily in relationships with friends, those who think that they *receive* all knowledge are more apt to think of authorities, not friends, as sources of truth. They equate receiving, retaining, and returning the words of authorities with learning—at least with the kind of learning they associate with school.

Ann, we saw, could learn verbatim what was right and wrong from the experts at the children's health center. Although Ann gained considerable confidence in her ability to receive, retain, and even pass on knowledge that others gave her, she still feels that she could not generate facts and ideas through reflection on her own experience. "I have to rely on the experts. I've never been one to make decisions. Whenever I need to know about something, I have to go to someone who knows. I have to rely on them because I don't know anywhere else."

Before, feeling "deaf and dumb," Ann depended on authorities to actually *do* things for her. Later, she heard "right answers" coming from authorities in words that she could understand. She depended on authorities to *tell* her what was right and wrong. Before, she wanted to be shown.

Angela entered a prestigious college as a received knower. When Angela sought "truth" she looked to authorities and imagined it being passed on from one person to another. "I tend to trust more what a professor says than what a student says. I have more faith in the teacher, that what he says is correct and concise. Whereas the student might be giving her opinion; it might not be the right one. The teachers are always more or less right." And why are professors always more or less right? Angela says, "They have books to look at. Things that you look up in a book, you normally get the right answer." As typical of received knowers, Angela did not realize that authorities have the capacity for constructing knowledge. In their view authorities must receive "truths" from the words of even higher authorities.

They assume that all authorities are infinitely capable of receiving and retaining "the right answer" with impeccable precision.

Wanting to do the right thing but having no opinions and no voice of their own to guide them, women in this position listen to others for directions as well as for information. A young woman from the community college found guidance in her brother. "My brother—he is a person who will talk and reason with you. He's calm. He's calm and he will talk things out. I listen to him—whatever he tells me. Whatever my brother tells me, I do. I do it because I know that he has thought it out and he's not going to tell me nothing but the best that's for me. I trust him." It was not her own but her brother's voice that this young woman heard and followed as she searched for the ideas that would give shape to her life.

Maria, too, had always looked to her elders for the "right answer." As a foreign student entering a progressive early college, she was faced with many changes, most prominent of which was the lack of adults willing to guide her every move. She was accustomed to being told everything. "In my old school, they give the courses they want to give. You don't choose your courses. And my parents—you know, they told me that it is wrong when whatever I was doing was wrong. Then if something was right, they would tell me." In her new school Maria had to make her own choices and be responsible for those choices. She worried how she would do that. "At the beginning, I wasn't so sure that I was gonna be bossing myself, doing whatever I wanted, and [still be able] to choose what was right and wrong. Still—you know—I still have a long way to go. [Laughs.] I don't know." "Bossing" herself without the guidance of adults' dictates, while facing cultural diversity, made the task seem overwhelming: "I really don't know. I really don't know—[long pause]—what's right and what's wrong yet. I mean, anything can be wrong or anything can be right. [Little laugh.] Anything!" No matter how contradictory, "truth" is still absolute to Maria. She has no way to determine "truth" without the aid of an authority.

Being recipients but not sources of knowledge, the students feel confused and incapable when the teacher requires that they do original work. Angela had a professor who burdened her with just such expectations. She said he was wrong—"wrong in his method of teaching," not, of course, "wrong because of what he said." Knowing all the "right answers" himself, the professor refused to pass them on. "He would make you feel stupid. He would make you find the answers on your own. And he wouldn't even give you any hints on what the right answers were." How could she learn if the teacher refused to pass along his knowledge?

Those who think of knowledge as received rather than constructed assume that the authorities can dispense only one right answer for each problem. As Rachel said, "In most cases, there is a right or a wrong answer. No matter how you say it, it is right or it is wrong."

Ann, who had learned so much from the agency staff she consulted, considered our question "What would you think if two of your advisers from the children's center gave you the opposite advice?" The possibility that her advisers might give her contradictory information filled her with amazement. Her teachers, who knew everything, could not possibly disagree. She exclaimed, "Oh, that's never happened!! I don't know what I would do. . . . Maybe I'd go eeny, meeny, miny, mo. I don't know really." If faced with this dilemma, Ann would have to choose between her advisers' views on the most arbitrary basis.

We posed a similar question to another woman, working out of the same perspective, about her child's teachers. She, too, seemed astonished at the idea that the authorities might disagree with one another. Equating status with truth, she would "go with the head teacher," the one who had authority over the other.

In response to the same question, Rachel said she would gather her facts by going "right to the studies." But then we asked her, "What if the studies disagreed with one another?" "I don't know," she responded. "They'd make two studies—and one is—?" Her voice trailed off in bewilderment. Her resolution to the unimaginable dilemma was: "I'd just have to go with what most people believe in." Bigger is better. The bigger in status or in number, the greater in truth.

For those who adhere to the perspective of received knowledge, there are no gradations of the truth—no gray areas. Paradox is inconceivable because received knowers believe several contradictory ideas are never simultaneously in accordance with fact. Because they see only blacks and whites, but never shades of gray, these women shun the qualitative and welcome the quantitative.

The women holding this outlook are never consciously ambivalent, never attracted and repelled by the same object. It is all or nothing with them. If a thing is partly wrong, it is worthless. The remarks of one young mother illustrate the point.

> I only like to read the books that LaLeche League [an organization supporting breastfeeding of infants] recommends. Because the other books—I know that there will be things in them that I might not agree with. And then it kind of ruins the whole book for me, even if it's just *one* thing in there that the doctor or author rec-

ommends that I don't agree with. Suddenly, the whole book is—
you know, not as interesting.

The received knowers are intolerant of ambiguity. They believe that
for every poem there is only one correct interpretation. They have trouble
with poetry. It is not clear to them why poets do not just say right out
what they mean. Literature is full of equivocation, and they do not see
why this is so. They are *literal*. They read the lines and follow the plot;
they cannot read between the lines. There isn't anything between the lines.
People who see things there are making them up. They add up the facts,
the numbers, and the items marked "correct." They like predictability.
They want to know what is going to happen when. They like clarity. They
want to know exactly what they are expected to do—what they are "responsible for." As a young college student said, "I think my mind is really
structured. I have to have things all clearly laid out in front of me."

In deciding whether to take a course, students in this position want
to know how many tests and papers there will be and how long the papers.
How many pages of how many books will they have to read? Exactly how
will their grade be computed? They think that grades should take the form
of hourly wages: The longer you work, the higher the grade.

These women either "get" an idea right away or they do not get it at
all. They don't really try to *understand* the idea. They have no notion,
really, of understanding as a process taking place over time and demanding
the exercise of reason. They do not evaluate the idea. They collect facts
but do not develop opinions. Facts are true; opinions don't count. As a
college student says,

> There are absolutes in math and sciences. You feel that you can ac-
> complish something by—by getting something down pat. Work
> in other courses seems to accomplish nothing, just seems so
> worthless. It doesn't really matter whether you are right or wrong,
> 'cause there really isn't a right or wrong. Um-hm. [Laughs.] You
> can't say. It's all guesswork.

She "learns" the material; that is, she stores a copy of it, first in her
notes and then in her head. She does not transform the material; she files
it "as is." She willingly reproduces the material on demand, as on an exam;
but she feels betrayed if the teacher asks her to "apply" it or to produce
materials on her own.

Unlike the silent women, who do not see themselves as learners at
all, these women feel confident about their ability to absorb and to store

the truths received from others. As such, they perceive themselves as having the capacity to become richly endowed repositories of information. They may be quite successful in schools that do not demand a reflective, relativistic stance.

Most of the women we interviewed who still held this perspective came into our study through the social service agencies or were very young students just beginning their college careers. In the highly selective colleges, where we were able to talk with the same students several times over a span of one to four years, it was exceedingly rare for a student to continue looking outside the self for the source of knowledge. In pluralistic and intellectually challenging environments, this way of thinking quickly disappears. If it is not rapidly dislodged, the student is likely either to drop out or to be pushed out early in the game (Clinchy and Zimmerman 1982; Goldberger 1981).

Many colleges, as well as some high schools, are becoming increasingly dedicated to dislodging this perspective and stimulating the development of more adequate conceptions of knowing. (See also Parker 1978; Perry 1970, 1981.) Reliance on authority for a single view of the truth is clearly maladaptive for meeting the requirements of a complex, rapidly changing, pluralistic, egalitarian society and for meeting the requirements of educational institutions, which prepare students for such a world.

Comparing Men and Women as Knowers

Perry's dualist position describes men who hold an outlook that is similar to the received knowledge position we found in women's data. Dualism, the simplest way of knowing that Perry observed, was held only briefly, if at all, among members of his elite college sample. Perry's men particularly dichotomize "the familiar world of Authority-right-we as against the alien world of illegitimate-wrong-others" (1970, p. 59). Indeed, in the 1950s when Perry first observed this way of thinking, he thought he had located at Harvard College the authoritarian personality type that T. W. Adorno, Else Frenkel-Brunswik, Daniel Levinson, and R. Nevitt Sanford (1950) had recently depicted in *The Authoritarian Personality*, a most important study of that era, because deference to authority and ethnocentrism was central to both accounts.*

While some of the women we interviewed most certainly saw authorities as the source of the "right answers" and "truth," they did not align themselves with authorities to the extent Perry described occurring among men. This world of "Authority-right-we" was quite alien to many women.

The women in our sample seemed to say "Authority-right-they." They were as awed by but identified less with authorities than did Perry's men. This might be accounted for by the fact that the women were, on the whole, less privileged in terms of social class than were the men Perry studied. To test this notion we examined the interviews of the young, privileged women attending elite colleges who held the perspective of received knowledge. While these women also seemed to be awed by authorities, they appeared to identify more with outsiders than with the authorities, as did their less privileged peers.

That women identify less with authorities might be accounted for by the fact that the authorities they meet do not include women in their "we." The women we interviewed spoke, for instance, of science professors who communicated their beliefs that women were incapable of making science. They spoke, all too often, of authorities who wielded their power to extract sexual favors. Women are much less likely than men to find authorities of either sex who are willing to act as sponsors and mentors for them (Hall and Sandler 1983; Speizer 1981). Even in the modern age in which these women are living, it is still relatively rare for them to find authorities of their own sex as models. Leadership in public life still rests predominantly on male shoulders. The schools that these women attended were very likely to have ignored the works and achievements of women in developing the curriculum. Their male classmates were more likely to have taken and held the floor for presenting their views and to have received a greater amount and more effusive public praise for their achievements than were the women (Hall and Sandler 1982; Richardson, Cook, and Macke 1981; Treichler and Kramarae 1983). Some of the colleges we studied had few or no women as senior administrators and few or no women as senior tenured faculty, and the female faculty members that were hired had to scramble for temporary, annual appointments, year after year.

That women are less inclined to see themselves as separate from the

* On observing authoritarian attitudes disappear on subsequent reinterviews as students progressed through college, Perry concluded—as did Nevitt Sanford (1956, 1962) and Jane Loevinger (1976) when following still other populations—that it would be better to consider authoritarianism as a function of the individual's level of development rather than as a personality type per se.

"theys" than are men may also be accounted for by women's rootedness in a sense of connection and men's emphasis on separation and autonomy—the major themes that theorists like Carol Gilligan (1982), Nancy Chodorow (1978), and Jean Baker Miller (1976) evoke to understand gender differences in human development. Men, valuing distance and autonomy, are more exclusionary. To them, "we" clearly means "not they." Women valuing connection and intimacy are much more likely to be inclusionary, finding "they" and "we" to be intertwined and interdependent.

One of the reasons that we call this position "received knowledge" is that these women focus on listening; Perry's dualistic men seem to lecture more than listen. Given the women's tendency toward conformist thinking and their subordinate status, it is not surprising that women cultivate their capacities for listening while encouraging men to speak.

Studies on gender differences in the use of language suggest that the world is commonly divided into two domains: speaking and listening. Studies repeatedly, but not always consistently, find that it is the men who do the talking and the women who do the listening (Argyle, Mansur, and Cook 1968; Aries 1976; Bernard 1972, 1981; Fishman 1983; Swacker 1976; Thorne and Henley 1975; West and Zimmerman 1983; Zimmerman and West 1975). These sex differences are large and persistent and have been noted in private as well as in public domains.

The observed behavior is markedly discrepant with the commonly held stereotype that men remain silent while women gab. That the actual behavior of the two sexes can be so discrepant from the stereotype is puzzling. As Gloria Steinem (1981) suggests, it may be that when women talk, their behavior is not compared with men's but is assessed against a standard that holds that women should be seen but not heard. When women deviate from a standard of absolute silence, they are thought to be loquacious and out of line.

Entering into the Moral Community

Feeling capable of hearing, understanding, and remembering, women at the position of received knowledge have faith that if they listen carefully enough they will be able to do the "right thing" and will get along with others. Because they look outward for moral knowledge, their moral judgments conform to the conventions of their society—or to the dictates of the nonconventional they choose to emulate (see, for example, Kohlberg and Gilligan 1971).

While the moral language of the silent women centers around such concepts as "mine," "I want," "I feel," "I had to," and "they made me," the received knowers have a different vocabulary. In trying to grasp moral ideas, they substitute such words as "should" and "ought" for the words "would" and "have to" when trying to solve a moral problem. They strive to subordinate their own actions to the symbolic representations of the good that they are able to hear in the voices of others.

Sharp dichotomies and intolerance of ambiguity mark the moral thinking, as well as the thinking in general, of the received knowers. An act is right or wrong, good or evil. A person is a leader or a follower, a shepherd or a member of the flock, a speaker or a listener. (We note in passing that the Protestant Reformation focused on the right to speak and listen to God directly.)

Thinking that everything must be "either/or," the received knowers assume that in times of conflict between the self and others, they must choose one or the other but not both. Women worry that if they were to develop their own powers it would be at the expense of others. Not only are they concerned to live up to the cultural standards that hold that women should be the listeners, subordinate, and unassertive; but they also worry that if they excel, those they love will automatically be penalized (Gilligan 1982; Horner 1972; Miller 1976; Sassen 1980). Conventional sex-role standards establish a routine for settling self-other conflicts when they occur. Men choose the self and women choose others.

One theme emerges in the moral thought of these women, a theme Miller and Gilligan find central in the women's voice: They should devote themselves to the care and empowerment of others while remaining "selfless." Accepting that the world is and should be hierarchically arranged and dualistic, the received knowers channel their increasing sense of self into their growing capacity to care for others. A college freshman's comment illustrates the point. "I think that I'm a nice person, but I want to be even better to people. I don't mean nice, like I am in love with myself, but I mean that I am nice—polite to people, that kind of thing. I like to be nice to people—to help people." She did not want anyone to think that she might be the object of her own care. The fear of diminishing others by acting on one's own behalf suggests a destructive power that cannot be tolerated by those whose emerging identities center on being nice, caring for others, and refraining from inflicting hurt.

The women who hold the perspective of received knowledge feel quite comfortable with advancing themselves, only if it is clear that self-advancement is also a means of helping others. A college student describes how she finally decided to act on her own behalf: "A turning point came when I decided to get off welfare and go out to work, so I could show the children that I tried to make things better for them. I always felt put down when I was on welfare. If I got a decent job and I could do the things for my children that I always wanted to do, I think I might stop putting myself down."

That they can strengthen themselves through the empowerment of others is essential wisdom often gathered by women. Many of the women we interviewed cited empowering others, either by helping them, by listening and understanding, or by teaching others what they know as an important experience; but it was particularly important to women at the received knowledge position. As one woman said about the self-help group she worked with, "Being in this group and helping others has given me more confidence. I wouldn't have been able to help someone cross the street before, let alone solve any kind of real problem, you know."

For the received knowers, being thrust into roles of responsibility for others helps erode the belief that they are dependent on "them" for "truth." For these women it is the act of giving rather than receiving that leads them to a greater sense of their capacity for knowing and loving. A woman who arrived at college following a long stint with Alcoholics Anonymous describes the transformation she experienced when two different people asked her to be their sponsor: "Helping others, I think, is the one thing that really helped me. I think that that was, bar none, probably the greatest experience I have had in my life. . . . When someone is baring their soul to you, it is hard not to like them. For the first time, I found friends."

A community college student describes her journey from juvenile delinquent to prison inmate, to paid prisoner advocate, to mother, to college student, and to a person with a carefully detailed career line spread out before her. She accounted for the changes. "Being on the outside but helping those on the inside; taking on the responsibility of dealing with a child; paying the bills; not slighting the landlord. All those things have changed me. Sticking to the grindstone and going by the books. I care about all of them. It's been beautiful. I love helping people."

One of her classmates who had also scraped bottom told a similar story about a relationship with a friend. "There is one person who really had something to do with helping me to get where I am. She was a person who had no confidence in herself. If I had very little, she had none." She and her friend had consulted the same psychiatrist. The doctor told her that the friend was mentally ill and without hope. That he had written off her friend violated a human trust. That he had shared his pessimism violated a professional trust as well. She invited this woman to room with her and they lived together for many years.

> I decided then and there that I was going to prove him wrong. I decided that I was going to help her become a person and to really love life. I encouraged her to go to school, to follow her interests, to meet people. Now she has met someone she loves very much, and she is going to be married. I feel that she has become a total person. She is happy now. She is not as crazy as the psychiatrist thought she was. To see her happy . . . the idea that she knows what love is. . . . We both came from a loveless background. It has made me feel, hell, one day that will happen to me, too, if I want it to happen.

She imagines that some day her life might also "begin to soar," and that she, too, "will become a total person."

Women typically approach adulthood with the understanding that the care and empowerment of others is central to their life's work. Through listening and responding, they draw out the voices and minds of those they help to raise up. In the process, they often come to hear, value, and strengthen their own voices and minds as well.

Conceiving the Selfless Self

Because women at the position of received knowing believe that all knowledge originates outside of the self, they must look to others even for self-knowledge. Thus, the conscious attempts at identity formation that these women make are often expressed in such questions as "What do they think of me?" and "What would they want me to become?" As a college freshman said, "Everything I say about myself is what other people tell me I am. You get a pretty good idea of yourself from the comments that other people are saying about you."

If one can see the self only as mirrored in the eyes of others, the urgency is great to live up to others' expectations, in the hope of preventing others from forming a dim view. Thus, women of received knowledge listen carefully and try hard to live up to the images that others have held up to them. They are especially at the mercy of authorities' judgments. If someone in a powerful position tells such a woman that she is wrong or bad or crazy, she believes it. One woman recalled the experience. "Before, I would have said, 'I am no good. I don't know how to think. I don't know how to do anything right.' Whatever bad things people could say about me were true. If *they* thought it, it had to be true."

That others can have such power in defining how people see themselves undoubtedly helps to account for the fact that people born with all their senses intact and with a reasonable share of gray matter can be discouraged so completely from recognizing, utilizing, and developing their intellectual powers. However, if the authority seeks out and praises the intelligence of those who hold the position of received knowledge, it may alter their whole way of seeing themselves.

> I never used to think of myself as smart. I really didn't. Most people have never really said anything about it, because I'm quiet. My mother doesn't know how smart I am. My sister never thought I was very intelligent. I never had evidence of it before. So coming here I see myself reflected by other people, what they think of me. It really boosted my ego—I needed that, I think.

Authorities hold considerable leverage and can be in particularly strategic positions to help these women find the power than can reside in their own minds, as well as in the minds of others. A student at a community college felt transformed by a mentor who acknowledged her intelligence and competence:

> I've been through the mill. I've been on public assistance. I got myself off public assistance. I've been in jail. I got myself out of jail. I am a twenty-three-year-old who is pushing forty-five and who has come a long way. Now I am the sort of person who sets pretty high goals.

She traveled the distance from jail to college because she had found a boss through a prison work-release program who really believed in her.

> From the beginning, when I didn't even know one end of a sentence— you know, I am supposed to be a clerk-typist. I didn't know anything. He pushed me and he pushed me. He was behind me. In the beginning, I didn't know what he was doing. I came to know

that every time he said something, it meant something. I would go about in some way trying to correct whatever was wrong and trying to improve whatever was right. He has given me—I can't explain. He told me to never say he's given me anything. That it is me who has done it. Okay, I know that I've done it, but he has given me the ability to say "I've done it!" [Laughs.]

In looking outward for self-knowledge, received knowers organize their attempts at self-definition around the social expectations that define concrete social and occupational roles. One says, "I am a mother," while another says, "I'm going to be a highly placed official in the Department of Corrections."

Conceptions of right and wrong are likely to be as black and white when defining the self as when defining the moral. The either/or thinking that these women confine themselves to makes it difficult for them to express notions of "becoming"—evolution, growth, or development. One woman, when asked if she could describe herself fifteen years into the future, said, "I don't think so. I could be anywhere. I don't want to think about that. That's like opening a Christmas present in October." The self-descriptions offered by these women seemed relatively static. On the rare occasions when the women tried to describe how they saw themselves changing, they focused on how the social and occupational roles they expected to occupy would be different from those they currently held. For example, a student's success in her community college encouraged her to imagine the possibilities of becoming upwardly mobile. She seems to equate occupational change with changes in the self, as do others who hold this perspective. "I am going up the ladder. I am ready for the next step and I want to go on to better things. I want to change from a dull job and go into a career." Passing grades in academic or corporate structures seem to give these women rather literal rungs on a ladder for providing firm benchmarks for gauging their own progress.

A sharply contrasting image of growth and change is provided by a classmate who operates out of a more complex perspective. This woman, locating the agent of reflection, self-evaluation, and change more clearly within, said, "I could be a better person. I can do whatever I want to do. I can think about what I want to become. I can change my mind backwards and forwards. I can become what I want to become." Unlike those who assume that all knowledge is received, this woman has begun to see her own thoughts orchestrating the changes that govern her life.

Women who are unable to see themselves as growing, evolving, and changing are at a particular disadvantage in a rapidly changing technological society. Indeed, as we will see in the next chapter, when their social arrangements collapse and demands for change are imposed, many women must look inward for self-truths, abandoning the notion that they can and should rely on others for knowledge, direction, and care.

The women discovering the limits of received knowing bring this era to an end with critiques of their tendency to subordinate their own perceptions and judgments to those of others, of their selflessness, and of their voicelessness: "I don't think I'm in control. I'm very easily influenced by either side. My counselor told me about something, and I'm very influenced by it. A friend may say something else, and I'm influenced by that! I'm not really in control of that. It's something that I have to work on." This woman saw that she had to find the means to make decisions if she was to have direction in life, a goal that was just beginning to assume importance. "I have no direction so it's easy for me to be pushed this way and that. I get stuck in indecision."

Rachel also struggled to hear what others said, convinced that they had all the right answers. She, herself, was quite speechless. Rachel's critique of her muteness and dependence harbingers its demise: "Well—I have a lot inside, but I have a difficult time in getting it out. I think my main problem is that I have trouble communicating. Even if I have it straight in my head, it's very difficult for me to talk."

Another student, also buffeted by the slightest change in the wind, looked outward for notions of right and wrong. "When I read things, I get very frustrated. I can read one thing and it seems to make sense. Then I read something else and that makes sense, and it would be conflicting views. I don't trust what I believe—how can I trust what I read—or how to know what's valid?" She outlined for herself the work that she must do to find anchorage within her own self. "When I listen to others, I get confused. If I were to listen to my deep-rooted intuition, I might be able to say 'That's right and that's wrong.' But right now in my own life, I cannot find what the right answer is." She understands that she must begin to listen to her own voice if she is to become clear and confident and to move on in her life.

3

Subjective Knowledge:
The Inner Voice

> There's a part of me that I didn't even know
> I had until recently—instinct, intuition,
> whatever. It helps me and protects me. It's
> perceptive and astute. I just listen to the
> inside of me and I know what to do.
> —Inez
> Thirty-year-old mother of three

SITTING WITH US at a kitchen table in an abandoned mill town in the Northeast, Inez, an intense, dark-eyed Colombian-American woman of thirty, had just finished summing up the story of her childhood and young adulthood—a story filled with pain and intimidation. She had spent years as the "dummy on the bottom," a worthless child, then a worthless woman. For most of her life she had been looking for a "safe place to hide." Inez grew up in a family with an abusive and alcoholic father and a mother who, according to Inez, avoided the truth about her husband for thirty-five years. Inez had come to equate authority with physical power and assertiveness with destructiveness. For most of her life she felt unloved and unlovable; she doubted that anyone could ever care for her. Having been shown over and over again by her father and brothers that women were supposed to remain in a position of silence and servitude, she did not trust her own judgment nor did she believe that any woman could "think and be smart." She married a man much like her father. She depended on him, and he abused her and their children.

Inez told a story of a woman of silence trapped in a world of brutal and belittling external authorities—a story we often encountered as women talked to us, although this one stood out in its tragedy and drama. Then Inez's story changed and she began to talk in terms seldom used by women guided by fear of authority. She felt she had grown beyond the person she had been for twenty-some years, the person who passively accepted her lot and never asked questions. On the contrary, she described her current self as "stubborn, opinionated, mouthy, and generous."

What is more, she no longer adhered to a dualistic perspective on truth and knowing. She was no longer subject to the dictates and whims of external authorities and no longer agreed with what some people thought was a simple matter of right and wrong. Things for her were not so clear-cut as before. She no longer thought of herself as dumb, as a know-nothing. She told us how her way of knowing and understanding the world had changed. "I can only know with my gut. I've got it tuned to a point where I think and feel all at the same time and I know what is right. My gut is my best friend—the one thing in the world that won't let me down or lie to me or back away from me."

Attending to her infallible gut instead of listening to external authorities, Inez left her husband, took a job as a child-care worker, using the skills she had developed as a mother, and saved her money to buy a motorcycle to prove to all that she could learn by herself and for herself. With pride, she told us how she mastered the machine totally on her own and now felt competent to service and maintain it. "The thing about my motorcycle—If I could feel about the rest of my life the way I feel about the motorcycle, I'm unbeatable." Although her confidence in herself was still shaky, Inez's future was brighter.

> I'm just getting to the point where everybody else starts. Do you understand what that means? Most people, when they leave home or graduate from high school, already have an idea of what they are worth. An idea that they go out and conquer the world. I'm just getting to where everybody else is at.

Something clearly had happened to dislodge Inez's assumptions, carried with her through her twenties, about her worth, her life options, and the nature of knowledge, learning, and truth. Inez had changed radically.

The Emergence of Subjective Knowing

The kind of change that Inez experienced is the center of our discussion in this chapter: from passivity to action, from self as static to self as becoming, from silence to a protesting inner voice and infallible gut.

For many of the women, the move away from silence and an externally oriented perspective on knowledge and truth eventuates in a new conception of truth as personal, private, and subjectively known or intuited; thus, we are calling this next position *subjectivism* or *subjective knowing*. Although this new view of knowledge is a revolutionary step, there are remnants of dichotomous and absolutist thinking in the subjectivist's assumptions about truth. In fact, subjectivism is dualistic in the sense that there is still the conviction that there are right answers; the fountain of truth simply has shifted locale. Truth now resides within the person and can negate answers that the outside world supplies.

The shift into subjectivism is, we believe, a particularly significant shift for women when and if it occurs. Our reading of the women's stories leads us to conclude that as a woman becomes more aware of the existence of inner resources for knowing and valuing, as she begins to listen to the "still small voice"* within her, she finds an inner source of strength. A major developmental transition follows that has repercussions in her relationships, self-concept and self-esteem, morality, and behavior. Women's growing reliance on their intuitive processes is, we believe, an important adaptive move in the service of self-protection, self-assertion, and self-definition. Women become their own authorities.

We encountered women from sixteen to sixty for whom the discovery of subjective truth was the most recent and personally liberating event of their lives at the point when we interviewed them; thus, women themselves attached the notion of growth or developmental progression to the shift from silence or conformity to external definitions of truth into subjectivism. Developmentalists in the past (Blos 1979; Erikson 1968; Kohlberg 1969; Piaget 1952) have noted that this kind of shift in orientation toward authority—from external authority, which binds and directs our lives, to an adherence to the authority within us—is one of the central tasks of adolescence. Other psychosocial theorists, including Abraham Maslow (1962) and David Riesman (1961), cite transcendence of social conventions and

* The "still small voice" is a biblical reference from 1 Kings 19:11–12, denoting the voice of God; Maimonides uses the phrase to refer to intuition.

pressure as an achievement of the mature or "autonomous" personality. What is remarkable in the stories of our women is that this seeming move toward greater autonomy is not tied to any specific age. Many of the women described listening to other voices for most of their lives, only to move into the subjectivist perspective at age forty or fifty, after years of raising children, managing households, or working outside the home. For Inez, the change began at thirty. For women, the freedom from social convention and definitions implied in the shift into subjectivism represents a move toward greater autonomy and independence. However, as we will show, it is also another step toward the kind of maturity that we call connected knowing, an orientation toward understanding and truth that emphasizes not autonomy and independence of judgment but a joining of minds.

Of the 135 women we interviewed, almost half were predominantly subjectivist in their thinking. It was not easy to absorb and generalize about the diverse stories we collected from this large group of women we categorized as subjective knowers. They appeared in every educational and agency setting included in the study. They cut across class, ethnic, age, and educational boundaries. At first it was difficult to see what linked the women in so diverse a group, but upon delving into their stories, we began to see how the subjectivists' assumptions about intuitive and private knowing can act as guideposts for our understanding the developmental pathways and byways in other facets of their lives.

Since the nature of thought and the ways of knowing associated with subjectivism have much in common with myths and stereotypes about women's thought in that it is intuitive and personalized, we must consider what the adaptive utility and drawbacks of subjective knowing are for women living in our society and times. In many non-Western and non-technological societies, subjective knowledge and intuitive processes hold a more esteemed place in the culture.* In a world that emphasizes rationalism and scientific thought, there are bound to be personal and social costs of a subjectivist epistemology. Women subjectivists are at a special disadvantage, as we shall see, when they go about learning and working in the public domain.

---

* In Western philosophy in the nineteenth and twentieth centuries, positivism gradually replaced the classical intuitivism represented by the work of Spinoza and Henri Bergson. Both of these philosophers held that it is *only* intuition that leads to the apprehension of ultimate reality. In Eastern religions and mystic philosophy, inner contemplation and intuitive understanding are primary routes to basic knowledge, if not to God.

WOMEN AND FAILED AUTHORITY

The majority of the women we classified as subjective knowers did not come from supportive, stable, and achievement-oriented families but grew up in families that were either less advantaged, more permissive, or frankly more chaotic than average. These women were not usually students in prestigious colleges but were in more experimental or community educational settings. Many had been school dropouts as younger women who only recently returned as adults to complete degrees or acquire new skills. Some of the women were not in school at all but were clients in social agencies—the "invisible colleges"—where they had come to seek help in and learn something about parenting. Many had been married and raised children. For these women, the shift into subjectivism seemed tied to factors that had little to do with their academic experience or with exposure to diversity of opinion that Perry sees as the main catalyst of the shift out of authority-dependent dualism. For these women, the shift in perspective on knowing was associated with recent changes in their personal lives outside the classroom or the college dorm.

Of course, there were a number of women subjectivists who could not tell us much about how they came to think the way they did. Sometimes the woman we were interviewing found it impossible to reflect on that period in her life in which she asked no questions and felt she had no answers, almost as if she had existed without language or voice or self in a kind of fugue state. She might say, "I've just changed," or "I'm just different now." Or she might be able to tell us when she changed but not why. The turning point often was a vividly remembered, precise moment in time—late one afternoon sitting on the porch after the chores were done or, for one woman, on a particular morning while looking at herself in the mirror. Some women, however, gave us detailed and explicit accounts of transformations in their understanding of the nature of truth and authority.

We can elaborate on the process of change and a common path of female development by returning to the story of Inez. We left Inez saying that she had radically changed from the passive, silent victim to the assertive woman who had discovered her "infallible gut." Throughout her twenties, Inez had been depressed. She had married young and borne three children in her late teens. Her husband, whom she married so she would feel less alone, also grew up in a Latino culture in which men were dominant, women submissive. There was considerable violence in her new family, a repetition of her childhood home, with much shouting and physical intimidation. The turning point for Inez occurred during a visit to her parental home in California, where she had retreated to escape the misery of her marriage. She reported that she was jolted out of her passive silent state (at age twenty-five) after being told by an aunt that her father was a child molester and was known in the community as "someone who fucked little girls." This discovery about her father reawakened memories of her own incestuous relationship with him when she was younger, which she had accepted as "the way things were." Suddenly her past fell into place—the jealousy between her and her mother, her brother's hatred of her, the innuendos of terrible things happening between her father and her girl cousins.

Inez told us that it was at this point, upon this visit home, that she became enraged at "the audacity of these people to treat me like that." "Something inside" her told her that she would have to "walk away from the past." By listening to this voice within (which was experienced more as an inchoate urging than as part of the self), and in rage and disappointment, Inez precipitously left her family and old community for good, divorced her husband, and with her children settled in an area remote from those old authorities—her father and her husband—who had taught her obedience and self-sacrifice. It was only later that Inez began to feel good about herself, after she had found a job, bought her motorcycle, joined several self-help groups, and entered therapy with a woman who represented for Inez a model of how to be powerful and also feminine. The affirmation she received that she was worth something was reinforced in a relationship with a boyfriend who introduced her to a part of herself that "I didn't even know I had—intuition, instinct, what I call my gut." The process of discovering her inner power—her subjective self—transformed her view of herself and her future. There was no school, no teacher, no book that taught her these lessons.

We met other such women who believed they were stupid and helpless. They had grown up either in actual physical danger or in such intimidating circumstances that they feared being wrong, revealing their ignorance, being laughed at. A large number of women we classified as subjectivists or as moving into subjectivism grew up without the protection of a father due to early divorce, neglect, or abandonment. Many subjectivists had had parents or husbands who belittled them or squelched their curiosity or chastised them for questioning. Remembering back, their world had felt unpredictable and fragile, insecure and impermanent. They had spent their lives looking for some faithful authority to whom they could attach themselves—if not this father, perhaps this boyfriend or this husband.

What comes through most strongly in these stories from women is the picture they paint of *failed* male authority. Society teaches women to put their trust in men as defenders, suppliers of the economic necessities, interpreters of the public will, and liaisons with the larger community. Women learn that men hold the power and in society's eyes have the ultimate authority. They are the esteemed teachers, the religious spokesmen, the medical, the military, the corporate, the respected creators. But, for many subjectivist women we interviewed, there was an absence of stable male authority in their personal lives. Their sense of disappointment and outrage was pervasive. Black women told us that their men had been "wasted" in wars, on the street, and in prison; now they had to go without men or to share them with other women. Black and Hispanic women spoke of disenfranchised men, men who themselves found no place in American society. Poor women talked of the years of trying to cope with the anger, despair, and eventual disappearance of the men on whom they and their children were hanging their hopes. Middle-class women talked about the emotional defections of their fathers or husbands who left to "find themselves" or start a new life.

It seemed as though education per se played a minor role in the shift into subjectivism for the majority of women. Instead of opening the world up to them, the kind of education and educators they encountered as children and adolescents were alienating and irrelevant to their lives. To us, it appeared that it was only after some crisis of trust in male authority in their daily lives, coupled with some confirmatory experience that they, too, could know something for sure, that women from these backgrounds could take steps to change their fate and "walk away from the past." For them, a return to education followed the onset of subjective knowing; it did not usher it in.

SEXUAL HARASSMENT AND ABUSE

A pervasive background theme in the women's stories of loss of trust in male authority was that of sexual harassment and abuse. Although we did not initially intend to collect information on sexual abuse, it became clear to us, after we started interviewing, that women spontaneously mention childhood and adolescent sexual trauma as an important factor affecting their learning and relationships to male authority. Midway into the study we began to survey the women systematically on their history of sexual and physical abuse. Our statistics are based on seventy-five women (fifty-five from the in-school sample and twenty from the social agencies).

Based on our data, sexual abuse appears to be a shockingly common experience for women. In our sample of seventy-five women, 38 percent of the women in schools and colleges and 65 percent of women contacted through the social agencies told us that they had been subject to either incest, rape, or sexual seduction by a male in authority over them—fathers, uncles, teachers, doctors, clerics, bosses. Abuse was not limited to any particular epistemological grouping of women in our study, nor was it limited to any specific class, ethnic, or age group; but the sense of outrage was most prominent among the subjectivists, who angrily recalled their past naiveté and silent submission. For them, their abuse was a current and vivid memory that they had not yet worked through. They tended to locate the trauma in time at an earlier period during which they had no sense of voice and an unquestioned trust in the authorities of their life.

Our statistics on incest are particularly alarming. Among the college women, approximately one out of five women described a history of childhood incest. Among the high-risk women from the social agencies that draw clients from families in which drug and alcohol abuse and violence are commonplace, almost one out of every two women reported a history of incest. We have no reason to doubt the veracity of the women's accounts, but even if some were to be discounted as doubtful or fanciful (as some clinicians claim), we believe that sexual trauma among women is a far more serious problem than is acknowledged by the medical and psychiatric establishment and the public at large.*

Some women indicated to us that their sexual history made them cautious around male professors, confused about "what was really going on," and consequently conflicted about receiving praise (see also Dzeich and Weiner 1984). Often the denial and silence that had been imposed upon them in the incestuous relationship carried over into present interactions with teachers who had power over them. As one woman observed, "My whole response to praise, my sense of what I can achieve and how I should achieve it is all wrapped up in my past [experience of incest]. I know it has affected my relationships with men and male professors. Maybe there are things in the professional relationship that ought not be there."

* Our findings confirm the findings from other recent research showing that sexual abuse of girls and women is far more frequent than earlier reports and clinical data indicated. Judith Herman (1981) reviews five major surveys since 1940 that report statistics on the incidence of sexual assault in childhood in the general population (Finkelhor 1979; Gagnon 1965; Kinsey et al. 1953; C. Landis 1940; J. Landis 1956). Herman reports that the results of these surveys are remarkably consistent. Between 20 percent and 35 percent of women reported a childhood sexual encounter with a male family member (father, stepfather, grandfather, uncle, or brother). Herman believes that the incidence of childhood sexual abuse is actually higher due to underreporting and a "conspiracy of silence" (Butler 1978). Diane Russell (1986), in her recently completed scientific survey of a representative sample of 930 women, reports an incidence level of 16 percent of women sexually abused by a relative before the age of eighteen, and 4.5 percent of women abused by their father before the same age. Given these new studies, it is astounding that, as late as 1975, one prominent psychiatric textbook (Freedman, Kaplan, and Sadock 1975) still estimated that the incidence of all forms of incest was only one in a million!

We believe that a kind of cognitive cloudiness pervades the thinking of many such women—they are literally unsure if they really know what they know and if their achievements are genuinely deserved. Not all these women, but some, like Inez, identify the eventual reaction to sexual abuse as one precipitating factor in their changing epistemology and move out of silence.

MATERNAL AUTHORITY AND THE WOMAN IN TRANSITION

Looking back on their childhoods, many of the women like Inez told us they had experienced themselves as outside or at the bottom of the power hierarchy. In their eyes, the public world was controlled by men, the experts with the credentials and the clout, those who seemed to know what they were talking about and could argue others down. They described the public truth these experts held as remote, mysterious, and inaccessible.

When such women are just beginning to make the transition into subjectivism, they are no longer willing to rely on higher status, powerful authorities in the public domain for knowledge and truth. Instead they consider turning for answers to people closer to their own experience—female peers, mothers, sisters, grandmothers. Although the women may still think of these people as authorities, they draw them from the private world of family and friends. Truth for these transitional women is particular and grounded in the firsthand experience of others most like themselves.

When we asked transitional women who they considered experts, they told us about grandmothers and mothers who "have lived a long time and experienced a lot" and who, therefore, "know about life" and "dealing with problems you're having day to day." Sometimes, when a benevolent mother or grandmother had been missing in her life, a woman would tell us about relying on a good friend who was like a sister to her or even on a "maternal" social agency that made her feel that she had some wisdom about raising babies. For example, Inez's female therapist was an important authority for her during her period of transition.

As we indicated earlier, an important step on the route to subjective knowing is the affirmation these maternal or nurturant authorities can provide for women in transition. Some of the women told us that agency staff were the first people *ever* to listen to them or to show an interest in what they had to say. By sharing reactions and solutions, whether about child-rearing, domestic problems, or weight reduction, by being given the opportunity to talk things over with a sympathetic, nonjudgmental person with similar experiences, a woman can begin to hear that maybe she is not such an incompetent, a dummy, or an oddity. She has *experience* that may be valuable to others; she, too, can know things.

The discovery that firsthand experience is a valuable source of knowledge emerges again and again in the stories of subjectivist women. Suddenly all they experienced in the course of living takes on new meaning—pleasing others sensitized them to people's moods and needs, placating family members or close friends taught them much about negotiation and groups, managing households taught them organizational and financial skills, raising children taught them about growth, health, and illness. Although they have not yet realized the power of their own minds and are reluctant to generalize from their experience to advise others, they begin to feel that they can rely on their experience and "what feels right" to them as an important asset in making decisions for themselves.

A nineteen-year-old mother who was a client in a health program for mothers and children described the discovery as follows:

> When my daughter was first born, there wasn't anybody that really had the right knowledge, the right answers. I would worry about it. . . . Do I raise her the way I want to? But I'd have questions, and if there wasn't an answer, I'd sit there and worry about it. And six more problems would come up and there was no one there to answer them. But it's changed a lot in the last year because Marcia, my counselor, was there, a sounding board. It made me realize that I'm all right. And sometimes now I think of something before somebody else thinks of it.

A Catholic woman of forty-eight who had returned to school out of a need to develop skills to support her children found support and affirmation in a women's discussion group provided for all reentry women in her college. She remembered the moment at which she knew she must change.

> I always thought there were rules and that if you followed the rules, you'd be happy. And I never understood why I wasn't. I'd get to thinking, gee, I'm good, I follow the rules. I do everything they tell me to, and things don't go right for me. My life was a mess. I wrote to a priest that I was very fond of and I asked him, "What do I do to make things right?" He had no answers. This time it dawned on me that I was not going to get the answers from anybody. I would have to find them myself.

So, she started back to school, discovered other women like herself who had lived through similar experiences, and began to think of herself as a knowing person.

One remarkable woman, age sixty-two, mother of six children and nurse for many years to a husband who was a stroke victim, knew that she was the person in the family on whom everyone leaned. Nevertheless, she felt that all the things she had done in her life were inconsequential; she saw herself as a "big negative." Her husband, before his illness, had "spent his life telling me how stupid I was." After his transfer to a nursing home, her fright over being alone and her depression drove her to a therapist, a woman who helped her see that what she had been doing all her life had some value. A door opened for her. "A man's advice to his son is that whenever he feels the need of a helping hand to look at the end of his arm and he'd find one. That's where I've been very blind. I haven't looked at the end of my arm. I've been giving myself a helping hand all my life. I can lean on me."

Whomever a woman finds to turn to—social agency, female relative, girlfriend, even a nurturant boyfriend—the significant educational action is the reassurance and confirmation that "maternal authority" provides her that she, too, can think and know and be a woman.

Perry's View of Men and the Shift Out of Dualism

Before turning to a more detailed description of subjective knowing that emerged for us from the stories of women, we want to examine the position of multiplicity that William Perry describes, which is similar to subjectivism in its emphasis on personal truth. We chose the term "subjectivism" as a more apt description of women's experience of inner knowing than Perry's term "multiplicity"; however, in most cases, the terms are interchangeable.

Perry implicitly locates the shift into multiplicity/subjectivism as occurring in early adolescence and explicitly links it to the process and impact of a liberal education and exposure to cultural pluralism. According to Perry (1970, 1981), the catalyst for the move is the simple and profound discovery that there is a diversity of opinion about what is good and what is right. With multiplicity, truth is no longer conceived as absolute and singular but multiple and infinite. The perception of multiple perspectives on truth and values is almost unavoidable for advantaged children growing up today, given their opportunities for international travel, discussions and debates with worldly parents and diverse friends, the popular media, and challenging liberal education and educators. Among the advantaged, only adolescents from the most culturally isolated and protected homes can easily remain naive dualists who believe that a benevolent authority out there holds the "right answers." In fact, Perry notes that dualists are rare at Harvard.

Based on his work with advantaged men, Perry observes that young people today realize that controversy and uncertainty are everywhere; even experts can disagree. Although at first the young person assumes that some opinions and some experts must be wrong if there is truly one right answer, this secure dogmatism collapses as first teachers, then professors and dormmates batter away at one's naiveté and outdated morality. What the young person has assumed to be "the right way," heretofore bolstered by an unexamined trust in authorities, is revealed to be only "my way" or "your way." Some people avoid the unsettling period of multiplicity by turning back to the safety and security of old authorities; but, for many others, authority begins to lose its potency as it loses its hold on "absolute truth."

The basic dilemma for the dualist who is moving into multiplicity, as Perry sees it, is how to position the self vis-à-vis defrocked authority. With the progression to multiplicity, the individual develops the capacity to carve out a domain in which all opinions are equally valid; everyone, including the self, has the capacity and the *right* to hold his or her own opinions. Early in multiplicity, the student expresses this as a belief that "in areas where authority doesn't have the right answers yet, I have a right to my own opinion." Eventually, when controversy and disagreement are seen as inevitable, there is a change in the nature of truth itself. Absolute truth will never exist, and the right-wrong criterion is irrelevant since, as one student put it, "Anyone's interpretation is valid if that's the way they see it. . . . I mean nobody can tell you that your opinion is wrong, you know." As Perry says, at this position "an opinion is related to nothing whatsoever—evidence, reason, expert judgment, context, principle, or purpose—except to the person who holds it" (1981, p. 85).

Unlike dualists, Perry's multiplists no longer mimic the teacher's opinion or memorize verbatim the words of the textbook; now they often insist that their opinion is as good as the teacher's. By the time he reaches college age, the average advantaged child, like Perry's Harvard men, has learned that everybody is different, everybody has opinions, and the business of the classroom is to express loudly what you believe and feel. Or so it goes in the stories of male multiplists as told to Perry.

In our reading of the male stories (as reported in Perry 1970), the male child begins to doubt the authority of his elders and to wrest power away from them, somewhat like the Freudian disposal of the fathers by the primal horde. His actions are cast in terms of *reason* and *right*, as he operates under the assumption of a natural order and the centuries-long belief in the "correctness" of male supremacy. He foresees his own future as an authority and stakes his claim to the intellectual terrain that has been falsely and unreasonably held by the fathers. It is his duty and right to do so. The boy's perception of the multiplicity of truth becomes a tool in the process of his separation and differentiation from others. His opinion distinguishes him from all others and he lets them know it. He maneuvers himself into the unassailable castle of subjective truth and defies anyone to challenge his position. He generalizes his belief in personal truth to mankind—"Each man is his own expert"—and becomes a protector and defender of the abstract right of others to believe what they want. It is only later, in the position that Perry sees as the next step beyond multiplicity, that sons rejoin fathers as equals by incorporating as their own the analytical methods and objective procedures for isolating truth that the intellectual elite value. As we shall see, the female stories are somewhat different.

Hidden Multiplists: Stories of Advantaged Women

Some of the women in our study were propelled into subjectivism in the same way as Perry's young men. We call this group of female subjectivists "hidden multiplists." These young women have backgrounds and values similar to Harvard men, that is, from middle-class to upper-middle-class families whose investment in liberal arts education is obvious. They are attending "good" schools, living out the parental expectation that scholastic achievement and higher education are desirable for the female as well as the male children. Often the family structure follows traditional stereotypes of the aspiring middle class: the successful, somewhat remote though admired father and the mother whose central and clearly expressed concern is caring for the family, even though she might have a job outside the home. The daughters from such families enter college with an unquestioned acceptance of family standards and ambitions only to find themselves confronted on all sides by alternative viewpoints and life-styles that open up a Pandora's box of possibilities.

Unlike the male student, who takes up the banner of multiplicity with vigor, the young woman usually approaches multiplicity much more cautiously. Although she may be exhilarated inside that she, too, can be freed from the stricture of external authority, she also feels at times overwhelmed with options and fearful of ultimately being alone in her choices. To take a stand against others means to isolate herself socially. She fears that engaging in combative measures in support of her opinion may antagonize and jeopardize her connections to others.

As Gilligan (1982), Miller (1976), and others have shown, separation and individuation can leave women feeling vulnerable and unconnected. Unlike the advantaged adolescent male, who has had years of practice in exploring and testing social limits, the adolescent female from a similar background has frequently been rewarded for her quiet predictability, her competent though perhaps unimaginative work, and her obedience and conformity. This kind of "good girl," when confronted with diversity and what seems to be the arbitrariness of truth and values, suddenly begins to feel that her world is unanchored. As one young women put it, "I never could have predicted the changes that I've made in this past year. Sometimes I feel like I'm on a speeding freight train and I have no control over events."

Life appears to be rich in opportunity, yet the "good girl's" own life may seem suddenly dull and impoverished. Although she senses that she is free to control her destiny, she does not feel in control nor able to take the risks that experimentation entails. Neither her parents nor society seem to her to support risk taking in women. This is the kind of woman whose parents tell her to develop enough marketable skills so that she will have something to fall back on if her husband loses his job, dies, or divorces her.

Erica's story is an illustration of this scenario. An academically talented sixteen-year-old in her first year of college study, Erica talked about the disjunction between her family's view of her and her own inner dreams.

> It seems like there are some things I want to do and I feel I'm going to disappoint them. Just like I might want to disappear for a year, or join the Peace Corps, or something. Maybe just go off and climb a mountain sometime. My parents have always given so much to my life that I would feel guilty not giving it back. . . . I think I mean a lot more to them than I want to right now.

To Erica, others appear to be much stronger, more assertive; she feels tentative, hesitant, unable to articulate her desires for fear of inadvertently offending or losing the other. She muses over whether she really wants people to get to know her well, and she tends to keep silent in groups, even though, like others who are predominantly subjectivist in their thinking, she firmly believes that "everyone should do and say what he wants."

One solution for hidden multiplists like Erica, who seem on the brink of letting go of their pasts and their dependence on external authorities, is to retreat into anonymity and surface conformity by adapting a wait-and-see attitude. They become the polite listeners, the spectators who watch and listen but do not act. In the classroom, they keep quiet while performing adequately.* Erica told us that she preferred to observe rather than reveal to others that she sometimes felt critical of their ideas. The ethic of the hidden multiplists seems to be that they should hear people out, since everyone has their own opinion of things and should be allowed to speak, but that they are under no obligation to accept or even consider others' ideas seriously. This ethic carries over into the dorm, where these women often find themselves in the role of sounding board: "I guess a lot of times I try to find my identity through someone else. So I like to be an ear, for me to listen."

These women reveal that their epistemology has shifted away from an earlier assumption of "truth from above" to a belief in multiple personal truths. The form that multiplicity (subjectivism) takes in these women, however, is not at all the masculine assertion that "I have a *right* to my opinion"; rather, it is the modest, inoffensive statement, "It's *just my opinion*." Their intent is to communicate to others the limits, not the power, of their own opinions, perhaps because they want to preserve their attachments to others, not dislodge them.

As responsible and serious as these young women appear from the outside, they often harbor unspoken desires to be free from prescriptions of others. They dream of escape and release. They can be intensely subjective, spilling out the truth about themselves, about their views on life and living, in their diaries and daydreams. Rarely do they voice these private thoughts in public, although they may share them with friends.

The loneliness of these hidden, reticent, yet proud women is striking. Their isolation and distance from others place them in sharp contrast to the women we described in chapter 2, who are embedded in conformity

---

* Eleanor Maccoby and Carol Jacklin (1974) analyzed the psychological literature on the differential socialization of boys and girls and reported that girls tended to conform more readily than boys to directives from parents and teachers. Boys, particularly in early childhood, showed more curiosity and exploratory behavior.

and community. The tragedy is that hidden multiplists still their public voice and are reluctant to share their private world; ultimately this hinders them from finding mentors who might support their intellectual and emotional growth. Hidden multiplists can be silently alienated from the educational process, knowing somehow that their conformity is a lie and does not reveal the inner truth or potential that they have recently come to value. One college junior, an honors physics major, told us that she had been secretly working out a scientific thesis which she dared not share with the male science faculty for fear of their ridicule or skepticism. Stating that "men don't think women have any place in science," she told us that she was contemplating dropping out of college to seek a nonacademic community where she might feel freer to express what she feared were unorthodox scientific views.

Erica, limited in her options for escape, told us when she was a freshman that she was a loner who always went off by herself in the woods. In later interviews that took place over her first three years of college during which several developmental transitions took place, we saw how Erica's initial embeddedness in the subjectivist position—that is, in her private conviction that authorities could be wrong and that everyone should do as he or she wants—led her gradually into an essentially private intellectual escape into anarchistic and solipsistic philosophy. She pursued a rebellious course—the upending of social form, values, and reality—via her choice of academic reading matter and secret plans. For Erica, intellectual daring predated overt action and rejection of her parents' wishes for her. For two years Erica struggled quietly with the impulse to leave school, which did not feel like real life—a move that implied for Erica that she must break connections with her parents.

Other hidden multiplists talked about occasionally yielding to their impulse to live a carefree and unrestrained life. They sometimes courted danger by disappearing to nearby cities for the weekend, by becoming involved in "one-night stands," by befriending strangers. They usually returned to campus by Monday. Why they remained so long in environments that felt stifling to them was not always clear. Perhaps there was some lingering trust in old authorities; perhaps they did not perceive any societal permission to live a nonstereotypical life; perhaps they did not feel within themselves a strong enough conviction that they could make it on their own. Nevertheless they nurtured a strong sense of defiance and a trust in their subjective truth to which they sometimes gave voice in diaries or poetry. They might even have expressed a feeling of omnipotence vis-à-vis authority, described by one woman as "an intuitive feeling. I just know. And when I do, fifteen experts won't change or affect me."

Thus all subjectivist women, whether they have come from a back-ground of oppression and disappointment in male authority or have grown up as obedient and cautious children in a world that emphasized conformity to cultural norms, ultimately come to disregard the knowledge and advice of remote experts. They insist on the value of personal, firsthand experience; and, as we shall see, if they listen at all to others, it is to those who are most like themselves in terms of life experiences. Let us now look more closely at the way subjectivist women reason, set standards for themselves, and make sense of the world.

"Just Knowing": The Inner Expert

Once the modest and often belated process of reliance on the self is initiated and supported, women typically move full speed into the subjectivist position on knowing. Subjectivism is for women a position from which they redefine the nature of authority. It is the position at which their views of experts and expertise undergo radical change. The orientation to authority shifts from external to internal. Along with the discovery of personal authority arises a sense of voice—in its earliest form, a "still small voice" to which a woman begins to attend rather than the long-familiar external voices that have directed her life. This interior voice has become, for us, the hallmark of women's emergent sense of self and sense of agency and control.

Early in the transition into subjectivism, women can have a difficult time identifying the new source of knowing and articulating the process. One woman communicated a sense of inner conviction in the words "I just know," and described a process that bypasses awareness. "I try not to think about stuff because usually the decision is already made up inside you and then when the time comes, if you trust yourself, you just know the answer."

Subjective knowers may be shaky about their own judgment but are proud if others affirm their conclusions and opinions. Some told us they were mystified that they could know something before others and had no idea where their own good ideas came from. One woman said she relied on her own experience and "prayed that she was right," an indication that she must still have feared that ultimately her subjective assessment would be evaluated against some external criterion.

Other women were better able to describe this newly recognized power of subjective knowing. It was as if there were some oracle within that stood opposed to the voices and dictums of the outside world.

> It's like a certain feeling that you have inside you. It's like someone could say something to you and you have a feeling. I don't know if it's like a jerk or something inside you. It's hard to explain.

> There's a part of me that I didn't even realize I had until recently— instinct, intuition, whatever. It helps me and protects me. It's perceptive and astute. I just listen to the inside of me and I know what to do.

Truth, for subjective knowers, is an intuitive reaction—something experienced, not thought out, something felt rather than actively pursued or constructed. These women do not see themselves as part of the process, as constructors of truth, but as conduits through which truth emerges. The criterion for truth they most often refer to is "satisfaction" or "what feels comfortable to me." They do not mention that rational procedures play a part in the search for truth.

Occasionally women distinguish between truth as *feelings* that come from within and *ideas* that come from without. This differentiation between thinking and feeling thus appears for the first time during the period of subjective knowing. This split, for women, may be a consequence of their belief that thinking is not womanly or that thought will destroy the capacity for feeling. Thus they relegate ideas to male authority and, as such, the ideas may or may not have relevance to their lives.

They view truth as unique to each individual, an accident of personal history and experience.

> Every person has her own unique body of knowledge that's been given to them through their life's experiences. And realizing that mine is as valid as the next person's, whether or not that person has gone through six or seven years of college, I feel that my knowledge is as important and real and valuable as theirs is.

For women at the positions of silence and received knowledge, there is absolute truth that is true for everyone; at the position of subjective knowing, truth is absolute only for the individual. The subjective knower takes a huge step: She sees truth as subjectified and personal. The subjec-

tivist discovers that each person's life experience gives a different view of
reality from that of any other person. What is more, truth is necessarily a
private matter and, at least from the point of view of these women, should
not be imposed on others.

Two very different women—one black from an urban ghetto, the other
white from a rural backwater, both enrolled in a college program—had
essentially the same way of expressing their perspective on private subjective truth, a point of view held by other women as well.

> I think what one person sees to be a fact is not necessarily a fact in
> the eyes of another. So I tend to weigh anything in light of how
> I feel about it. I am only searching for what is valid to me.

> I don't try to suffocate people with my ideas or anything like that. I
> only know for myself. That is a truth for me. I believe in myself
> and my powers.

Truths can converge; however, in case of disagreement, subjectivist
women's own experience and inner voice are the final arbiters. Although
so-called experts may have done more thinking on a subject, subjectivists
feel that they don't have to accept what the experts say. Another person's
opinion may be misguided or disagreeable; but they have a tolerance for
differences, since others "must obviously believe in their opinion." Subjectivist women recognize that others may disagree with them but seem to
be less concerned than men in persuading others to their point of view.
For most, resolution of disagreement is impossible; attempts at resolution
only lead to unpleasant battles and threaten to disrupt relationships.

When faced with controversy, subjectivist women become strictly
pragmatic—"what works best for me." They refer back to the centrality
of their personal experience, whether they are talking about right choices
for themselves or others. They insist that, since everyone's experience is
unique, no one has the right to speak for others or to judge what others
have to say. "You have to be in a situation to know what is right or wrong.
You can't look at someone from a distance and say, 'Well, they should do
this or that.' Maybe it wouldn't work for everybody."

In situations in which the inner voice is silent and personal experience
is lacking, subjective knowers adopt a cafeteria approach to knowledge,
an attitude of "let's try a little bit of everything until something comes up
that works for me." There are no thought-out procedures in the search for
lurking truths. The process is magical and mysterious: "It's like the truth
hits you dead in the face, and it knocks you out. When you come to, that
is it."

Alien Expertise

Subjectivist women distrust logic, analysis, abstraction, and even language itself. They see these methods as alien territory belonging to men. As we listened to subjectivist women describe their attitudes about truth and knowing, we heard them argue against and stereotype those experts and remote authorities whom social institutions often promote as holding the keys to the truth—teachers, doctors, scientists, men in general. It was as if, by turning inward for answers, they had to deny strategies for knowing that they perceived as belonging to the masculine world.

The fervor with which subjectivist women draw sharp lines between intuitive knowledge and what they assume to be the impersonality of abstract thought harks back to the dogmatism and either/or thinking characteristic of the women we described in earlier chapters. It is not that these women have become familiar with logic and theory as tools for knowing and have chosen to reject them; they have only vague and untested prejudices against a mode of thought that they sense is unfeminine and inhuman and may be detrimental to their capacity for feeling. This antirationalist attitude is primarily a characteristic of women during the period of subjectivism in which they value intuition as a safer and more fruitful approach to truth.

The passionate rejection of science and scientists, while not true of all subjective knowers, was very common. Whereas silent and authority-oriented women often perceived scientists as ultimate authority and looked to science for final answers, after the onset of subjective knowing women often became alienated from things scientific. In many of our interviews with women currently in school, the shift into subjectivism was accompanied by a shift in academic major from science to the arts or humanities. They expressed their distrust of and alienation from science in a variety of ways.

What's missing in science is a whole sort of human element. It doesn't seem to be infused with any morality. It doesn't even seem to be a world about people anymore.

I'm having a hard time with the premise that truth is scientific knowledge, because for me it isn't that at all. For me, truth is internal knowledge. I don't think we need scientific methods to ascertain what's right at all. I think we need internal exploration and knowledge of self to know what's right and what is true.

I think women have been cowed by science. We've been told, "That's unlogical, that's unscientific. Anything you can't prove is not worth talking about." They're saying if you can't prove your sensations, you don't got 'em. Our society is trying to suppress the senses in favor of what goes on from the eyes up. That's so destructive.

Over the past decade, there has been considerable feminist academic debate over just these issues, that is, the equation of the masculine with objectivity, science, and the scientific method in its emphasis on manipulation, control, and distance from the objects of study (Bernard 1973; Duras 1975; Elshtain 1982; Keller 1978, 1985; Sampson 1978). Because of the high value Western technological societies have placed on objectivity, rationalism, and science, women and modes of thought cultivated by women have had relatively little impact on the values and directions of modern-day society (Ruddick 1980). However, as Evelyn Fox Keller has recently pointed out, there is a temptation for feminists "to abandon their claim for representation in scientific culture and, in its place, to invite a return to a purely 'female' subjectivity, leaving rationality and objectivity in the male domain, dismissed as a product of a purely male consciousness" (1982, p. 593). This extreme antirationalist attitude to which Keller refers was strikingly echoed, in a simpler version, by many of the female subjectivists we interviewed.

The point at which individual women begin to express negative attitudes toward abstraction, theory, and science differs from person to person, although in many cases it is anchored in a concrete interaction with a specific teacher or doctor or male acquaintance from the past. Some of the young students we interviewed recalled their frustration with a particular instructor; mothers often looked back on their struggle with a doctor over the proper treatment for a child.

Anna Jean's story illustrates the antirationalist conclusions that some women come to. Anna Jean, a thirty-three-year-old, white, divorced mother of three young children, had returned to college two years before we interviewed her. Being pregnant, going through childbirth, and "living with kids" made her feel much stronger; her experience in childbearing demonstrated her own strengths to her. She recalled how her sense of herself as a woman was changing, how she was beginning to grow away from a stereotyped view of women and her old view of experts.

> You know, I always used to keep things inside because I would think it might be stupid or it wouldn't have any meaning and that no-body would care what I said. But now I can speak out. You know, women are always known as relatively stupid. If you're sitting in a room with men and women, the men are the ones that know what they are talking about. And women are listening and more or less looking silly. . . . And so, my only source of learning was men, which one to believe.

Anna Jean resisted her doctor's advice to have her baby in a hospital and decided to go through childbirth in her home. This was the first time that she recalled resisting authority. Although she went through a long and difficult labor, she "learned a lot about having faith in myself. . . . I always thought doctors were like God and knew the answers to everything. But now I'm glad I know it myself. I can figure things out for myself and I don't need them. I ended up learning that it was *me* that knew it all and they didn't."

As Anna Jean began to trust her own conclusions, she decided to return to school to pick up the college education she had abandoned many years before. There, to her surprise, she discovered new things about herself as a student. Her attitudes toward teaching and learning began to change and so did her willingness to take for granted the truth value in the words of professors and textbooks. "Now I do my own thinking instead of reading someone else's theory and memorizing who said what. That doesn't interest me anymore." She became aware of the intuitive, experiential base of her knowledge, valued it above all else, and was quite dismissive of what she called "theorizing," a way of knowing that baffled her and in the past had intimidated her: "I think of theories as intellectualism. I think there's other ways of learning the same things. In more basic ways, like tuning into yourself. Say I'm reading a book and I don't understand the words but I may already know that in a different way. Know what they are saying without even knowing it." An antimedical bias was apparent as she explained why she did not value the words of scientists.

> Scientists seem to lack a whole feeling of things, that other perception of nonmaterial, nonconcrete things. . . . A lot of books in psychology, especially in medicine, seem to have a whole separate

vocabulary than normal thinking. Reading books when I can't understand them makes me not want to read them. I've talked to other women and they find it hard, too.

In place of books and theories, Anna Jean found a new way to learn. "Reading books is not enough. I really want to talk to people and watch them."

Many other women subjectivists like Anna Jean expressed a distrust of books and the written word in favor of learning through direct sensory experience or personal involvement with the objects of study. In contrast to the women at the position of received knowledge, who allowed the words of others to guide them, subjectivists described themselves as avoiding the words of others: "I make up my mind based on my own feelings most of the time. When you read someone else's words, they may influence you." Some women become almost word-phobic and will even classify the written word as an instrument of oppression that has too often been used against them—an echo of the theme of "words as weapons," which we discussed in the chapter on silent women. Subjectivists often prefer to express themselves nonverbally or artistically so as to bypass the categorizing and labeling that the use of language implies.

Needless to say, these attitudes profoundly affect the behavior and reception of subjectivists in academic circles. Faculty often perceive subjectivist students as arbitrary, emotional, overly personal, concrete, and unmanageable. A teacher may occasionally be intrigued and challenged by their intensity and elusiveness, but faculty interest is apt to turn to frustration when the student seems unwilling to acknowledge that classic texts or winning arguments are relevant to her learning. In some cases, subjectivist women's alienation from the words and influence of their professors was dramatically stated. A college senior was highly critical of a male professor: "I never knew what the man was talking about. It was the way he spoke or the words he used or just the way he put words together that was hard for me to understand. You can't learn things from teachers and books like you can from experience."

Another student who strongly believed that truth is personal and private found the idea of the expertise of professors ludicrous. "Experts don't know what they are talking about. They just like to hear themselves talk. What people who are experts say is always general, never specific. And each situation is different."

A woman in her sixties stated the subjectivist viewpoint on language, learning, and knowing most dramatically.

If I read something, and if it agrees with my senses, then I believe it, I know it. If it doesn't, I'll say, "Well, you may be right but I can't corroborate that." For me, proof is usually a sensory one. If you say, "Water falls," yeah, I believe it because I've seen it happen. If you call it gravity, then I say, "Oh, is that what you call it?" One doesn't have to be told in words. That's the point. That's the thing that's very hard for word people to believe—that there are other ways of telling.

Some women will probably hold to these antirationalist attitudes and to a subjectivist epistemology for the remainder of their lives. Others, particularly women who return to academic settings, will move on to another position in which they manifestly embrace objectivity and logical analysis as important tools for knowing. Still others will develop distinctive procedures that may be more characteristic of women than men in our culture for sustaining connection with and promoting understanding of the unknown. We will describe these new positions and procedures in coming chapters.

4

Subjective Knowledge:
The Quest for Self

Right now I'm busy being born.
—Teresa
Twenty-four years old

Wʜᴀᴛ ꜰᴏʟʟᴏᴡꜱ a woman's discovery of personal authority and truth is, of course, a blend of her own unique life circumstances and attributes. But as we listened to many stories, we began to hear how a newly acquired subjectivism led the woman into a new world, which she insisted on shaping and directing on her own. As a result, her relationships and self-concept began to change.

Severance of Connections: "Walking Away from the Past"

Over half of the large group of subjectivists had recently taken steps to end relationships with lovers or husbands, to reject further obligations to family members, and to move out and away on their own. They seemed to be saying to us that if firsthand experience was the route to knowing, then they were going to amass experiences. Although subject to an extraordinary range of emotional pushes and pulls—anxiety, anger, insecurity, guilt, depression, exhilaration—most of the women were making these changes with a stubborn determination. Some realized they faced loneliness ahead, but they did not seem to care. It was easy to be impressed by the courage of some, by the recklessness of others. Certainly it was clear that as they began to think and to know, they began to act. Some were even driven to action by their inner voice.

There were almost no women in this group who were not actively and obsessively preoccupied with a choice between self and other, acting on behalf of self as opposed to denying the self and living for and through others. In younger, single, advantaged women, this took the familiar turn of an adolescent push for freedom from "oppressive" or "stagnant" parental and community influences, bolstered by going away to school. For some of the women from close-knit ethnic communities, it meant moving out of the old neighborhood to avoid the pressure to conform. Although a few of the older women with established families felt unable to leave the economic and emotional security of home, most were planning to retreat or actually had retreated from old responsibilities and connections to others. They had thrown out husbands or left home themselves, usually but not always taking the children with them.

In many ways, these women are like the youths in fairy tales (as we recall, usually male) who set out from the family homestead to make their way in the world, discovering themselves in the process. Our women set out on this developmental journey with a sense of power in their intuitive processes and a newfound energy and openness to novelty.

We see in the women's stories the dilemma that Gilligan alerted us to as central in women's morality. Women are drawn to the role of caretaker and nurturer, often putting their own needs at the bottom of the list, preceded by other people, husband, and children. At the position of received knowledge, using the either/or thinking so characteristic of the position, women believe that "to get something for oneself" is abhorrent and selfish because others are bound to be deprived as a result. Gilligan believes that for people operating within a responsibility orientation, the initiation of actions on behalf of the self signifies the transition into mature moral thought, a late-occurring developmental shift in which the self is included as an equal claimant in any moral decision. We, however, disagree with Gilligan on this point, having examined the stories of subjectivist women who were beginning to get something for themselves but who did not yet appear to be developing a coherent, reflective moral maturity in Gilligan's terms.

With subjectivist women, there is minimal forethought and reason in their decision to "walk away from their pasts." The claims of others, for years so salient for them, are often suddenly disregarded when the women begin to assert their own authority and autonomy. They leap at the first chance to escape and go it alone without thinking much at all about the consequences; perhaps, for some, the escape is an overly eager promotion of the self at the expense of others.

It is important to keep in mind the broader cultural context in assessing the meaning of such changes in women's priorities. During the 1970s there was a widespread cultural sanction of self-indulgence, self-actualization, and opportunism. Promotion of self was in vogue and assumed the status of a new social phenomenon, being tagged a symptom of the "me-decade" by Tom Wolfe (1976) and the "cult of narcissism" by Christopher Lasch (1979). The time was ripe for the development of subjectivist thought and the severance of ties and responsibilities to others.

Some of the women we interviewed had both the financial resources and the personal willfulness to launch themselves into the world at large. They were the will-o'-the-wisps, the wanderers, the world travelers. As-sertive and self-absorbed, they had thrown themselves into life, taken risks others would not, tried out new selves as their contexts changed. By the time of the interview, many of them had already changed their contexts several times in their quest for self—they had shifted schools, lived in communes, traveled to foreign countries, taken wilderness trips, worked a variety of jobs.

One young woman we call Abby related the change in her assessment of her responsibilities in her marriage after the birth of her child.

> Being married to him was like having another kid. I was his emotional support system. After I had my son, my maternal instincts were coming out of my ears. They were filled up to here! I remember the first thing I did was to let all my plants die. I couldn't take care of another damn thing. I didn't want to water them, I didn't want to feed anybody. Then I got rid of my dog.

Two events—the birth of her child and a solitary month-long wilderness trip—had put Abby in touch with "the divine forces" within her and changed her "whole way of looking at the world." Abby divorced her husband, moved to a new community with their son, and had just entered into a lesbian relationship at the time of the interview.

Looking more closely at some of the life stories, we saw that often the subjectivist's escape from parents or inhibiting marriages and relationships had all the aspects of what Erik Erikson (1968) calls a "negative identity," that is, a definition of yourself primarily in terms of opposition to others or what you are not. One woman from a small midwestern community and religious family quietly and with considerable trepidation began to redefine herself in opposition to her family's values. She first chose a liberal eastern arts-oriented college over her state university and, at the time of her interview, was contemplating leaving college with her black boyfriend to live in the rural southern town from which he came. Another college student, who described her uneducated parents as stagnant and banal, was about to set out to find herself by moving to Europe and establishing a career in the theater, entertaining a vision of herself that her parents would find unfathomable and shocking. Yet another woman related with bitter humor how she considered herself to be a careless, impetuous slob who was the exact opposite of what her perfectionistic and methodical father expected her to be.

The eventual path a woman takes is, in large measure, a function of the familial and educational environments in which she is struggling with these problems. Families and schools differ tremendously in the degree to which they reinforce risk taking or conformity behavior in women. Erica's options might have been broadened significantly by her hard-working, self-denying mother who communicated to her daughter her own unrealized wish to go to Spain. Certainly the college Erica chose for herself was an optimal environment for intellectual and psychological awakening in its explicit support for questioning and adventurous thinking and exploring. Abby was brought up in a very traditional, male-oriented family in which she sought paternal approval and was "geared to pleasing men." She was given money to explore the world but not the paternal sanction to step out of the stereotyped female role as nurturer.

All too often neither the family, whether the family of origin or of reproduction, nor the educational institution she attends, recognizes or nurtures the budding subjectivist's impetus toward change, redefinition, and application of her new ways of knowing and learning. The family's reaction to a woman's return to school can be painful for her. One woman described her tearful daughter berating her: "You used to stay home to do needlepoint." Another told us how her angry husband had first hidden then burned her schoolbooks.

As women begin to act on their new conceptions of truth and to forge new rules and boundaries in their relationships, some become distinctly antimale. Negative attitudes toward specific men in their pasts—lovers, fathers, husbands, teachers—become generalized to all men, whom they perceive as controlling, demanding, negating, and life suppressing. Their attitude is not so much that of retreating from others—the attitude "I will go it alone"—as it is the attitude "I will go it without men."

Other subjectivist women we interviewed assumed a much more antagonistic stance toward men.

There are men who can't stand the fact that I am female, as young as I am, doing the things that I do. I sometimes feel that they are trying to pull me down but I am not going to let that happen. . . . I'm going to be my own person. I don't have to live with and depend on men.

I deal with men when I have to, when I can't avoid it. I'm not friendly nor am I unfriendly. I'm just eager to get it over with. I have no desire to waste any time or energy on men at all.

I find I can do better without men. Definitely better without men! I have to let them know that I'm not the sweet little girl from the all-girls' college that you think I am. If you walk on me, then I'll get up and walk back on you. I won't be rude but I'll give you a taste of your own medicine.

We heard a number of stories from women who spoke in these terms and who turned all men out of their lives, and many other stories from women for whom heterosexual relationships and intimacy were on hold. For most, there was the early adherence to traditional sex roles; the stress of never getting anything for themselves; the angry, even dismissive feelings toward others whom they experienced as clinging tyrants; the impulsive yet determined throwing out and breaking ties; and the launching of new intentions and new directions. Yet throughout this turmoil and tumultuous effort to claim the self, we saw many signs that women were still invested in connections to others: their children, their reliable and supportive friends (usually female), new groups and organizations that "understood" their motives and objectives, and, for some, a new man "who is on my side."

Nevertheless, there is something tentative and unsettled in the view of the self that is characteristic of women at the subjectivist position. They sense the enormity of the steps they have taken. Relationships feel unstable and the future is dim. As Abby put it, "It's hard to foresee anything, because the whole structure of our lives can change overnight. I can say, 'Now I see myself changing in this way or that way,' but I really don't know what's going to happen to me." These women sojourners have been propelled into action and are committed to continuing their developmental journey; the way ahead appears foggy.

Concepts of the Self

The instability and flux that subjectivist women experience when they con-template their future is due, in part, to the lack of grounding in a secure, integrated, and enduring self-concept. Whereas in the position of received knowledge, women derive a sense of "who I am" from the definitions others supply and the roles they fill, subjectivist women shift away from this perspective and experience a wrenching away of the familiar contexts and relationships within which the old identity has been embedded. Their place in life is no longer a matter of adopting the values of the community and fulfilling the expectations of those they care about. The women in subjectivism often seemed bewildered over the sense of loss of themselves once they distanced themselves from the feedback and reinforcement that family and community provided. If, as Gilligan and Miller claim, women tend to define themselves in the context of relationships, then it is not surprising that women making a break with their pasts and former rela-tionships may enter a period in which there is considerable flux in self-concept. If new relationships and new self-definitions have not yet emerged or been articulated, past images or labels that others supplied may have a peremptory hold on the woman's experience of herself. Sadly, some women looking back on their lives recalled themselves in painfully negative terms, revealing as they talked how little the people with whom they lived valued them. They felt trapped by the negative images from the past or splintered into vaguely sensed parts and subject to kaleidoscopic shifts in self-picture that kept them off balance.

A young, unmarried woman with two sons, having just begun the transition into subjective knowing, revealed such a negative self-image. "Unfortunately, I've never felt much about myself. I guess I was brought up to think everybody else was better than I was, and unfortunately I kind of still feel that way, you know. If I'm walking down the aisle and meet someone, I'll get out of the way." Another early subjectivist had an equally hard time believing that she had a self other than vaguely sensed negative traits: "How would I describe myself to myself? I—I—that's really just a blank. I wouldn't know what to say. I can pretend something or try to portray something, but I never really think of myself. I never talk to myself. If I did, it would be a negative type of thing."

No matter what their pasts were, most subjectivist women found it difficult to reflect upon or even describe themselves clearly. Like so many other aspects of their lives that were changing, so, too, was the image they held of themselves. Having entered the era of subjective truth, in which knowing is a matter of internal groping and intuition, these women had few words available to them to communicate something about an inner self that still was so novel, so hidden from public view. At best they resorted to a string of images or metaphors when asked to describe themselves, leaving the job of integration to the listener. A young college student revealed the private and connotative language often used during the period of subjectivism.

> The easiest way for me to see myself is in images. Images of flowers, in Winnie the Pooh, sea gulls. I don't know if I could ever do it using words. A lot of times you see something in your own mind. Other times you see it and there's no word connection. It's just ... bonk ... and it's there and it's really a true form of understanding. It's hard to use words.

She did, in fact, use words as she talked to us, but like many women in this group she reported that she found talking about herself an almost impossible task.

The majority of women we interviewed and classified as subjective knowers, even though they experienced fluctuations in their sense of who they were, which contributed to their uneasiness, also valued this instability as a sign that they were now open to novelty. We heard again and again how openness to change and novelty had become the fulcrum around which their new identities revolved. Some women used the imagery of birth, rebirth, and childhood to describe their experience of a nascent self.

> The person I see myself as now is just like an infant. I see myself as beginning. Whoever I can become, that's a wide-open possibility.

> I actually think that the person I am now is only about three or four years old with all these new experiences. I always was kind of led, told what to do. Never really thought much about myself. Now I feel like I'm learning all over again.

> I've never had a personality. I've always been someone's daughter, someone's wife, someone's mother. Right now I'm so busy being born, discovering who I am, that I don't know who I am. And I don't know where I'm going. And everything is going to be fine.

These were women for whom the birth of the self was occurring as late as thirty or forty, even fifty. Along with their reported sense of being newly born were significant indicators of an impetus toward action, change, and risk taking. They seemed propelled by an inner fire, communicating to us a feeling of exhilaration and optimism as they plunged ahead toward some dim future.

> It's hard to say who I am because I don't really think about more than tomorrow. In the future I'll probably have a better understanding, because now I simply don't know. I think it will really be a fun thing to find out. Just do everything until I find out.

> I'm a different person each day. It's the day, I guess, depending on how it is outside or how my body feels.

> I'm only the person that I am at this moment. Tomorrow I'm somebody different, and the day after that I'm somebody different. . . . I'm always changing. Everything is always changing.

New Connections: The Role of Inward Watching and Listening

For all women the shift into subjectivism is an adaptive move in that it is accompanied by an increased experience of strength, optimism, and self-value. Nevertheless, we were concerned, as we heard their stories, about maladaptive consequences.* Paradoxically, in spite of their basic commitment and responsiveness to others, their fervent insistence on "going it alone" contributed to their isolation from others. We wondered how trapped women might become in their subjectivist philosophy, how lonely they would become if they excluded others from their lives in an attempt at self-protection. We also wondered what or who might engage them in further questioning their assumptions about truth and knowing, propel them into further growth, and lead them to move beyond their distrust of external influence.

Certainly a few of the women impressed us as entrenched in their subjective world. They were stubbornly committed to their view of things

* The linguist George Lakoff and the philosopher Mark Johnson discussed the limitations of either a purely objectivist or subjectivist epistemology in their book *Metaphors We Live By* (1980). Their description of what they call the myth of subjectivism corresponds to our concerns about a strictly subjectivist epistemology.

and unwilling to expose themselves to alternative conceptions. Although they might have described themselves as generous and caring, they could be, in fact, impatient and dismissive of other people's interpretations. They easily resorted to expletives when faced with others' viewpoints—"That's bullshit!" "That teacher was an asshole. He didn't know what he was talking about!" These were women at their most belligerent, oppositional, and argumentative. They were similar to the males whom Perry called "oppositional multiplists," who were adept at turning the tables on authorities by bludgeoning them with wordy, offensive arguments. In the classroom as in life, they warded off others' words and influence via ploys to isolate, shout down, denigrate, and undo the other.

It was difficult to imagine how such entrenched subjectivists might advance to a more adaptive and differentiated way of knowing. Perry speculated that perhaps oppositional multiplists become "entrapped by their own argumentativeness" (1970, p. 99), implying that the route to further development was the pressure others exerted to provide reasons and evidence for opinions recklessly thrown about.

In our study, few women were as outspoken and confrontative as Perry's male multiplists. Even when the women held strongly to their own way of doing things, they remained concerned about not hurting the feelings of their opponents by openly expressing dissent. They reported that they were apt to hide their opinions and then suffer quietly the frustration of not standing up to others. Some women described feeling either a petulant, private resentment of others or self-admonishment for being so unassertive. Once again we saw that sustaining connections with others prevail in the stories of women.

An additional consequence of the entrenched subjectivist position appeared in only a few of our cases. A kind of existential loneliness and despair pervaded the interviews of these few women who had not found bridges back to other people. One depressed college sophomore told us about her discovery that there were multiple truths and multiple realities. She had concluded that, since no one could know anything for sure and each person was locked in her own world, there was no way and no reason for people to try to reach each other or communicate. She believed that "it's a case of knowing too much. . . . My question to you, Why do people live?"

Most of the subjective knowers we interviewed were neither entrenched and oppositional nor depressed and despairing. They were, as we described earlier, forward-looking, positive, and open to new experiences. They were curious people and, from the moment they turned inward to listen to the "still small voice," found a new and fascinating object for study: the self. When we asked subjectivists how they learned best, they frequently mentioned knowledge obtained by observing the self as well as observing others. Women at the position of received knowledge, in contrast, were limited to listening to others and imitating because there was little inner experience of self. During the period of subjectivism, the predominant learning mode is one of *inward* listening and watching. The women associated this mode with a sense of change.

> I'm turning in. I try and watch myself more. Like if I had watched myself years ago, it would have been pretty boring because I really wasn't doing anything. I wasn't changing.

> I keep discovering things inside myself. I am seeing myself all the time in a different light.

Given the unsettled sense of an ever-changing self, it is not surprising that observation and listening serve an important function for these women. They are the primary means they have available for articulation and differentiation of the self. They watch and listen to themselves and begin to notice inner contradictions; they watch and listen to others and begin to draw comparisons between their own and other people's experience. They become aware of other as "other" in contrast to the more conformist women who diffuse distinctions between self and other and perceive people primarily in stereotypic terms.

To some extent listening to others is self-serving. It is a way of learning about the self without revealing the self; however, good listeners draw others to them. Watching, listening subjectivists attract other persons' trust, in part because they listen and in part because they seem nonjudgmental. Many of our women told us about this important skill and how it kept them connected to others. Yet some also clearly indicated that it was the knowledge they gained about themselves that they valued rather than the mutual exchange of experience.

Women's emphasis on beginning to hear themselves think, while gathering observations through watching and listening, is the precursor to reflective and critical thought characteristic of the other positions we will discuss. During the period of subjective knowing, women lay down procedures for systematically learning and analyzing experience. But what seems distinctive in these women is that their strategies for knowing grow out of their very embeddedness in human relationships and their alertness to the details of everyday life. Subjectivist women value what they see and hear around them and begin to feel a need to understand the people with whom they live and who impinge on their lives. Though they may be emotionally or intellectually isolated from others at this point in their history, they begin to actively analyze their past and current interactions with others. Although they may not have taken the next step of speaking out to others about their perceptions of the world, of acquiring a public voice, they engage in self-expression by talking to themselves, talking to their diaries, and even, with one woman, talking to her cats about her inner secrets. These women are "gaining a voice" and a knowledge base from which they can investigate the world. We will see as we consider the rest of our story how significant "really listening" and "really talking" can be for women.

5

Procedural Knowledge: The Voice of Reason

This year I realized that I can use my mind.
—A college junior

I N MAY SARTON'S *The Small Room*, a novel about a women's college, a professor reflects ruefully upon the "art" her students are required to practice: "Learning is such a very painful business. It requires humility from people at an age where the natural habitat is arrogance" (1951, p. 110). Most of the women we meet in this chapter are well practiced in the art of being students; they are attending or have recently graduated from prestigious colleges, many from a women's college much like the one Sarton describes. Most are privileged, bright, white, and young, ranging in age from late teens to mid-twenties. They form a more homogeneous group than the women in previous chapters, and they inhabit a narrower world, an academic world that may feel claustrophobic to the reader, as it sometimes feels to the women—a "small room" indeed.

In a small room one tends to speak softly. The voice we hear in this chapter is much humbler, although ultimately more powerful, than the voice we heard in the previous chapter. It is the voice of reason.

Steps toward Procedural Knowledge

We know from earlier interviews with the women in this chapter or from their own retrospective accounts that most of them once relied on a mixture of received and subjective knowledge, looking to feeling and intuition for some of the answers they needed and to external authorities for others. But by the time of the final interview they had abandoned both subjectivism and absolutism in some areas of their lives in favor of reasoned reflection. We cannot be sure why some women make this move and others do not, but we can identify some common sources of challenge and support in the lives of the women who do.

First, all the women encountered situations in which their old ways of knowing were challenged. The stories many women told began when authorities attempted to inflict their opinions in areas in which the women believed they had a right to their own opinions. The conflict was between the absolutist dictates of the authorities and the women's own subjectivism. At the time the women experienced the conflict not as an invitation to growth but as an attempt to stifle their inner voices and draw them back into a world of silent obedience. They struggled not to move beyond their subjectivism but to defend it. The stories of Patti and Naomi, which thread in and out of this chapter, are cases in point.

For Patti the story began as a typical conflict between a high school student and her parents. Looking back after several years, Patti recalled that in high school she was "a wild kid" who cared about nothing but having a good time. Patti believed she knew what was right for her, and she tried to act in accordance with her gut; but her parents believed otherwise, and they tried to constrain her. If she obeyed her impulses she had a good time, but she had to endure her parents' punishment. If she obeyed her parents' dictates, she had no fun at all.

At home, increasingly unable either to listen or to speak to her parents, she was driven to a life of "lies, secrets, and silence" (Rich 1979). When her father "preached" to her about the folly of her ways, Patti closed her ears. She could not—and still cannot—stand preaching. A feisty adolescent, she tried to fight with her father, but she was no match for him. Six feet tall, weighing nearly 300 pounds, and as "stubborn and headstrong" as she, he was "the type of person you don't talk back to." He did not even need to speak. When he got "that look," Patti "cleared out." Patti could not talk to her mother, either. She was always hiding something from her, because she was afraid of how she would react.

So far, Patti had gone her subjectivist way, ignoring and evading the authorities in her life as best she could and using her own intuition as a guide to action. But the tension between Patti and her parents became insufferable by her senior year, and she didn't know what to do.

Naomi, too, had a problem. At about the same age as Patti, she entered an elite women's college and almost immediately encountered the dilemma with which colleges commonly confront their subjectivist students: If truth and value are matters of purely personal opinion, how can teachers presume to judge students? Specifically, what right do teachers have to grade students' opinions?

For Naomi the dilemma appeared in starkest form in an introductory art history class. When we interviewed her during her first year at college she said that although she was willing to reproduce the historical facts provided by the teacher and the textbook, she believed that "in a subjective course like art history, there are certain questions that you have to answer for yourself, where there isn't just a right and wrong. You can like a piece that someone else doesn't like, and you have to decide for yourself."

But the art history professors insisted that she *write* about her reactions, that she put her feelings into words and justify her intuitions. Left to herself, she simply might have gazed at a Van Gogh and enjoyed it—mute, except, perhaps, for a murmured "Wow!" But "Wow!" did not make a paper. The inner voice convinced Naomi, but she feared it would not convince the teacher. She did not know what to say in her paper. The professors provided a five-page guide. "They give us a way to analyze paintings. Then we analyze the painting and come to a conclusion. There are certain criteria that you judge your evaluation on—the composition, texture, color, lighting, how the artist expresses his feelings, what the medium is." These criteria are "objective" in the sense that they pertain primarily to the *object*—the painting. Naomi preferred to explain her responses to paintings in terms of herself—her background, moods, feelings, and tastes—but the teacher deflected her attention from herself to the painting. Naomi could feel as she pleased about the painting, but she had to justify her response in terms of the painting. Teachers were not interested in her subjective feelings. Or so it seemed.

To Naomi, who had only recently staked out for herself a territory free from the heavy hand of authority, it felt like "academic prostitution" to comply with the teacher's request. She had just begun to acquire a voice of her own when the teacher asked her to suppress it and to adopt a new and alien vocabulary containing words such as *composition*, *texture*, and, as many students said, "all that garbage." Naomi was struggling to hear her own inner voice, but the authorities seemed to be saying, "Listen not to yourself but to us, the experts who know about painting. Forget your so-called knowledge and memorize ours." Naomi did not know what to do.

She could have ignored the art history guidelines, written papers full of feeling, and flunked out of college. Or she could have left voluntarily, as many women in her position did. But Naomi wanted to make it within the system. She planned to be a linguist, and she needed a college degree. Unlike Patti, but like many women, she preferred to conform rather than rebel. She had formed habits of obedience, and so far they had served her well, enabling her to graduate at the top of her high school class and to be admitted to an elite college.

Patti, on the other hand, could have left home, perhaps through marrying and then becoming pregnant (or becoming pregnant and then marrying) as many of her classmates did. But the thought of breaking with her parents scared and saddened her. Both women perceived real costs in leaving and real benefits in staying. They were not society's rejects; they had a lot to lose. Patti wanted to maintain a relationship with her family; Naomi wanted to get a college degree.

Unlike many of the women we met in the previous chapter, Patti and Naomi retained some trust in authority. The presence of fairly benign authorities may be critical to the development of the voice of reason. The authorities in these two women's lives did not utterly fail them; they were neither vicious nor absent. They meant well. The art history teachers intended their guidelines not as instruments of oppression but as aids to understanding paintings. And, as Patti came to realize—and perhaps dimly sensed all along—her father's sermons and tantrums were inept expressions of genuine concern. Both Naomi and Patti found in their lives enough support to move on rather than out.

A sign of Patti's residual trust in authority was her decision to enlist the help of a family counselor. She assumed that the counselor would serve as her advocate, and she hoped that her parents could be made to "see reason." She wanted her parents to understand her feelings, and she expected the counselor to explain her position to her parents; but the counselor told Patti that she would have to state her own case. It was up to her to help her parents understand by explaining to them how she felt. She had to struggle to translate her inner voice into words her parents could understand.

In the midst of this struggle Patti began to question whether she really knew what she wanted. From the counselor Patti learned that "in order to really explain to somebody how you're really feeling, you have to know yourself. I had to find out what I really wanted to do."

Before going into counseling Patti acted on impulse, never pausing to consider the consequences of her behavior, even to herself. She construed her situation in dualistic terms: Either she could obey her own impulses and do what she felt like doing, or she could submit to the dictates of authority and do what her parents wanted her to do. The counselor taught her a third way, the way of reason, which allowed her to "make her own choices" while still considering her parents' needs: "She [the counselor] said, 'Well, if that's how you feel, you have to do it. But think of why these other people don't want you doing things, and weigh things out, taking their interests into consideration.' "

In order to consider her parents it was necessary to understand them. Before counseling it had not occurred to Patti that her parents required understanding; they simply *were*. But now, as she began to articulate her feelings and even to divulge her secrets, her parents' reactions surprised her. She began to listen *hard*, actively and effortfully, and she saw that she really had not understood them at all. Her first guesses about why they behaved as they did often turned out to be wrong. The counselor helped Patti and her parents understand each other. She taught them how to talk to and hear each other. Patti's mother became more predictable. As for her father, Patti felt that she could finally understand his viewpoint and realized that she was the same kind of person he was. Patti's world became understandable. Having felt for years "blown by the wind," anchored only by rules imposed by others, she finally felt her feet touch the ground.

Naomi, who seemed by her own account to have been a "hidden multiplist," keeping her subjectivist side secret from the authorities, dealt with the demands of the art history professors as she had dealt with authorities' demands in the past. Outwardly, she did her best to comply with them. Naomi reserved the right to disagree, but she did not exercise it in her academic work. She used the strategy many students use: Find out what the guy wants and give it to him. Composition and texture and "all that garbage" seemed meaningless and unreal to her; but if that was what he wanted, that was what she would try to deliver.

When Naomi set out to discover what her teachers wanted, she discovered that unlike dictators of the past, they did not want to tell her what to think. Like Patti's counselor, they did not offer answers, only techniques for constructing answers. In writing an essay about a painting, Naomi learned, you had to do it "the way they said."

> But you're the one who's placing the judgment on it and as long as you're substantiating your argument, they can't—they're not going to disagree with—They can't—It's not a matter of disagreeing, as

long as you substantiate what you're saying. They're teaching you a method, and you're applying it for yourself.

Naomi expresses here an essential new insight. She realizes that her teachers do not presume to judge her in terms of her opinions but only in terms of the procedures she uses to substantiate her opinions. They do not insist that she agree with them but only that she use the proper procedures, and they are willing—indeed eager—to teach her the procedures. They do not seek to silence her but to teach her a new language.

Although Naomi quickly became adept at using this new language, she used it only to compose messages to her teachers. Alone and in the company of close friends she clung to a private voice that did not need to justify itself. In an interview at the end of her sophomore year Naomi made a distinction between "opinions" and "arguments." Opinions, she said, were based on intuition and all opinions were equally valid. Arguments, on the other hand, had to be "reasonable." When you presented an opinion to authority for purposes of evaluation, you had to back it up with an argument; and the teacher had a right to evaluate the validity of your argument. Naomi made a similar distinction between judgments of "liking," which remained intuitive, and judgments of "artistic merit," which had to be supported with "reasons." Naomi felt that people could keep their intuitions as long as they kept them to themselves.

In forming her private opinion of a Picasso painting, Naomi did not analyze its composition and texture. Left to herself, she still stood there murmuring "Wow." In Naomi's view opinions required no knowledge beyond the immediate experience of the painting. Public interpretations, on the other hand, required further knowledge. If a professor asked her to interpret or evaluate a painting by Picasso, Naomi felt that there were certain things she should mention. "What things?" the interviewer asked. "Well," Naomi answered, "you talk about composition in cubism. And color—If it's the Blue Period, that's important. These things should be included, 'cause they're necessary." "Why?" asked the interviewer. "I guess that's just convention. If you didn't know about cubism, and you were asked to look at a painting by Picasso, obviously you couldn't use that." Asked if her opinion of the painting would, then, be valid, she said "I don't think you could give a substantial interpretation. You could give an opinion, but you couldn't analyze why all the bodies are broken up into little parts."

Naomi's words suggested that she was not quite sure why someone should analyze a painting in this way: "I guess that's just convention." She spoke the language, but she was not sure what the words meant. At the same time, she was beginning to suspect that these words did mean something, that they were not just garbage. Compared to the substantial interpretations she prepared for professors, her intuitive opinions began to appear thin. Naomi's position was painful. She was developing a new voice, but it was not yet hers, and the older inner voice was fading.

It seems likely that in order to achieve the voice of reason one must encounter authorities who are not only benign but knowledgeable, like Patti's counselor and Naomi's teachers. All the women we classified as predominantly procedural knowers, with the exception of Patti, were attending or had graduated from college. Most (including Patti) described actions teachers or counselors had taken that seemed to them critical in promoting their powers of reasoning. In a later chapter we will look at educational interventions that help and hinder development at all positions of knowing. At the moment we simply want to suggest that the development of the technical know-how, the procedural knowledge that emerges at this position, requires formal instruction or at least the presence of knowledgeable people who can serve as informal tutors.

Aspects of Procedural Knowledge

Patti and Naomi had come to embrace assumptions about knowing that were very different from those they once held. Earlier, according to their own testimony, they believed that at least on some matters truth was intuitive, personal, and essentially incommunicable; that they could know what was right only for themselves (but could know that for sure); that all opinions were equally valid; and that firsthand experience was the only reliable source of authoritative knowledge. Now, they argue that intuitions may deceive; that gut reactions can be irresponsible and no one's gut feeling is infallible; that some truths are truer than others; that they can know things they have never seen or touched; that truth can be shared; and that expertise can be respected. The change in voice is striking.

SPEAKING IN MEASURED TONES

Unlike their more subjectivist sisters, Patti and Naomi engage in conscious, deliberate, systematic analysis. They have learned that truth is not immediately accessible, that you cannot "just know." Things are not always what they seem to be. Truth lies hidden beneath the surface, and you must ferret it out. Knowing requires careful observation and analysis. You must "really look" and "listen hard." Looking back in her senior year, Naomi gave credit to the art history handout for first "forcing" her to "look closely" and showing her "how to be thorough. . . . Those basic underlying principles have worked their way into the way I look at other things." She reads literary passages "closely and intensely," and she gets "a lot of satisfaction" from writing short papers analyzing in specific detail brief passages of Latin text.

Several years after the counseling sessions, Patti, married and the mother of a toddler, tried to apply the lessons learned in counseling to her faltering marriage. "I think I have learned more about trying to understand people than I have learned about any other subject, even though I am not an expert in it at all." Among the lessons Patti learned was that "not everybody thinks on the same train." Her husband, Mick, in particular, did not think as she did. She devised strategies for getting Mick to talk. "I try to get him to give me some answers, but you can't come right out and demand them. You have to think about how you want to say it. I'm learning new things all the time about how he feels."

Things that had once appeared simple now seemed problematic. Patti and Naomi recognized and respected the complexity of the objects they sought to understand. Aware that some events (a husband's behavior, a literary passage) were open to more than one interpretation and that some interpretations made better sense than others, they were careful not to jump to conclusions. Patti studied her husband's words. She tried to find ways to coax more words from him, to elicit more data from which to infer the "logic" of his behavior. Concerned about possible "bias" in her own interpretations, she suggested that they enlist professional help. Similarly, Naomi closely scrutinized the words of the Latin text, reading and rereading, utilizing the techniques of structural analysis her teachers taught her, constructing, comparing, and discarding possible meanings.

To most women, the first steps on this journey do not feel like progress. The voice diminishes in volume; it lacks authority. These women lack even the derived authority of those who, having faith in received knowledge, can assume as they parrot their elders that they speak the truth. Lacking, also, the inner authority of the subjectivist, they cannot cheerfully blurt out the first idea that springs to mind. The inner voice turns critical; it tells them their ideas may be stupid. Women at this position think before they speak; and, because their ideas must measure up to certain objective standards, they speak in measured tones. Often, they do not speak at all. But this is not a passive silence; on the other side of this silence, reason is stirring.

KNOWING HOW

All the women who appear in this chapter were absorbed in the business of acquiring and applying procedures for obtaining and communicating knowledge. Some (like Patti) were passionately involved in this process, while others (like Naomi) treated it primarily as a game; but the emphasis on procedures, skills, and techniques was common to all.

We asked one of Naomi's fellow students, a sophomore whom we call Faith, what she thought would stay with her about her experiences at college. Like most of the women at this position, she responded with a list of skills: "I'm learning to reason, learning how to write decently, learning how to speak concisely and to say what I mean." Faith told us about a course in moral philosophy that she took in her first year. "I couldn't tell you right now the philosophies of most of the people we studied, but I can tell you how you would set about criticizing their arguments and what types of things you should look for."

Form predominates over content. "It does not matter," said one young woman, "whether you decide to have your baby or abort it. It matters only that you think the decision through thoroughly." There is a chillingly academic quality to this position. Surely it does matter whether or not you have your baby. Listening to these women we were reminded of meetings of committees evaluating research proposals, in which the entire discussion centers on the methodology and no attention is paid to the significance of the problem. The curious dissociation between means and ends at this position also arouses more sinister associations: One thinks of seminars on "war games," for instance, in which military strategists seriously debate the cost-benefit ratios of various modes of extermination.

Sometimes the emphasis on procedure verges on *methodolatry*, a term coined by the feminist theologian Mary Daly (1973). Methodolatry may be especially dangerous for women, because women, after all, have not participated in designing the procedures developed by the various disciplines for acquiring knowledge; and the procedures may make it difficult or impossible for women to acquire the knowledge they need. Daly writes,

The tyranny of methodolatry hinders new discoveries. It prevents us from raising questions never asked before and from being illumined by ideas that do not fit into preestablished boxes and forms. The worshippers of Method have an effective way of handling data that does not fit into the Respectable

Categories of Questions and Answers. They simply classify it as nondata, thereby rendering it invisible. (P. 11)

The methodolators, although ostensibly basing their decisions upon form, implicitly decide upon content, as Daly makes plain. When a government funding agency insists upon a particular methodology in the research it supports, it outlaws questions that cannot be answered in that fashion. In learning to "do philosophy," Faith learned how to formulate questions; but the questions had to be of a particular kind, and the questions she might have formulated on her own might have been quite different from those she was being taught to ask. The philosopher Sara Ruddick, "burdened for years by a timid professionalism," writes,

> Harvard's training, and the identity it allowed, had become intimately, unconsciously connected with lessons of respectability I had learned as a child. . . . Even now, I can surprise myself, wondering whether a question is "really" philosophical, whether I should ask questions I haven't been trained to answer. (1977, p. 137)

Faith's own experience, from which her own questions might have arisen, was so different from the experience that led philosophers such as Locke and Hobbes to formulate their questions that it might well have been considered "nondata" and rendered invisible. Were a woman to invent philosophy, she might, like Janice Moulton (1983), have come up with a "non-adversarial paradigm."

Still, as these women become increasingly skillful at executing procedures for obtaining and communicating knowledge, many of them experience an increasing sense of control. The world becomes more manageable. Several undergraduates remarked that earlier, when faced with a problem, they were helpless unless the solution sprang instantly to mind. Clara, an undergraduate, said she used to "panic" during exams if she didn't know just by looking at the question what the answer was, but she had learned that she could "think about it and then come up with an answer." And a middle-aged Irish woman said that until recently much of the world had seemed to her "magic," beyond comprehension. Now that she had entered college, she was learning things she would not have believed she could learn, and the world had become reasonable. She told us there were many things she did not understand, but there was nothing she could not understand eventually, because "there are reasons for it, logical reasons that I can understand. I don't have to think that somebody out there has to figure these things out for me anymore, because if I want to, I can."

PERSPECTIVE TAKING

The world that procedural knowledge reveals is more complex than the world revealed through received or subjective knowledge. In formulating her answer to an exam question, Clara learned to ask herself how many different ways she could look at it. The notion of "ways of looking" is central to the procedural knowledge position. It builds upon the subjectivist insight that different people have—and have a right to have—different opinions, but it goes beyond the idea of opinions as the static residue of experience. Women like Clara conceive of knowledge as a process. They believe that each of us looks at the world through a different lens, that each of us construes the world differently. They are interested not just in *what* people think but in *how* people go about forming their opinions and feelings and ideas.

At first the insight that each of us looks through a different lens can be profoundly disturbing, because it suggests that each of us is profoundly alone. At the onset of the procedural knowledge period of development, women may despair. They see no way to get out from behind their own spectacles and enter another perspective. Recall Patti's dismay when she learned that she did not understand her parents. But women like Patti develop procedures for understanding where others are "coming from" and how they are communicating with them.

Subjectivists sometimes espouse two contradictory beliefs: that communication is impossible and that in some cases people can achieve an easy, wordless communion based on intuitive understanding, "that certain rapport when you just have to look at each other, and you know what the other one's thinking, not having any of the pressure of having to talk." Women who put their trust in procedural knowledge believe that communication can occur, but that it requires talk. Patti interviewed her husband in an attempt to discern the track of his thinking. Clara, studying for the exam, interviewed the material. She imagined the questions her teacher might ask, and she asked them herself. The point was not to hit upon the exact questions the exam would contain, but rather to ask the *kind* of questions the teacher asked, to think as the teacher thought.

Clara credited a professor in her introductory English course with teaching her to "think more." At first, to think more meant to generate a series of ideas instead of stopping with one; but by her sophomore year it had evolved into a technique for generating a variety of perspectives. No longer stuck with a single answer, no longer stuck behind a single pair of spectacles, Clara assumed that certain phenomena have many potential meanings, depending upon the way she viewed them, and that in order to fully understand the phenomenon, she had to view it from a variety of angles.

OBJECTIVITY

Procedural knowledge is more objective than subjective knowledge. In the previous chapter we saw that although women who relied on subjective knowledge professed to be open to anything, they were, in fact, stubbornly immune to other people's ideas. They saw what they wanted to see and ignored the rest, listened to the inner voice and turned a deaf ear to other voices. In contrast, women who use procedural knowledge pay attention to objects in the external world. Naomi and her classmates were told to attend to the painting itself, not just to the feelings it aroused in them. In an attempt to placate the authorities, they tried to do so, although many resented it, feeling that their old intuitive approach led to deeper understandings of poems and paintings than the clinical dissections they were forced to undertake. Their teachers' wordy analyses ("Seventy minutes of lecture on *one line*—can you believe the guy?") struck them as pretentious nonsense. Still, they tried to imitate them, straining to impose interpretations of their own.

It takes time to learn to attend truly to the object, to wait for meanings to emerge from a poem, rather than imposing the contents of your own head or your own gut. Faith told us that it was in an introductory poetry class that she came to understand that all interpretations are not equally valid, that a good interpretation of a poem is firmly grounded in the poem itself, while a bad interpretation contains too much of the reader and too little of the poem.

> We were discussing a Robert Frost poem. The title was "A Dust of Snow"—something about a crow sitting in a hemlock tree shaking down the snow. And one of the students said, "Well, you know, this poem has very, very evil connotations to it." And the teacher said, "What are you *talking* about?" And the student said, "Well, a crow is a bird of evil, and hemlock is what Socrates drank." And the teacher was so flabbergasted that for a couple of minutes she couldn't say anything. "On Stopping by Woods on a Snowy Evening," another Frost poem, somebody said, "Well, the author is clearly contemplating suicide," because of "the woods are lovely, dark, and deep." There's nothing really in the work that would lead you to believe that, unless you're actually searching for it.

A college senior spoke scornfully of critics who used their "so-called interpretations" as "an excuse to get their own ideas off the ground." She felt that to understand a text, you had to treat it as you would a friend. You had to "accept" it as "real," as "independent of your existence," rather than "using it for your own convenience or reinforcement." This gifted and privileged young woman was grateful that she had finally emerged from a period in which she was so caught up in her own self-styled "identity crisis" that she could not acknowledge the reality of other persons. Now she has become capable, in Simone Weil's words, of "a way of looking" that "is first of all attentive. The soul empties itself of all its own contents in order to receive into itself the being it is looking at, just as he is, in all his truth" (1951, p. 115).

Toward the other end of the social scale, Minna, who had recently enrolled in a community college and was studying to be an occupational therapist, was just beginning the struggle toward procedural knowing. She, too, experienced an identity crisis when her husband deserted her, leaving her with an eight-year-old daughter, no money, no friends, and, according to Minna, no self. She told us that never during her marriage did she face a problem squarely. "I was confused about everything. I was unrealistic about things. I was more in a fantasy world. You have to see things for what they are, not for what you want to see them. I don't want to live in a dream world."

Minna and others have discovered that the inner voice sometimes lies. It tells you something is right for you that turns out to be disastrously wrong for you. It tells you that you have met Mr. Right, for instance, and nine months later you find yourself alone, raising his child. Minna wants to see things "the way they really are," so that she can figure out what goals are realistic for her and what steps she must take to reach those goals. Procedural knowers are practical, pragmatic problem solvers. Far from will-o'-the-wisps, their feet are planted firmly on the ground. They are trying, with more or less success, to take control of their lives in a planned, deliberate fashion. As Minna said, "I think everything out, and I want to make sure I understand exactly what's going on before I do anything."

6

Procedural Knowledge: Separate and Connected Knowing

> I never take anything someone says for granted. I just tend to see the contrary. I like playing devil's advocate, arguing the opposite of what somebody's saying, thinking of exceptions to what the person has said, or thinking of a different train of logic.
>
> —A college sophomore

> When I have an idea about something, and it differs from the way another person is thinking about it, I'll usually try to look at it from that person's point of view, see how they could say that, why they think that they're right, why it makes sense.
>
> —A college sophomore

THE PROCEDURES Patti and Naomi use for making meaning, although similar and equally reasonable, are not identical. Their stories illustrate the evolution of two distinctive forms of procedural knowledge. The theme of understanding is more prominent in Patti's story than in Naomi's, and the theme of knowledge is more prominent in Naomi's story than in Patti's, although both themes are present in both stories.

By *understanding* we mean something akin to the German word *kennen*, the French *connaître*, the Spanish *conocer*, or the Greek *gnosis* (Lewis 1983), implying personal acquaintance with an object (usually but not always a person). Understanding involves intimacy and equality between self and object, while *knowledge* (*wissen, savoir, saber*) implies separation from the object and mastery over it. Understanding, in Patti's view and the view of other women at this position, entails acceptance. It precludes evaluation, because evaluation puts the object at a distance, places the self above it, and quantifies a response to the object that should remain qualitative. (Many women who hold this view at one point in their lives come to take a different view. We shall meet some of them in the next chapter.)

In Perry's (1970) account of intellectual development, the student discovers critical reasoning as "how They [the upper case "T" symbolizing authority—here, the professors] want us to think," how students must think in order to win the academic game. The student uses this new mode of thinking to construct arguments powerful enough to meet the standards of an impersonal authority. This is Naomi's story, and most of the women in this chapter tell a similar story. Viewed from a distance, at least, these women might almost be men.

Patti's story is different. Her new mode of thinking emerges not out of a need to conform to the demands of external authorities but out of a need to understand the opinions of other people, opinions that seemed at first obscure, alien, even threatening to her. We saw in chapter 4 how some of the subjectivist women were beginning to really listen in order to discover what other people were thinking. Patti goes further. In an attempt to achieve a kind of harmony with another person in spite of difference and distance, women like Patti try to enter the other person's frame to discover the premises for the other's point of view. The other may be a teacher but is more likely to be a peer and may be a long-dead poet. The focus is not on how They want you to think, as in Perry's account, but on how they (the lower case "t" symbolizing more equal status) think; and the purpose is not justification but connection.

Naomi, like Perry's prototypical male undergraduate at this position, asks herself, "What standards are being used to evaluate my analysis of this poem? What techniques can I use to analyze it?" As with the small boys Piaget (1965) observed playing marbles on the sidewalks of Geneva fifty years ago, the orientation is toward impersonal rules. Borrowing a term from Gilligan (1982), we call this epistemological orientation *separate knowing*. Women at the same position who think more as Patti does ask instead, "What is this poet trying to say to me?" The orientation, as with the little girls Piaget observed playing hopscotch, is toward relationship. We call this epistemological orientation *connected knowing*.

Gilligan (1982) and her colleague Nona Lyons (1983) use the terms *separate* and *connected* to describe two different conceptions or experiences of the self, as essentially autonomous (separate from others) or as essentially in relationship (connected to others). The separate self experiences relationships in terms of "reciprocity," considering others as it wishes to be considered. The connected self experiences relationships as "response to others in their terms" (Lyons 1983, p. 134).

People who experience the self as predominantly separate tend to espouse a morality based on impersonal procedures for establishing justice, while people who experience the self as predominantly connected tend to espouse a morality based on care (Lyons 1983). Similarly, we posit two contrasting epistemological orientations: a separate epistemology, based upon impersonal procedures for establishing truth, and a connected epistemology, in which truth emerges through care. As the philosopher Nel Noddings says, "In the intellectual domain, our caring represents a quest for understanding" (1984, p. 169). Although our use of the terms *separate* and *connected* is similar enough to Gilligan's to warrant our adopting them, when we speak of separate and connected knowing we refer not to any sort of relationship between the self and another person but to relationships between knowers and the objects (or subjects) of knowing (which may or may not be persons).

The relationship between a person and an idea seems doomed to be one-sided, since an idea cannot reciprocate the care lavished upon it by a thinker. But, as Noddings says, "When we understand, we feel that this object-other has responded to us" (p. 169). We hear it speak to us. The joy attendant upon intimacy with an idea is not so different from the joy we feel in close relationships with friends.

The voice of separate knowing is easy to hear. Developmentalists like Piaget, Kohlberg, and Perry have tuned our ears to it, and it rang out loud and clear in our interviews, especially with women from highly selective, rigorous, and traditional colleges like the one from which Perry drew his sample. The voice of connected knowing was harder to hear, because our ears were not tuned to it and because we never before listened with such care to relatively unschooled women, like Patti, who speak it most eloquently. We heard the voice, once identified, as at least a minor theme and sometimes the major one in the lives of even the most gifted and privileged women we interviewed, especially at the less traditional colleges. Connected knowing is not confined to the poor, the uneducated, or the soft-headed.

Nor is it exclusively a female voice. We all encounter men, in person and in print, who speak in this voice. Separate and connected knowing are not gender-specific. The two modes may be gender-related: It is possible that more women than men tip toward connected knowing and more men than women toward separate knowing. Some people, certainly, would argue that this is so, but we know of no hard data (to use a favorite separate-knowing term) bearing directly on the issue, and we offer none here because we interviewed no men.

The women we interviewed were not limited to a single voice. Most of them spoke sometimes in one voice, sometimes in the other. In the next chapter we will see how some women moved to integrate the two orientations into a single, more balanced voice. For the moment, however, the developmental moment recorded in this chapter, each of the women spoke in two distinct voices, and each tipped toward one orientation or the other.

Separate Knowing

Most of the women who leaned heavily toward separate knowing were attending or had recently graduated from a traditional, elite, liberal arts college. The majority attended a women's college. We will say more in a later chapter about different types of institutions as contexts for development; here, a brief description is necessary to set the stage.

Teachers at traditional, rigorous, liberal arts colleges are bona fide experts with Ph.D.'s in respected disciplines who believe that it is their responsibility to teach their students methods of critical thinking, especially the methods peculiar to their disciplines, and to provide students with regular feedback on the degree to which their work meets the high standards of the institution. In such a setting students may be expected to discover separate knowing as "the way They want you to think" and to learn how to do it.

Some of the separate knowers, in having chosen and having been chosen to attend such institutions, already showed a penchant for separate knowing. In one sense, these were highly conventional women. They met the standards of academic achievement and conformed to the expectations set by their parents and their teachers. But they also violated conventional feminine stereotypes. Many reported that as children they were tomboys. Naomi said that she sometimes wished she were a boy so she could do things that boys did, and some women said that they used to dress up in boys' clothes and play boys' games. These women conformed to a pattern

observed in a study by Norman Livson and Harvey Peskin (1981): Girls
who behaved like tomboys in early adolescence exhibited high intellectual
competence in late adolescence. Livson and Peskin suggest that "sex-
inappropriate behavior in early adolescence is an expression of protest
against the incompetency 'demands' of the conventional feminine role"
(p. 191). "Most people," said one young woman, now a student in medical
school, "do not look at women as people, certainly not intellectual people."
Separate knowers refuse to play the conventional female role, choosing
instead to play a game that has belonged traditionally to boys—the game
of impersonal reason.

DOUBTING

At the heart of separate knowing is critical thinking, or, as Peter Elbow
(1973) puts it, "the doubting game." Elbow, a teacher of writing (who,
incidentally, designed an imaginative writing program for incoming students
at one of the colleges in our sample), appends his essay on the believing
game and the doubting game to a book about writing. Although the essay
does not refer to writing, it is easy to see why a teacher of writing may
come to value both games: In order to produce a first draft, writers need
to believe their own words; but in editing the final draft, they need a more
doubtful eye.

Separate knowers are tough-minded. They are like doormen at exclu-
sive clubs. They don't want to let anything in unless they are pretty sure
it is good. They would rather exclude someone who belongs to the club
than admit someone who does not. As Elbow says, the doubting game
involves "putting something on trial to see whether it is wanting or not"
(p. 173). Presented with a proposition, separate knowers immediately look
for something wrong—a loophole, a factual error, a logical contradiction,
the omission of contrary evidence.

Separate knowing is in a sense the opposite of subjectivism. While
subjectivists assume that everyone is right, separate knowers assume that
everyone—including themselves—may be wrong. If something feels right
to subjectivists, they assume it to *be* right. Separate knowers, on the other
hand, are especially suspicious of ideas that feel right; they feel a special
obligation to examine such ideas critically, whether the ideas originate in
their own heads or come from someone else. (Francis Bacon advised men
to avoid "whatever the mind seizes and dwells upon with peculiar satisfaction" [quoted by Michael Lewis 1983, p. 171].)

LISTENING TO REASON

"I'll not listen to reason," says a woman servant in Elizabeth Gaskell's novel *Cranford*. "Reason always means what someone else has to say" (1894, p. 242). The women in this chapter, like all the women we interviewed, were wary of other people's words and reasons, because people had battered them with words and reasons. Separate knowers remain suspicious; but as they develop techniques for analyzing and evaluating arguments, they become less vulnerable to attack. Because other people's reasons threaten them less, they are more able to listen to them. They can detect specious reasoning and find rational grounds for disagreement; but, like hidden subjectivists, they find it difficult to give voice to their disagreement, unless they can couch it in the method. Some said they could argue only with strangers; others said they could argue only with their most intimate friends. In both situations, we think, arguing feels relatively safe because it does not threaten the dissolution of relationships. Some women said, for perhaps the same reason, that they could argue only about things that did not matter; argument was possible only if pointless.

In general, few of the women we interviewed, even among the ablest separate knowers, found argument—reasoned critical discourse—a congenial form of conversation among friends. The classic dormitory bull session, with students assailing their opponents' logic and attacking their evidence, seems to occur rarely among women, and teachers complain that women students are reluctant to engage in critical debate with peers in class, even when explicitly encouraged to do so. Women find it hard to see doubting as a "game"; they tend to take it personally. Teachers and fathers and boyfriends assure them that arguments are not between *persons* but between *positions*, but the women continue to fear that someone may get hurt.

A woman may avoid debates with peers, but her professors force her to construct arguments. Sometimes they invite her to argue with them. Faith, in her sophomore year, said, "Last night, the professor gave us his interpretation of Henry James's *Turning* [sic] *of the Screw*, and after it he said, 'All right. This is my interpretation. You should be ripping it apart. You're sitting there. Come on, start ripping at it.'" The interviewer asked, "Did you?" and Faith replied, "Well, I did a little, but basically I agreed with what he was saying." Faith had not yet learned how to play the doubting game. It does not matter whether you agree with an interpretation or not; you must still try to find something wrong with it. In fact, as Elbow (1973) says, the more believable the interpretation is, the harder you must try to doubt it.

Separate knowing is essentially an adversarial form. If played among peers, the game is fair; but in the "games" the women described, as in Faith's case, the woman was nearly always pitted against an authority, usually a professor and usually male. These were unequal contests. The teacher wields very real power over the student, although masked with genial camaraderie; and it is dangerous for the relatively powerless to rip into the interpretations of the powerful.

Teachers, being professionals, are much more skilled than students at playing the game. Daphne, in her sophomore year, said, "It seems like he's up on Cloud Nine, and you're way down on the ground floor, and there's just no way you can get on common ground. A lot of the time I don't agree with his interpretation of the poetry, but I can't come up with anything he could consider worthy of notice."

When we asked Faith to tell us about an important learning experience in her life, she recalled a time when she successfully challenged her seventh-grade physics teacher's assertion that Mount Everest was the highest mountain on earth. This seemingly trivial incident stuck in her mind, she thought, because it taught her that "you don't have to accept people's words." But seven years later Faith continued to wrestle with issues concerning acceptance of teachers' words. "Teachers are in such a powerful position at any level. I think it's important for students not to take everything they hear at face value." But she admitted that she often did, especially in an area with which she was not familiar. Just beginning to trust her own reasoning, she was easily intimidated by displays of brilliance. "Whenever I'm around anyone I perceive as being very, very intelligent, I'm always afraid of saying something stupid. And so I tend to be silent."

This loss of voice is common, especially when separate knowing is the only voice allowed and especially when that voice is just beginning to emerge. Faith had trouble doubting her teacher's polished interpretations, but she had no trouble doubting her own. Lines from Marge Piercy's poem "Unlearning to Not Speak" come to mind.

> Phrases of men who lectured her
> drift and rustle in piles:
> Why don't you speak up? (1973, p. 38)

Faith believed that the only way people could say something important was by weighing its importance in advance. But how could she help but think before she spoke? She knew her thinking was inadequate; teachers told her so in person and in the margins of her papers. Again, from Marge Piercy's poem,

> You have the wrong answer,
> the wrong line, wrong face . . . (p. 38)

Faith had adopted for herself the standards teachers used in evaluating her thoughts. The "phrases of men who lectured her" reverberated inside her head whenever she picked up a pen to write, whenever she opened her mouth to speak. In Piercy's words, "she grunts to a halt" (p. 38).

Although the process of learning can be painful, many students become adept in playing the academic game of separate knowing. Daphne is one of them. As a sophomore, Daphne despaired over writing anything that "the guy on Cloud Nine" could tolerate, but a year later she devised a surefire formula for constructing successful papers. "You take a point of view, and then you address the points of view that might most successfully challenge your point of view. You try to disqualify those." Using this procedure, she consistently received A's on her papers and occasionally reached "common ground" with her teachers, at least to the degree that she could engage in friendly arguments with them. This is not the common ground of genuine colleagues. The teacher has not, in the words of radical educator Paulo Freire, become a genuine "partner of the students," a "student among students" (1971, p. 62). The teachers still wield the power: They write the rules of the game and rate the players' performances. But teachers and students can now speak a common language, and they can at least play at being colleagues.

Separate knowers use these new skills to defend themselves against the authorities in their lives. As students, they use their new skills to construct essays that they submit to authorities for evaluation in an attempt to demonstrate that they have mastered the requisite skills and so defend themselves against the teacher's doubts. In their academic lives students sometimes come to feel like pawns in the doubting game. They are the "something" put on trial to see whether or not "it" is wanting. (And, as we shall see, even when they succeed and are found not wanting, something may seem to them to be wanting.)

In accepting authorities' standards, separate knowers make themselves vulnerable to their criticism. The authorities have a right to find fault with the reasoning of separate knowers; and since there is nothing personal in their criticism, the separate knowers must accept it with equanimity. On the other hand, separate knowers move toward a collegial relationship with the authorities. Armed with new powers of reason, separate knowers can criticize the reasoning of authorities. Laws, not men, govern the world of separate knowers, at least in theory. Authority is nonarbitrary; it rests on reason rather than power or status. Anyone who speaks with the voice of reason—even a peasant or a student—has a right to be heard; and anyone who does not, whether a king or a professor, has no right to be heard. Experts are only as good as their arguments. According to Perry (1970), the paradox is that, although attempting merely to conform to authorities' standards, the student is developing the capacity for independent thought. A process that begins with mere "lip service" and parroting ultimately leads to a real voice.

But the voice is specialized. At this point in development the woman exercises her capacity for independent thought only at the behest of authority. Separate knowers speak a public language. They exhibit their knowledge in a series of public performances, and they address their messages not to themselves or to intimate friends but to an audience of relative strangers. Often, the primary purpose of their words is not to express personally meaningful ideas but to manipulate the listener's reactions, and they see the listener not as an ally in conversation but as a potentially hostile judge. Faith, who spoke proudly of having learned to say what she meant, in the next breath added, "You learn how to sound like you know what you're talking about, even if you don't."

We asked another student, Simone, what she thought the purpose of class discussion was. We meant what purpose it served for *her*, but she answered from the teacher's perspective: "It helps to see if the students are doing the reading. There's not much else to grade on." According to Simone, the purpose of discussion was to provide data that authority could use for evaluation. No wonder Simone rarely spoke in class.

Simone's professors forced her to put words on paper. She complied dutifully and even successfully, but her heart was not in it. "I write good papers when I try," she said, and we have no reason to doubt her. She was an able student with a verbal SAT score of 780 and a grade point average around A−. "Good papers" to Simone were papers teachers liked. Simone, herself, did not like them much: "I can write a good paper, and someday I may learn to write one that I like, that is not just bullshit, but I still feel that it's somewhat pointless. I do it, and I get my grade, but it hasn't proved anything to me."

Simone reminds us of the two Ivy League women students in Joan Bolker's (1979) composition class, who got good grades on their papers but sensed in them "a lack of personality" and felt a "sense of nonownership and of disappointment at not being able to make [themselves] heard." According to Bolker, although these young women "have both learned how to write papers, they have not yet learned to write—that is, to be able to communicate by expressing their own ideas, feelings, and voices on paper" (p. 906). Simone and her separate knowing sisters have developed a public voice that aims to please the teacher and pays no attention to the speaker. Their papers are so "highly polished . . . that it is hard to catch a human voice in them" (p. 907).

SELF-EXTRICATION

One of the meanings of *objectivity* is that people do not project the contents of their own heads into the external object. Both separate and connected knowers are wary of projection, but they avoid it by different means. Separate knowers avoid it by suppressing the self, taking as impersonal a stance as possible toward the object. Separate knowers try to "weed out the self" (Elbow 1973, p. 171) so that the flowers of pure reason may flourish.

Separate knowers' procedures for making meaning are strictly impersonal. Feelings and personal beliefs are rigorously excluded. These procedures have been most highly elaborated and explicitly codified in the sciences, but they exist in some form and with some degree of specificity in all disciplines. Faith, interviewed in her first and second years, articulated especially clearly the view that in order to really analyze an event you had to divorce yourself from your emotions about it. In writing a paper about *Wuthering Heights*, she said, "The hardest thing to do was to separate my personal opinion of Heathcliff from the issue of whether or not Heathcliff was a fully developed, rounded character." When Faith first read the novel she just plain hated Heathcliff. Upon the third reading she could see how Emily Brontë had developed the character; and this, she saw, was what the teacher wanted her to write about. He did not care how she personally felt about Heathcliff as a person; he wanted her to explain how Heathcliff worked within the system of the novel.

In her political science class Faith began to apply this mode of objective analysis outside the classroom to issues of world affairs. She said, "I personally am very appalled at the Iranians taking Americans hostage. However, when analyzing it, I can't say, 'Well, that's awful because they're harming Americans, and I sympathize with the hostages.' I have to say, 'Well, this isn't really smart of the Ayatollah Khomeini to do this, because it causes world opinion against Iran,' and so forth."

To be objective, here, means to speak dispassionately, to exclude your own concerns and to adopt a perspective that your adversaries may respect, as in their own self-interest. It also means to exclude *all* feelings, including those of the adversary, examining the issue from a strictly pragmatic, strategic point of view. In treating the Iranian crisis, like *Wuthering Heights*, as a technical problem, Faith reminds us of the boy Gilligan calls Jake, who treats a moral dilemma as "a math problem with humans" (1982, p. 28). Faith has surely succeeded in "weeding out the self."

Disinterested reason is, of course, one of the highest of human achievements, and separate knowers appreciate it. They deplore the egocentricity of their earlier judgments. They believe that they can see more and see more clearly than they could when blinded by their own passions and opinions. But some of the young women we interviewed carry disinterest too far; it degenerates into absence of interest, anomie, and monotony. These women used mechanical or biological metaphors to describe their paper writing. Daphne loved reading her English novels and discussing them in class, perhaps because these activities allowed her to engage in connected knowing; but writing papers felt like "just cranking." Simone called her papers "shit," because she did not care about what she was writing about, and reason in the absence of feeling "is bullshit."*

"The problem," Simone says, "is that I don't feel terribly strongly about one point of view, but that point of view seems to make more sense. It's easier to write the paper, supporting that point of view than the other one, because there's more to support it. And it's not one of my deepfounded beliefs, but it writes the paper." Simone did not write the paper; *it* wrote the paper. Reasons wrote the paper, and words and reasons seemed unrelated to personal truth. Forced to choose between a personal belief she could not reasonably articulate and a position she did not believe but could defend, she felt she had to choose the reasonable, the "acceptable lie" (Rich 1979, p. 239).

Simone's A-minus arguments seemed to her unrelated not only to personal truth but to objective truth. It seemed to her that you could write a good argument in support of a bad interpretation. Simone could tell a well-reasoned argument from a poorly reasoned one, but she remained suspicious of reason. "It's just rhetoric," she said. "It's just a game. It doesn't prove anything." The person who won the argument was the person with the greater rhetorical skill, not the person closer to the truth.†

Some of the women we interviewed were proud of their rhetorical skill, but for many it was an empty exercise that did not, as Simone said,

---

* We are reminded of a comment made by Dorothy Smith, the feminist sociologist: "In the social sciences the pursuit of objectivity makes it possible for people to be paid to pursue a knowledge to which they are otherwise indifferent" (1974, p. 9).

† "Rhetoric," writes the poet Adrienne Rich, is a "masculine adversary style of discourse," developed, according to Walter Ong, as a rational form of masculine ceremonial combat, requiring the use of Latin at a time when Latin was used almost exclusively by males. Rich quotes Ong as follows: "During the romantic age, academic education was all but exclusively focused on defending a position (thesis) or attacking the position of another person—even medicine was taught in this way" (1979, p. 138).

"prove anything." Ceremonial combat, to women, often seems just silly. The exercise of rhetoric seemed to be experienced as especially futile by undergraduates, who used it mainly to prove their worth to the authorities. The content of the academic arguments hardly mattered; what did matter was proving that you had mastered the form.

These young women had little sense that their words and reasons could have powerful effects. Their arguments did not convince them; why should they influence anyone else? We asked one undergraduate what she would do if she were opposed to nuclear power and her boss ordered her to write a report favoring it. She saw no problem in writing the report. "Just saying I'm in favor of it would never change my idea," nor, she implied, would it change anyone else's.

But when they leave school and enter the real world, many of these women find themselves in situations in which it is necessary to fight; and they are grateful, then, to find themselves equipped with words that they can wield effectively as weapons of attack. One alumna said, "I think I can set up an argument very well, so that I've got a much better chance of winning it. I'll start one out from a position of offense, rather than all the time trying to get back on my feet."

Daphne's father, whom she dearly loves, used to "deflate" her with "his voice and his words." But three years out of college, she could "prick his bubble. . . . It's something I learned out in the big world, that you don't have to be polite and concede the other person's point. You're much better off if you deal from a position of strength. That way you're going to be less of a victim. And I proceed to do that in my relationships all over the place."

Gretchen repeatedly and publicly objected to sexist misinformation dispensed by her professors at medical school, although she knew her classmates would jeer at her.

> The professor was saying that sanitary pads cause more vaginal in-
> fections, so that you should use tampons. Then he said something
> about how women shouldn't wear pantyhose because they cause
> vaginal infections. The dilemma was, Do I sit here and let this
> bastard give us all this false information? Do I just sit there and
> listen to this? Or say something about it and have an argument
> with the guy?

She decided to have the argument.

I pointed out that tampons encourage infection because intestinal organisms sometimes ascend the string and that the problem with pantyhose is with the ventilation and absorbance of fluids in that area. With the proper materials, if cotton were used, then the problems would be decreased. People in the class said, "Oh, my God! I can't believe she's bringing this up—to talk about cotton-crotch pantyhose!"

In her sophomore year, Faith took a philosophy course on feminism, which helped her to formulate her own feminist convictions and to articulate her own anger about the position of women. In addition, she felt the course taught her to argue "without getting too emotional."

On the first part of the midterm exam we were given this article that, for me at least, inspired nothing but blind rage. I was so infuriated reading it. And then I had to sit down and write a critique of it. And it teaches you to have the anger there, but also the reasoning. And not lose the reasoning. So people can't tell you, "You're just being overemotional—typically female."

Faith's last sentence suggested that she still tailored her messages to withstand the doubts of powerful authorities; but this passage has a very different flavor from the ones taken from her earlier interview. Although she was careful not to get "too emotional," she did not extricate herself entirely from the argument. She argued in favor of her own convictions; and she allowed herself to "have the anger there." It was rare, in our experience, for undergraduates at this institution to do this. More often, like Naomi, they kept their feelings out of the classroom. But Naomi, like most of her fellow students, was strongly tipped toward separate knowing; while in Faith the two modes were more evenly balanced. And in connected knowing, the self is allowed to participate.

Connected Knowing

Connected knowing builds on the subjectivists' conviction that the most trustworthy knowledge comes from personal experience rather than the pronouncements of authorities. Among extreme subjectivists this conviction can lead to the view that they can know only their own truths, access to another person's knowledge being impossible.

Connected knowers develop procedures for gaining access to other people's knowledge. At the heart of these procedures is the capacity for empathy. Since knowledge comes from experience, the only way they can hope to understand another person's ideas is to try to share the experience that has led the person to form the idea. A college senior, discussing *The Divine Comedy* with us, said, "You shouldn't read a book just as something printed and distant from you, but as a real experience of someone who went through some sort of situation. I tend to try and read the mind of the author behind it, and ask, 'Why did he write that? What was happening to him when he wrote that?' "

Connected knowers know that they can only approximate other people's experiences and so can gain only limited access to their knowledge.* But insofar as possible, they must act as connected rather than separate selves, seeing the other not in their own terms but in the other's terms. Elbow (1973) calls this procedure the "believing game,"† and he says it is very hard to play. Although it may be difficult for men, many women find it easier to believe than to doubt. An undergraduate we interviewed said, "I'm not superanalytic. It's easy for me to take other people's points of view. It's hard for me to argue, because I feel like I can understand the other person's argument. It's easy for me to see a whole lot of different points of view on things and to understand why people think those things."

And, while women frequently do experience doubting as a game, believing feels real to them, perhaps because it is founded upon genuine care and because it promises to reveal the kind of truth they value—truth that is personal, particular, and grounded in firsthand experience. This comes through most clearly in their accounts of conversations.

---

* The feminist sociologist Shulamit Reinharz writes, "I will never know the experience of others, but I can know my own, and I can approximate theirs by entering their world. This approximation marks the tragic, perpetually inadequate aspect of social research" (1984, p. 365).

† The distinction between separate and connected, believing and doubting procedures for knowing is an old and recurring one. For instance, John Stuart Mill, comparing Jeremy Bentham's and Samuel Coleridge's approaches to the questions, "What is true?" or "What is the meaning of it?," wrote, "The one [Bentham] took his stand *outside* the received opinion, and surveyed it as an entire stranger to it; the other [Coleridge] looked at it from within, and endeavored to see it with the eyes of a believer in it" (1962, p. 121). More recently, Jerome Bruner has distinguished between "paradigmatic" and "narrative" modes of thought, reminiscent, he says, of Dilthey's *Naturwissenschaften* and the *Geisteswissenschaften*, "the sciences of nature and of humanity, the first seeking generality and the second uniqueness, one guided by the methods of science and logic, the other by a search for the meaning of historical and personal events in their full comprehensive richness" (1985, p. 101).

CONVERSING IN THE CONNECTED MODE

A first-year student recalled a "wonderful conversation" with a student from Ethiopia who explained why her people had accepted communism and described the effects of the new regime: "It was great to get another view on it from someone who's right there in the situation and who can see it differently from the American view that communism is bad, although I still feel it is."

We have in our records innumerable reports of conversations like this, especially among students in their first year of college. These conversations differed in both form and substance from the competitive bull sessions mentioned earlier. These young women did not engage in metaphysical debate. They did not argue about abstractions or attack or defend positions. No one tried to prove anything or to convert anyone. The Ethiopian articulated her reality, and the American tried to understand it. They did not discuss communism in general, impersonal terms but in terms of its origins and consequences among a particular group of real people.

The differences between the women's conversation and the male bull session were strikingly reminiscent of the differences Janet Lever (1976) noted between the play of fifth-grade girls and boys: intimate rather than impersonal, relatively informal and unstructured rather than bound by more or less explicit formal rules. Women have been practicing this kind of conversation since childhood.

An alumna recalled spending much of her first year "just sitting around and talking." Having lived in the same small town for eighteen years, she was dazzled by meeting "all kinds of people from all kinds of walks of life from all across the country and the world who have all kinds of different opinions and views of life. That made me really start listening to people and comparing and contrasting views." She began to engage in less facile and more energetic forms of listening, interviewing her new acquaintances. And she discovered that "if you listen to people, you can understand why they feel the way they do. There are reasons. They're not just being irrational."

The reasons mentioned here have to do not with propositional logic but with experience. "Why do you think that?" they ask, meaning not "What were the steps in your reasoning?" but "What circumstances led you to that perception?" This is not like an oral examination in which the respondent must prove that she knows what she is supposed to know. It is not like a courtroom interrogation in which the attorney fires off a series of highly specific questions and allows only brief responses so as to elicit only the evidence he or she wants. It is more like a clinical interview. By inviting the respondent to tell her story, without interruption, the questioner allows the respondent to control and develop her own response.*

These conversations occur with special frequency whenever women encounter people who hold and practice beliefs that seem exotic, intriguing, bizarre, alien, even frightening. Naomi, for example, was initially shattered when, late in her first year at college, a woman who had become a close friend revealed that she had discovered she was a lesbian. The friend talked, and Naomi listened until she understood.

If one can discover the experiential logic behind these ideas, the ideas become less strange and the owners of the ideas cease to be strangers. The world becomes warmer and more orderly. Sometimes, but not always, a woman adopts another person's ideas as her own. Through empathy she expands her experiential base; she acquires vicarious (secondhand, first-hand) experience and so expands her knowledge. "What I know," one freshman told us, "is very limited. I've grown up one way, and many people have grown up different ways; and if I don't know what they have to offer, I don't have those experiences."

Connected knowers begin with an interest in the facts of other people's lives, but they gradually shift the focus to other people's ways of thinking. As in all procedural knowing, it is the form rather than the content of knowing that is central. Separate knowers learn through explicit formal instruction how to adopt a different lens—how, for example, to think like a sociologist. Connected knowers learn through empathy. Both learn to get out from behind their own eyes and use a different lens, in one case the lens of a discipline, in the other the lens of another person.

Faith told us that deep relationships offered her a chance to really get to know another view of the world. Her close friends, she said, "have very different ways of looking at things, and my knowing them very well has shown me other ways of seeing the world." Discussions with one of these close friends led Faith to an entirely new conception of the purpose of a college education. She had thought that the purpose of college was to prepare for a vocation; but then she began to believe, with her friend, that it was to train and broaden the mind. If it is true, as Chodorow (1978), Gilligan (1982), Levinson (1978), Pollak and Gilligan (1982), Vaillant (1977), and others have suggested, that men fear intimacy, many men may find the mode of learning Faith used here as intimidating as Faith found the injunction to "rip into" her teacher's interpretation of Henry James.

* For an experimental investigation of "narrative" versus "fragmented" trial testimony by male and female witnesses, see Lind, Conley, Erickson, and O'Barr (1978).

SHARING SMALL TRUTHS

Conversations among intimates do not always concern such weighty matters as communism and higher education. More often they consist of what the literary critic Patricia Spacks calls "small shared truth[s] (1982, p. 24). Usually, women share these truths with other women, occasionally with friends and lovers of the opposite sex. Sometimes they talk directly about their own feelings, and sometimes they talk about other people. We call the latter gossip.

Spacks contrasts *gossip* with *discourse:* "People discourse *to* one another; they gossip *with.* . . . One discourses from a height, gossips around the kitchen table" (p. 24). Gossip concerns the personal, the particular, and frequently the petty; but it does not follow that it is a trivial activity. "Gossip, like poetry and fiction, penetrates to the truth of things" (p. 25). The explicit information gossipers share concerns the behavior of other people; but, implicitly, gossipers tell each other about themselves by showing how they interpret the information they share. In gossip, as Spacks says, "responses to news matter more than news itself." As the gossiper observes her friend's responses she learns about the friend's ways of making meaning. And the gossipers collaborate in practicing this "special mode of knowing" (p. 28), which moves back and forth between large and small, particular and general.

REFUSING TO JUDGE

Spacks (1982) says that gossip proceeds from trust and builds trust. This is true of all conversations conducted in the connected mode: These conversations grow out of connection, and they cement connections. Connected knowers begin with an attitude of trust; they assume the other person has something good to say. This trustfulness builds on the subjectivist notion that because all opinions come from experience and you cannot call anyone's experience wrong, you cannot call the opinion wrong. Connected knowers do not measure other people's words by some impersonal standard. Their purpose is not to judge but to understand.

Women seem to take naturally to a nonjudgmental stance. In teaching undergraduates we have found it necessary to ask many of the males to refrain from making judgments until they understood the topic. On the other hand, we have often had to prod the females into critical examination: Even when they disagreed vehemently with an opinion, they hesitated to judge it wrong until they had tried hard to understand the reasoning behind it.

These women start, like the women Gilligan (1982) describes, from a premise of connection. Negative judgments seem to them to violate such a premise by asserting superiority. Ideally—although not always in practice—they take the stance that nothing human is alien to them. As one student said, she could not imagine a situation in which "I would feel morally above or separate from someone else to the extent that I wouldn't make the attempt to understand." Within their own frameworks, these women said that they could make moral judgments, but they did not wish to impose these judgments on others. When someone said something they disagreed with or disapproved of, their instinct was not to argue but to "look at it from that person's point of view, see how they could say that, why they think that they're right, why it makes sense."

It is easy to condemn women's refusal to make judgments as evidence of passivity or absence of agency, and indeed, in a sense, it is. Connected knowing belongs to David Bakan's (1966) "communal" mode (involving fusion and acceptance) rather than the "agentic" mode (involving separation and control). But, as the philosopher Carol McMillan (1982) reminds us, "Agency need not involve control over events" (p. 131). McMillan quotes the philosopher Georg von Wright.

> Action has a "passive" counterpart which is usually called forbearance. For-bearance can be distinguished from mere passivity, not acting, by being intentional passivity. . . . The immediate outer aspect of forbearance is, normally, a state of muscular rest or, exceptionally, muscular activity which one "lets go on" although one could restrain the movements. (Pp. 131–32)

McMillan cites as an illustration of the coexistence of forbearance and control the relaxation of the woman who refuses medication in order to participate as an active agent in the birth of her child.

Connected knowing requires forbearance. "Patience," says the writer Simone de Beauvoir, is one of those " 'feminine' qualities which have their origin in our oppression but should be preserved after our liberation" (1976, p. 153). Elbow (1973) says that while the doubting game requires a "combative kind of energy that feels like clenching a muscle. . . . The shape of the believing game is waiting, patience, not being in a hurry. . . . A kind of trying-not-to-try" (pp. 177, 180, 181). This idea is akin to Weil's notion of "attention," which she defines as "inactive action" (1972, p. 39). Trustworthy truths gestate slowly, and people must "fight the itch for closure" (Elbow 1973, p. 177). According to Noddings (1984),

> I let the object act upon me, seize me, direct my fleeting thoughts. . . . My decision to do this is mine, it requires an effort in preparation, but it also

requires a letting go of my attempts to control. This sort of passivity . . . is not a mindless, vegetablelike passivity. It is a controlled state that abstains from controlling the situation. (P. 163)

COLLABORATING IN CONNECTED-KNOWING GROUPS

It is helpful for both separate and connected knowers to meet in groups of two or more people. Separate knowers bring to their group propositions that they have developed as fully as possible and that they hope to sell in the free marketplace of ideas. Members must know the rules, but they need not know each other. In connected-knowing groups people utter half-baked half-truths and ask others to nurture them. Since no one would entrust one's fragile infant to a stranger, members of the group must learn to know and trust each other. In such an atmosphere members do engage in criticism, but the criticism is "connected." A sophomore we call Bess helped us understand connected criticism by describing her studio art course. She told us that everyone was scared and no one wanted to "cut up" anyone's work. As the class went along, although people became more and more supportive, they also grew more and more critical.

> But if you've gone along since the beginning with the same people it never comes across as this awful criticism. It's very supportive. You have to stand there and face something for four hours and know that you didn't solve anything. You're emotionally drained when you're finished. Then, the next day, people help you decide why or say, "No, I think it came out all right; don't be so upset," or "This is fantastic." You just keep picking each other up out of the pits and saying, "You've done something good here," or "Why don't you try this?" [The teacher] is more or less a conductor. He shouldn't dominate it. It's never just a grade scrawled across the top; it's a suggestion. This one professor always found something right with your painting. When you were about ready to chuck it, he always said, "No, look what you've done." That's really important.

People could criticize each other's work in this class and accept each other's criticisms because members of the group shared a similar experience. This is the only sort of expertise connected knowers recognize, the only sort of criticism they easily accept. Authority in connected knowing rests not on power or status or certification but on commonality of experience.

Bess said that she would be in a better position than we would to evaluate a sculpture produced by a classmate.

> Because I went through the same experience. I did the same thing. I did the work at the same rate and time as my fellow students. I understood the assignment. I knew what we were searching for. I knew that the problem was to use one piece of wood. We had to use the whole piece of wood in a sculpture. I knew how hard that was. I knew how the wood warped. It wasn't good wood. I knew that we didn't have much time, so most of them aren't finished. If you walked in there, you're not going to understand why it's that awful piece of wood. Physically, it's a gross piece of wood that's warped and has knots. You're not going to understand why it seems like this amount, why it's not bigger or smaller. Even though you have your right to your opinion, I'm in a better place to give one, because I know more facts about the situation.

Members of connected-knowing groups engage in collaborative explorations. A sophomore told us how she was enjoying class discussion of Mary Shelley's *Frankenstein:* "You can just read it on the top for the story. Then you can get underneath into Mary Shelley's life and all the hidden parts, and some people see some parts more than others, and they can explain them to you and show them to you. And you don't have to agree, but it's there."

Separate knowers try to subtract the personality of the perceiver from the perception, because they see personality as slanting the perception or adding "noise" that must be filtered out. Connected knowers see personality as adding to the perception, and so the personality of each member of the group enriches the group's understanding. Each individual must stretch her own vision in order to share another's vision. Through mutual stretching and sharing the group achieves a vision richer than any individual could achieve alone.

Connected knowing works best when members of the group meet over a long period of time and get to know each other well. One of the women we interviewed spent two years in a very small college where most of the classes were conducted as seminars. She then transferred to a larger college, where she enrolled in a seminar on modern British poetry, one of her favorite topics. "It was awful. The people didn't know how to talk about anything. They didn't know how to share ideas. It was always an argument; it wasn't an idea to be developed, to be explored." Although students at the smaller college sometimes rambled into irrelevancies, spoke incoherently, and interrupted, they knew each other's quirks and had developed strategies for working around them so that they could avoid trivial conflicts and confront important issues. "It was like a family group trying to work out a family problem, except it was an idea."

In most educational institutions there is no chance to form such family groups. Each course starts with a new cast of characters, runs for thirteen weeks or so, and then disperses. Often, members of the class do not even know each other's names, much less their styles of thinking.

Many women first experience collaborative connected knowing in their families. Bess, like Patti, believed that family crisis transformed her into a thinker. Her parents' separation, just after she entered high school, caused "a sudden awakening." Before that, she had been "just sort of floating along, feeling things. All of a sudden I became more aware of my personal situation, my family feelings, what was going on, what I had to think about." She and her three sisters stayed with their mother. "We started to verbalize problems. We felt very much that it was just the four of us. We bought our first car together. My father had always bought the car before. My mother had to say, 'You've got to help me. We've got to buy a car.' And I realized, yeah, I really have to know how to do these things. I have to help."

Bess's family has become a collaborative enterprise. Each member regularly asks for and receives support from each other member. "We've gone through enough problems together that we're always supporting each other." Bess's family sounds very much like her sculpture class. Indeed, her experience within the family may have enabled her to appreciate the class. We shall have more to say in a later chapter about the family as a context for knowing.

USING PERSONAL KNOWLEDGE

When we asked the women we interviewed "Why be objective?" they often answered that unless you were objective you could not help a friend. Suppose, for example, your friend is considering an abortion. You may find that horrifying, but you have to look at it in her terms, as one student said, "in terms of her situation and what *she* wants. Help her figure out what *she* wants, rather than tell her what you want for her." Women who act on knowledge received from authority know what a friend should do without consulting her; if they believe that abortion is wrong, they tell the friend to keep the child. Women who trust subjective knowledge, on the other hand, advise their friends to do whatever feels right to them. Connected knowers make it their responsibility to understand how their friends feel and to help them think the problem through. When we asked procedural knowers to tell us about moral dilemmas in their lives, they often told us about friends who were contemplating actions that they believed were not in the friends' best interests. Their own task, as they saw it, was to help their distraught friends think through their decisions.

Although connected knowing may begin as a procedure for understanding people, it does not end there. The mode of knowing is personal, but the object of knowing need not be. It may be a painting, for example (or even, as we shall see, an ear of corn [Keller 1983]). Connected knowers try to understand texts by imagining themselves into the author's mind. We asked a senior how she would evaluate two conflicting interpretations, and she replied,

> I'd read them both very closely and try to recreate that person's reasoning, see if I could follow the path. I try to think as the author does. It's hard, but I try not to bias the train of thought with my own impressions. I try to just pretend that I'm the author. I try to really just put myself in that person's place and feel why is it that they believe this way.

Another student talked about reading a poem as if she were eavesdropping on two people talking. In interpreting the poem, she said that she tried to discover "what he was trying to say to this other person."

Many women take naturally to connected knowing, finding it easier to follow authors than to attack them, easier to get close to them than to stand apart; but they do not always find it easy to enter perspectives very different from their own. This requires real skill and effort. It is important to distinguish between the effortless intuition of subjectivism (in which one identifies with positions that feel right) and the deliberate, imaginative extension of one's understanding into positions that initially feel wrong or remote. Connected knowing involves feeling, because it is rooted in relationship; but it also involves thought. Like Noddings's "care," it entails "generous thinking" (1984, p. 186) and "receptive rationality" (p. 1).

Connected knowing is just as *procedural* as separate knowing, although its procedures have not yet been as elaborately codified. Faith, in her first year at college, saw what her history professor wanted her to do, but she could not see how to do it.

> He's trying to get us to divorce ourselves from modern ways of thinking and look at it as it was, say, in 1700, when the event occurred.

Which is fine. But I have difficulty doing that, because I can't place myself back in the proper time period. I come from a middle-class family, and back then you would either have been peasantry or aristocracy. And I can't imagine being either. Now that we've gotten into the late 1800s I'm doing a little better, I think.

We know that Faith succeeded (perhaps beyond her teacher's desires) in extricating herself from interpretations of *Wuthering Heights* and the Iranian hostage crisis. Her problem in the history course was not so much to extricate herself from the situation as to connect with it. Elbow would say that Faith must "insert" herself into the seventeenth-century mind: "It takes practice over time to learn not to 'project' in the bad sense—not to see only your own preconceptions or preoccupations; and to learn to 'project' more in the good sense—to see more of what's really there by getting more of the self into every bit of it" (1973, p. 171).

Elbow's notion is close to *The Oxford Universal Dictionary*'s definition of *empathy*: "the power of projecting one's own personality into, and so fully understanding, the objective of contemplation." This phallic imagery may capture the masculine experience of empathy, but it strikes many women—Nel Noddings, for example—as a peculiar description of "feeling with." Empathy, for Noddings, "does not involve projection but reception." "I do not project," she says. "I receive the other into myself, and I see and feel with the other" (1984, p. 30).

In describing connected knowing the women we interviewed used images not of invading another mind but of opening up to receive another's experience into their own minds. One undergraduate said, "When I'm reading a book, I can open my mind to the point where I see what the author was all about, see the *isness* of what he was trying to say." And another said, "You must let the poem pass into you and become part of yourself, rather than something you see outside yourself. . . . There has to be some parallel between you and the poem." Similarly, Faith needed to find some point of connection between her own experience and the experience of the seventeenth-century peasant.

Faith had done quite well in overcoming "bad" projection. Her schooling had given her plenty of practice, and indeed, women have had centuries of practice in self-effacement. But Faith had not learned how to *use* herself as an instrument of understanding. This requires self-knowledge, and Faith's teachers had offered her little opportunity for self-knowledge. Faith needed practice in constructing metaphorical extensions to span the distance between her own and others' experiences. She needed to learn to respect her own reactions, not as final truths but as starting points for understanding, just as therapists learn to use their reactions to a client to help them understand the client.

Reinharz describes how she came to invent a method of "experiential analysis" for studying families in an Israeli town subject to intermittent rocket shelling.

> As I began the study I discovered to my surprise that before I could examine the families, I had to attend to my own security needs. Early in the process of doing so, I uncovered my previously unknown and unexamined responses to potential disaster. I found myself recording my own feelings to the same problem to which the families' responses were being studied. . . . I no longer considered these personal reactions internal noise that disturbed the research process. Rather, I looked to my reactions as an indicator of general patterns for coping with the continuous threat of potential destruction. (1984, p. 336)

Judging from the stories Faith and her classmates told, the kind of self-analysis required for complex connected knowing has been largely excluded from the traditional liberal arts curriculum and relegated to "counseling." In institutions that are more progressive, or less rigorous (depending upon one's point of view), students may be encouraged to develop their own curricula, exploring their own self-interests, and to use their own personal experience as a source of knowledge. Under these circumstances, women find it easier (although still not easy) to identify and articulate their needs and desires and preoccupations. We will say more about these educational issues in chapter 9.

Beyond Procedural Knowledge

Some of the women we interviewed seemed content, for the moment at least, with procedural knowledge as a mode of approaching the world. Others had begun to chafe against the constraints of the position.

Procedural knowledge is "objective" in the sense of being oriented away from the self—the knower—and toward the object the knower seeks to analyze or understand. In Piagetian language, procedural knowledge is tilted toward "accommodation" to the shape of the object rather than "assimilation" of the object to the shape of the knower's mind. This is true of both the connected and the separate forms; connected knowers seek to understand other people's ideas in the other people's terms rather than in their own terms.

Although this selfless aspect of procedural knowledge is its glory, some women began to experience it as alienation. This was especially and perhaps exclusively true of our most separate knowers. They no longer felt any personal involvement in the pursuit of knowledge. They felt as though they were answering other people's questions, and they could not make themselves care about the answers. Connected knowers, on the other hand, were attached to the objects they sought to understand; they *cared* about them. This being so, it seems likely that connected knowers can make the transition beyond purely procedural knowledge more smoothly than those who are tipped toward separate knowing. But this speculation is based on very little data, because we have in our sample very few highly reflective women who relied more heavily on connected than separate procedures.

In any case, the following section mainly describes the travails of transition the more separate knowers experience. These women hear themselves speaking in different voices in different situations. They hear themselves echoing the words of powerful others. And, like so many women, they feel like frauds (Clance and Imes 1978; McIntosh 1985). They yearn for a voice that is more integrated, individual, and original—a voice of their own.

SEARCHING FOR A SINGLE VOICE

In the institutions of higher learning most of these women attended, the subjective voice was largely ignored; feelings and intuitions were banished to the realm of the personal and private. It was the public, rational, analytical voice that received the institutions' tutelage, respect, and rewards. Most of these women profited from the tutelage, respect, and rewards, and most were grateful to their colleges for nurturing their analytical powers. In acquiring the skills of separate knowing, women at this position did, indeed, transcend the stereotypes of women as creatures ruled by instinct and emotion, incapable of reason; but they also adopted a stereotyped view of reason as detached from feeling and remote from everyday experience.

Naomi is a case in point. Although she took pride in her analytical skills, she exercised them only on academic tasks, only when required to submit material for judgment. She told us that she would be "stretching it" to try to apply her analytical skills to her personal life. "I don't impose a method of analysis on my personal life. I think when you're trying to analyze human beings there is nothing concrete to base your analysis on. I think it's subjective." Naomi felt that it was appropriate to be objective and unbiased in academic life, but in personal life it "would be like being a robot, having no feelings."

Just as Naomi found no room for dispassionate reason in personal life, she found no place for passion in academic life. In an interview during her third year of college she reported a disconcerting experience with a distinguished guest at a meeting of the Shakespeare Society. Naomi had read the guest's article criticizing *Henry VIII* as an inferior work and arguing that Shakespeare did not write it. Naomi questioned the scholar about the criteria he used and the reasons he gave for his judgment. The scholar told Naomi that "the bottom line was his subjective response to that piece of literature. He just had this gut feeling that it wasn't Shakespeare." Naomi found it bewildering that a noted academician, "a guy who clearly knows his stuff," would allow his feelings to shape his scholarly judgment.

But in the same interview there were signs that Naomi's two worlds— the public world of reason and the private world of feeling and unjustifiable insight—were beginning to intersect. For the first time, she spoke of bringing analysis to bear upon her personal life. "I want some time to think about myself," she said, and she resigned all her extracurricular posts in order to provide time for introspection the following year.

During her senior year Naomi did devote time to introspection; she grew more and more "emotionally distraught" until she was "unable to function." With the help of a counselor she began to *think* about personal issues, to "take a very close-up look" at her problematic relationship with her mother—something she had never mentioned in her three previous interviews. She told us that her mother needed to believe that she and Naomi were identical. "She wants a merger of the two selves. If she cries, I have to cry. There just isn't any separateness. She's really confused about how to deal with emotions." She accused Naomi of changing, "as if," Naomi said, "change is bad."

Several other women who were searching for something beyond procedural knowledge told of being utterly submerged in relationships, sometimes, as in Naomi's case, in relationships with their mothers. Cynthia said,

> Most of my life I have had an unusual relationship with my mother, to whom I've always been very close and always followed her lead and always basically experienced things through her. I would experience something and then I'd relate it all to her and she would synthesize it and digest it for me, and then I'd get the final word on what really happened.

After graduating from college Cynthia moved back into her parents' home but left after a couple of years when she realized "it was not a culturally acceptable thing to remain dependent on one's family." She was still struggling toward

> trusting my own impulses and not questioning them and their adequacy and their rectitude. It's hard for me to know how I feel. I can rarely say honestly whether I like this or I don't like that, because I'm always trying to second-guess myself. I look forward to being fifty years old. I really do. I would like to be somebody who knew what she wanted, who could say I don't like this and I do like that. Most of my life has been spent in pleasing other people or in devising stratagems through which I could appear to have pleased them and fulfilled my obligations to everybody else but myself. One did one's best to oblige. And I'm finally realizing that that's an empty, swift way of leading one's life.

Another alumna told a less tragic, more typical story: "I would fall into relationships and just kind of subsume myself in what that person expected. I never developed a sense of who I was and what I needed." Recently, her lover and housemate of several years terminated the relationship, declaring that she had become his "clone." She agreed. "It wasn't like two equal people coming together. I was the little shadow following him around, doing what he wanted to do."

These women had treated their mothers and even their friends and lovers, as well as their teachers, as authorities whom they were obliged to please. They had never experienced active partnership in a truly equal relationship. Finally, they have begun to imagine such relationships with friends and lovers and even with mothers and teachers.

Again, Naomi's story illustrates the point. As she began to function again, she found that for the first time she was really enjoying her academic work, "maybe because I'm running ahead of the game, and I don't have to prove anything any more." (She was elected to Phi Beta Kappa during her junior year.) Although still "motivated to do well by traditional standards," she felt she was "putting more personal effort into it." She particularly enjoyed a seminar in modern drama, finding the professor "really exceptional," partly because of her fine credentials as a "noted scholar" who was "well published," but also because of the collegial atmosphere she established in the class.

> One learns a lot with and from her. She knows so much herself, but she still has lots of respect for whatever we have to offer in class. And she has a very special way of sort of elevating what a student says. It seems like a really reciprocal process. She gets a lot out of teaching us and learning from us, and we learn from her.

For the first time Naomi complained that her major adviser had never shown any personal concern for her. This woman, another noted scholar, spent hours advising Naomi about graduate programs and writing recommendations for her, but she had never asked Naomi why she chose to major in linguistics, nor had she ever told Naomi why she, herself, became a linguist. In the past Naomi portrayed her academic life as "sort of a battle" between two unequal and impersonal forces, "me and the professors." Now, she could imagine a student-teacher relationship of reciprocal care, built around a common concern for work. She could begin to envision an integration of thinking and feeling in a voice that spoke both in private and in public.

LEAVING THE SYSTEM

Women who rely on procedural knowledge are systematic thinkers in more than one sense of the term. Their thinking is encapsulated within systems. They can criticize a system, but only in the system's terms, only according to the system's standards. Women at this position may be liberals or conservatives, but they cannot be radicals. If, for example, they are feminists, they want equal opportunities for women within the capitalistic structure; they do not question the premises of the structure. When these women speak of "beating the system," they do not mean violating its expectations but rather exceeding them. Naomi, for example, told us that she beat the system by excelling both in academics and in extracurricular affairs, when "They" said it couldn't be done. Deborah remembered diving under water for an hour each day to escape the incessant demands of the college authorities. "The coach might yell, but once you had your head in the water you didn't have to listen to her." Deborah's tactics met with only limited success. She swam so well that the coach selected her for the swimming team.

In the past, these women felt secure only when they could tuck themselves into a niche within a structure. Most chose to attend highly structured
colleges that imposed busy agendas and rigorous standards of performance
and allowed little time for outside interests. These students complained
about the constraints imposed by the system; but, fearing they could not
function outside them, many took steps to ensure that a new structure
would be there to move to upon graduation. One young woman applied
to law school to give her life "some structure for the next two years." (Now
in law school and hating it, she complains that she has no time for herself.)
Another woman married one of her professors immediately after graduation, replacing the structure of school with the structure of marriage.
"From now on, whatever I do I will have to do within the framework of
Harold's life."

But some of the women we interviewed were taking steps toward
breaking out of the systems that had governed their lives. Naomi dropped
a busy agenda in order to allow herself time to think about herself. (Her
consequent collapse is not uncommon among women at this position. They
are so dutiful, so stubbornly responsible, that they can seek help only after
utter breakdown.) As graduation approached Naomi found herself shedding
old commitments and avoiding new ones. After a tedious summer spent
decoding cuneiform tablets in the attic of a museum, she withdrew her
applications to graduate programs in Assyriology. The gyroscope that had
steered her course since eighth grade had gone dead. To her "total surprise"
she had no idea what she would do after college. Earlier, not knowing was
frightening. Now, she welcomed it, "because I've always felt so directed.
Right now I have little direction. I feel like I'm at a point where I want to
become awfully selfish. I kind of look forward to living alone and not
answering to anyone and not being judged by anyone."

Women like Naomi found it especially difficult to take the initiative
in disengaging themselves from systems that they had struggled to maintain
in the past. Emily, daughter of a distinguished family and graduate of a
distinguished coeducational college, never spoke to anyone in the family
about the continual sexual assaults she suffered during childhood from her
father. Her mother tried repeatedly to commit suicide. Emily perceived her
mother as manipulative and her father as irresponsible; nevertheless, she
worked hard to keep the system going. "As a child, taking care of the
family unit was very, very important, making sure it survived. It was up
to me that this family was going to make it, that Mother wasn't going to
die one of these times and that Father wasn't going to leave her."

The week before our interview, Emily's mother made another suicide attempt, and Emily decided she had had enough. She marched into her mother's hospital room and, for the first time, told her off.

> The family operates in a very crazy sense where nothing is said, where everybody says that everything is fine and dandy. And that just didn't feel good. Somebody needed to start saying what they were thinking and feeling in this crazy milieu. My father began talking about the situation, how he really felt that he couldn't remain in this milieu much longer himself, which is a bit scary, because it's the fantasy I had as a child, that if I didn't take care of them then they would split up, that everything would disintegrate, and then when I do stop taking care of them, stop playing the game of never talking about anything, then he says that.

Emily, like Naomi and others beginning to break out of the systems in which they were embedded, described herself as "selfish." She felt, as many did, that she had swung from one extreme to another, from utterly selfless to utterly selfish, "very callous." The swing did not feel entirely good, but it did feel necessary.

"Selfishness" is required because the sense of identity is weak. Procedural knowers, many of them quite successful, feel much like other women we have met in this book who have also subordinated themselves to the demands of authorities. Procedural knowers feel like chameleons; they cannot help but take on the color of any structure they inhabit. In order to assume their own true colors, they must detach themselves from the relationships and institutions to which they have been subordinated. Like Naomi, many seniors decided to take a year off, a year apart from institutions and serious relationships. One of these seniors said, "I'm determined that what I'm gonna do is totally for myself, and I don't have to worry about what other people think about what I'm doing, 'cause if *I* think it's right, it's okay for me. At least for this year, that's what I'm gonna do." Although this woman may sound as though she is regressing into the sheer subjectivism she had earlier eschewed in favor of reason, we think she is not. As women move out of procedural knowing, they begin to put more faith in unjustifiable intuitions than they once did. But they do not abandon reason. They are aware that reason is necessary; but they know, too, that it is insufficient, that to ignore the role of feeling in making judgments is to be guilty of something like "romantic rationalism" (Noddings

1984, p. 3). What is needed is not reversion to sheer feeling but some sort
of integration of feeling and thinking. The task is clear, although the solution
is not. In the closing lines of "Unlearning to Not Speak," Marge Piercy
puts it this way.

> She must learn again to speak
> starting with I
> starting with We
> starting as the infant does
> with her own true hunger
> and pleasure
> and rage. (1978, p. 38)

7

Constructed Knowledge: Integrating the Voices

All this stuff accumulates to the point where it is possible to feel something different. . . . It's not dramatic. It's like a little voice— not even a real voice—it's like a voice of integration.

—Adele
A forty-six-year-old
musician/counselor

O KAY, what's real?'' asked Kay, a college senior, as she posed one of the most fundamental philosophical questions to herself.

Is the chair real? I would say, yes—the chair is sitting there. I can see it. I can touch it. I can feel it. Yeah, it's real. But when you move beyond and start thinking about the world philosophically rather than physically, it gets very complex. What is fact? What is not? It certainly changes things. It's very exciting to me—thinking that way—it opens up a whole new thing. It really makes the world of the mind become infinite.

Kay had just written her senior thesis on the theme of illusion and reality in modern fiction. For Kay, on the eve of her graduation from college, this topic was more than an intellectual brain-teaser. She was a writer, someone who knew she could manipulate reality with words. She could influence people and might choose to do so by becoming a journalist. In another arena of her life, Kay had also become aware of her part in constructing reality. After years of fighting her parents and their ideas, she finally saw that the family struggle was a matter of conflicting world views, not just a matter of domination and control. Her reality was not necessarily that of her parents, but she had learned to imagine their world. She thought she could finally understand her parents and wanted to include them in her life. Kay believed that her ability to connect with almost everyone had improved as she became more reflective about and accepting of herself.

Erica, whom we met during her first year in college when she was thinking as a subjectivist, said as a junior, "We can assume that something exists out there—but something is thinking that something exists. Our consciousness is part of the world. We are creating the world at the same time we think about it."

Erica was less sure than Kay of what she wanted for herself. She felt that the future was a "lot of confusion." Her epistemological transformations had paralleled shifts in her academic interests—from the authority and security of pure science and mathematics to the "freedom" of the studio arts, then to the disciplined study of art criticism, and finally to the mind-expanding topics of the origins of consciousness and the philosophy of aesthetics. Always an intellectual and reticent person, Erica saw her life task as "turning back on myself." She had become self-questioning and self-critical. "I feel like all the knowledge I'm getting here works very well, but as soon as I try to do something normal, I feel like I'm missing something." Erica felt the need to learn how to communicate and live with people outside the academic community while protecting her need for solitude. She wanted to find a way to balance her intellectual, creative, social, and practical interests rather than give up one for the other. Variety and complexity were both a part of and a plague in her life.

Adele, a forty-six-year-old divorced woman with four grown children, was feeling slightly depressed, finally acknowledging to herself that "there are things I'm not going to get, and things that won't happen, and things I can't do." For years a successful musician and more recently the recipient of a graduate degree in counseling, she felt exhausted by the period of graduate training and feared she had lost parts of herself. She was setting aside private time to let the "pieces of myself float back in." Adele related a history of being torn between the structure and stimulation provided by theoretical abstraction and an "unconscious creative process" that she believed helped her make decisions about life problems. Over time she had moved away from what she felt was cold intellectualizing to what she now considered to be a "trustworthy level of emotionality." Adele recognized that, although she could still get trapped by her own subjective world and still relied excessively at times on the judgment and evaluation of others, she tended to listen to what she called "a voice of integration" within herself that prompted her to find a place for reason *and* intuition *and* the expertise of others. She reported that her understanding of how answers were generated had changed as she had changed.

> I have come to see things in my own way. I feel that everyone has something unique to say, but some people know how to develop it. Some people can go even further—they can go outside the given frames of reference. Most people have something to say inside given frames of reference. But then you take someone like Freud or Darwin—they are able to jump outside of the given to create a whole new frame of reference. That doesn't happen too often. They stay with it. They create their whole life around it. They change everything for everyone.

Although Kay, Erica, and Adele differed markedly in age and life intentions, they shared a number of characteristics that we believe are central to the fifth epistemological position we will describe. These women were all articulate and reflective people. They noticed what was going on with others and cared about the lives of people about them. They were intensely self-conscious, in the best sense of the word—aware of their own thought, their judgments, their moods and desires. Each concerned herself with issues of inclusion and exclusion, separation and connection; each struggled to find a balance of extremes in her life. Each was ambitious and fighting to find her own voice—her own way of expressing what she knew and cared about. Each wanted her voice and actions to make a difference to other people and in the world. Although none of the three might jump so high as Freud or Darwin to invent new theories that "change everything for everyone," all three had learned the profound lesson that even the most ordinary human being is engaged in the construction of knowledge. "To understand," as Jean Piaget (1973) said, "is to invent."

Moving Outside the Given: The Reclamation of the Self

We have emphasized thus far that quest for self and voice plays a central role in transformations in women's ways of knowing. In a sense, each perspective we have described can be thought of as providing a new, unique training ground in which problems of self and other, inner and outer authority, voice and silence can be worked through. Within each perspective, although partial solutions are possible, new problems arise.

Silent women have little awareness of their intellectual capabilities. They live—selfless and voiceless—at the behest of those around them. External authorities know the truth and are all-powerful.

At the positions of *received knowledge* and *procedural knowledge,* other voices and external truths prevail. Sense of self is embedded either in external definitions and roles or in identifications with institutions, disciplines, and methods. For women in our society, this typically means adherence to sex-role stereotypes or second-rung status as a woman with a man's mind, but a woman nevertheless. These women seek gratification in pleasing others or in measuring up to external standards—in being "the good woman" or "the good student" or "the successful woman who has made it in a man's world." A sense of authority arises primarily through identification with the power of a group and its agreed-upon ways for knowing. As we have seen, however, an outcome at the position of procedural knowledge is the acquisition of the power of reason and objective thought, which provides women with a sense of control and competitive potential even though, for some women, real-life opportunities for exercising their authority may be hard to come by. Access to subjective sources for knowing are absent or lost at the positions of received and procedural knowledge. There is no sense of an authentic or unique voice, little awareness of a centered self.

At the position of *subjective knowledge,* quest for self, or at least protection of a space for growth of self, is primary. For women, this often means a turning away from others and a denial of external authority. Although the belief that truth is private and subjectively known often results in a sense of private authority, there is no public voice or public authority. Women at this position usually feel strongly that they "know" but have few tools for expressing themselves or persuading others to listen.

To learn to speak in a unique and authentic voice, women must "jump outside" the frames and systems authorities provide and create their own frame. Kay, Erica, and Adele have realized this. They told us that their current way of knowing and viewing the world—a way of knowing we call *constructed knowledge*—began as an effort to reclaim the self by attempting to *integrate* knowledge that they felt intuitively was personally important with knowledge they had learned from others. They told of weaving together the strands of rational and emotive thought and of integrating objective and subjective knowing. Rather than extricating the self in the acquisition of knowledge, these women used themselves in rising to a new way of thinking. As Adele described it, "You let the inside out and the outside in."

The paths taken by Kay, Erica, and Adele in the process of self-reclamation were as varied as their backgrounds; but all went through a period of intense self-reflection and self-analysis when they chose to "move outside the given" by removing themselves psychologically, and at times even geographically, from all that they had known. Erica, the young intellectual we have been following, took a year off from her studies to work at an A & P in order to immerse herself in a totally unfamiliar world. Adele left her life as a musician to become a novice in a new and very different field—counseling. Kay worked as a cook, up to her elbows in "flour and butter," so that she could sharpen the contrast for herself between the academic world and "real life." Erica, Adele, and Kay intentionally took time out to get to know the self and to reflect on the contexts that confined and defined them.

Another illustrative story comes from a woman who was not a member of our sample but was chosen nevertheless because she has written so directly about this period of transformation. Alice Koller, a woman in her thirties with a doctorate in philosophy, went alone to an island in search of "an unknown woman," herself. Like all the procedural knowers we met in chapters 5 and 6, she had been "taught a method," but she wanted to move beyond that method. She wanted to imitate "the doers," those

> who bridge the chasm that lies between the safe inadequacy of what they've been taught and the fulfillment that they uncertainly sense will exist on the other side. If I could learn how to see with my own eyes, I'd be able to make a comparable leap, leaving behind everybody else's rules. . . . I don't know what I want, or want to do. I don't know how to use my own evidence. I don't know what counts as evidence . . . I don't know what to look for inside me. I don't know how to identify *that* I'm feeling something, let alone give it a name. I think I've been anesthetized, deadened. (1983, pp. 94, 111–12)

For women like Koller, who are separate knowers, thinking and feeling are split asunder; they feel fraudulent and deadened to their inner experiences and inner selves.

Alice Koller planned to go after the inner self with the methods of her training. She planned to ferret out the evidence. It troubled her greatly that the skills of the philosopher seemed poorly matched for the task of knowing herself: "The part of me that never amalgamated with the philosophical is desperate for clues." Koller decided that she had "to find some way to set forth the data so that I'll be able to see the pattern of my behavior emerge" (p. 87).

It is at this point of transition into a new way of viewing the self and the world that women who are predominantly separate knowers describe looking for the "pattern" of their selves, whereas connected knowers refer to the lost parts of the self. The former emphasize the logic of the self, the latter the feel of it.

By "moving outside the given" and leaving the academic context that had dictated standards and methods for knowing, Koller hoped to turn inward, find herself, and construct her own ways of knowing. Koller's wish to be freed from the standards and reasons of others is reminiscent of the subjectivists' rejection of authority and the influence of others. Yet there is a difference between subjectivists and budding constructivists as they turn inward away from others. For subjectivists, the self is nascent and amorphous; the inner voice is a new experience. They must ignore other voices so that they can nurture the seeds of the self. They often dismiss or deny other people and other realities. For women shifting into the position of constructed knowledge, an inner voice and self exist but may have had a minimum of attention, particularly if the women have learned the lesson of "weeding out the self," which our academic institutions so often teach. During the transition into a new way of knowing, there is an impetus to allow the self back into the process of knowing, to confront the pieces of the self that may be experienced as fragmented and contradictory.

Women pose questions to themselves about themselves. Sometimes they frame the problem in terms of identity, asking "Who am I? What is my life to be about?" Sometimes this questioning is cast primarily in epistemological terms and the women ask, "In what way am I going to approach the world as a learner?" And sometimes the issue is seen more in moral terms. "What are the rights and responsibilities that I have to myself and others? On what basis can I choose when these conflict?" Whatever the focus, a thoroughgoing self-examination at this juncture leads to the construction of a way of thinking about knowledge, truth, and self that guides the person's intellectual and moral life and personal commitments.

During the process of self-examination, women feel a heightened consciousness and sense of choice about "how I want to think" and "how I want to be." They develop a narrative sense of the self—past and future. They do not want to dismiss former ways of knowing so much as they want to stay alert to the fact that different perspectives and different points in time produce different answers. They begin to express an interest in personal history and in the history of ideas. Cecily, a college junior, said,

> I think it's important to see why I think the way I do. Some people
> seem to think that their ideas belong to them, but a lot of things
> people believe have a long tradition of belief. It helps you to
> understand your beliefs if you understand where they come from.
> And it helps you to examine them and say, "Well, do I really
> agree with this?"

Women like Cecily become aware of how truths even within the self
are mutable—a matter of personal history, circumstance, and timing—and
how internal truths may conflict and change with time. Cecily spoke of
"truths colliding within" and was challenged by the clash.

Women constructivists show a high tolerance for internal contradiction
and ambiguity. They abandon completely the either/or thinking so common
to the previous positions described. They recognize the inevitability of conflict and stress and, although they may hope to achieve some respite, they
also, as one woman explained, "learn to live with conflict rather than talking
or acting it away." They no longer want to suppress or deny aspects of the
self in order to avoid conflict or simplify their lives. Erica would not, for
instance, turn away from the responsibilities of friendship so that the student in her could flourish. Kay knew she would not turn away from her
role as a daughter as she pursued a career. These women want to embrace
all the pieces of the self in some ultimate sense of the whole—daughter,
friend, mother, lover, nurturer, thinker, artist, advocate. They want to avoid
what they perceive to be a shortcoming in many men—the tendency to
compartmentalize thought and feeling, home and work, self and other. In
women, there is an impetus to try to deal with life, internal and external,
in all its complexity. And they want to develop a voice of their own to
communicate to others their understanding of life's complexity.

The Position of Constructed Knowledge

It is in the process of sorting out the pieces of the self and of searching for
a unique and authentic voice that women come to the basic insights of
constructivist thought: *All knowledge is constructed,* and *the knower is an
intimate part of the known.* At first women arrive at this insight in searching

for a core self that remains responsive to situation and context. Ultimately constructivists understand that answers to all questions vary depending on the context in which they are asked and on the frame of reference of the person doing the asking. In Piaget's terms (1952), there is a "horizontal décalage," in which a transformation in understanding of self begins to generalize and affect how women think about truth, knowledge, and expertise. Women become aware that questions and answers vary throughout history, across cultures, from discipline to discipline, and from individual to individual. One woman observed: "Circumstances change. Our way of looking at things change. Time may have given us what we think are right answers, but it also gives us a different set of problems." Whether separate knowers, who emphasize the relationship between the major ideas drawn from each discipline, or more connected knowers, who examine as well the relationship between the person doing the knowing and the nature of all thought, these women begin to see beyond limited compartments and advance their understanding of how all knowledge is constructed.

To see that all knowledge is a construction and that truth is a matter of the context in which it is embedded is to greatly expand the possibilities of how to think about anything, even those things we consider to be the most elementary and obvious. Theories become not truth but models for approximating experience; as one woman said, theories are "not fact but educated guesswork."

Elizabeth, a recent college graduate and a student of the humanities, understood that even "science is a moral art, dictated by the human heart and human mind. It was subjective and is subjective. Science is a creative evaluation of facts, of demonstratable [sic] happenings." A senior honors student in science said,

> In science you don't really want to say that something's true. You realize that you're dealing with a model. Our models are always simpler than the real world. The real world is more complex than anything we can create. We're simplifying everything so that we can work with it, but the thing is really more complex. When you try to describe things, you're leaving the truth because you're oversimplifying.

Such views are a far cry from the perception of science as absolute truth or as a procedure for obtaining objective facts, views women at other positions hold.

Once knowers assume the general relativity of knowledge, that their frame of reference matters and that they can construct and reconstruct frames of reference, they feel responsible for examining, questioning, and developing the systems that they will use for constructing knowledge. Question posing and problem posing become prominent methods of inquiry, strategies that some researchers have identified as a fifth stage of thought beyond formal-operational or logical thought (Arlin 1975; Kitchener 1983; Labouvie-Vief 1980). Women tend not to rely as readily or as exclusively on hypothetico-deductive inquiry, which posits an answer (the hypothesis) prior to the data collection, as they do on examining basic assumptions and the conditions in which a problem is cast.

For constructivist women, simple questions are as rare as simple answers. Constructivists can take, and often insist upon taking, a position outside a particular context or frame of reference and look back on "who" is asking the question, "why" the question is asked at all, and "how" answers are arrived at. They no longer dutifully try to come up with answers when questions are asked. "You're asking the wrong question!" we often heard them say. "Your question is out of context."

Experts and Truth in Context

When women accept the responsibility for evaluating and continually reevaluating their assumptions about knowledge, the attention and respect that they might once have awarded to the expert is transformed. They appreciate expertise but back away from designating anyone an "expert" without qualifying themselves. An evaluation of experts is not only possible but is an important responsibility that they assume. For most constructivists, true experts must reveal an appreciation for complexity and a sense of humility about their knowledge.

Lydia, for instance, said that the good expert was "somebody whose answers reflect the complexity I know the situation holds." Lydia recounted how important it was to her that the theories and recommendations of experts were grounded in real life and the data of the everyday. Experts had to reveal that they "listened" to people and gave equal weight to experience and abstractions. An expert's experience had to resonate with hers. Whereas at other positions ambiguity can be deeply troubling, constructivists such as Lydia are not troubled by ambiguity and are enticed by complexity. Lydia described, for instance, listening to a lecturer present his new ideas on infant development. He was "charting new terrain" by "taking into consideration thousands of pieces of information and weaving this new theoretical base." It was important to Lydia that he had listened to mothers—"something not many theorists about infancy do. This man had spent hours talking to mothers about what they did with their babies and how they did it and what felt good to them and what they noticed." Lydia was delighted, even awed, by his impressive performance and the way his mind worked.

> To hear him articulate what his theory was beginning to look like was like being on the edge of a new painting. He reminded me not to get caught up in the simplicity, because it isn't simple. I think that's one reason why I like paisley prints. I like the detail. I like the intricacy. I like the complexity!

When asked how they feel about experts disagreeing, many constructivists say that they are challenged, not daunted, by contradiction and conflict. If they are exposed to the methodologies of several disciplines, acquiring the analytical skills and methods of each, they experience themselves as investigators and search for truths that cut across the interests and biases that lie within a single disciplinary perspective. Unlike procedural knowers, who remain subservient to disciplines and systems, constructivists move beyond systems, putting systems to their own service. They make connections that help tie together pockets of knowledge. There is a new excitement about learning and the power of the mind.

> I am starting to *care* about academics. I'm beginning to feel that my courses have been connected. It's much more interesting once one discipline starts to interconnect with others. You can go through your own courses, pull together your own connections, figure out connections yourself.

There is also an emphasis on a never-ending search for truth, which is coordinate with a never-ending quest for learning. As Lydia explained, "It isn't the finding the truth that's so wonderful. It is in the looking for it, the exploring, the searching. If you were to ever think that you've finally arrived at it, you've blown it. Truth gets more elusive the older I get." She recalls the poem "Ithaca" in which Ulysses searches for home: "You don't want him to get home because it is the going that is important."

When truth is seen as a process of construction in which the knower participates, a passion for learning is unleashed. Bridget says she has experienced an "intellectual renaissance." Mildred marvels at a similar explosion she has noticed in herself and others—"I just think of the amazing yearning for knowledge that we have." We observed a passion for knowing the self in the subjectivists and an excitement over the power of reason among procedural knowers, but we found that the opening of the mind *and* the heart to embrace the *world* was characteristic only of the women at the position of constructed knowledge.

The Passionate Knower

Becoming and staying aware of the workings of their minds are vital to constructivist women's sense of well-being. Self-awareness aids them in setting the ground rules for their interactions with others and in self-definition. Constructivists seek to stretch the outer boundaries of their consciousness—by making the unconscious conscious, by consulting and listening to the self, by voicing the unsaid, by listening to others and staying alert to all the currents and undercurrents of life about them, by imagining themselves inside the new poem or person or idea that they want to come to know and understand. Constructivists become passionate knowers, knowers who enter into a union with that which is to be known. Philosopher Michael Polanyi writes about "personal knowledge" as being "the passionate participation of the knower in the act of knowing" (1958, p. viii). Feminist Barbara Du Bois writes of "passionate scholarship" as being "science-making, [which is] rooted in, animated by and expressive of our values" (1983, p. 113).

What we are calling passionate knowing is the elaborated form connected knowing takes after women learn to use the self as an instrument of understanding. In the earlier form of connected knowing described in chapter 6, opening up to ideas or people is stressed as a *procedure* for knowing, but the relative lack of self-knowledge prevents women from finding points of connection between what they are trying to understand and their own experience. Among women thinking as constructivists, connected knowing is not simply an "objective" procedure but a way of weaving their passions and intellectual life into some recognizable whole. For women, at least, once they include the self, they use connected "passionate" knowing as the predominant mode for understanding, regardless of whether separate or connected procedures for knowing had been emphasized in the past.

Sara Ruddick, in an autobiographical essay on the development of her thought and commitments (1984), described a "conversion" involving re-thinking and refeeling—in our terms, the growth of passionate knowing. Trained in philosophy, Ruddick prided herself on her "male mind" and her part in the "serious" intellectual endeavor of abstract thought. She learned well the procedures of separate knowing—detachment and abstract analysis. Nevertheless, after her marriage and the birth of her children, she began to feel that she was a foreigner among academic philosophers ("the charmed circle") and, for some time, was faced with a work block. Her passionate investment in her children's lives and "the parental work I shared with my husband and women friends" contributed to her fear that her intellectual life was being compromised by domesticity. She no longer felt a part of her academic peer group nor could she find any reason to continue trying to participate in a world "among people whose manner and ambition were increasingly strange." Out of desperation, she was drawn into a "secret world"—a private and totally absorbed study of Virginia Woolf, who showed her ultimately "a place outside the charmed circles where I could stand."

For Sara Ruddick, as for Virginia Woolf, and in fact for any number of the women we interviewed, the transformation in thinking began with a personal journal and a new alertness to the details of the everyday around her.

> For the first time since adolescence I attended to my days. I walked for hours, watching people watching each other and themselves; following Woolf, I imagined their inner life. In Woolfian rhythms, I heard the city's voices, personal conversations, and impersonal markers—subways, traffic, clocks. . . . I was discovering my eyes and ears. (1984, p. 142)

During this period of self-recovery, of learning about herself by immersing herself in the life and work of another, she began to realize that "my life, in its daily ordinariness, not in its labored cleverness, was worth attention. I began to imagine working without the ever-present curriculum vitae and my academic judges hanging over me. Woolf encouraged me to delight in female minds, to appreciate hers and my own" (p. 143).

Ruddick eloquently expressed the transformation of her thinking from separate and procedural to connected and caring.

> I play easily with abstractions, spontaneously searching out the general amidst the particular. Working on Woolf required relishing the particular for its own

sake, moving to generality only by tracing increasingly complex webs of connections and layers of meaning. . . . I seemed to learn new ways of attending
to the natural world and to people, especially children. This kind of attending
was *intimately concerned with caring;* because I cared I reread slowly, then I
found myself watching more cárefully, listening with patience, absorbed by
gestures, moods, and thoughts. The more I attended, the more deeply I cared.
The domination of feeling by thought, which I had worked so hard to achieve,
was breaking down. Instead of developing arguments that could bring
my feelings to heel, I allowed feeling to inform my most abstract thinking.
(Pp. 150–51)

Compared to other positions, there is a capacity at the position of
constructed knowledge to attend to another person and to feel related to
that person in spite of what may be enormous differences. As we have
seen in chapter 6, empathy is a central feature in the development of connected procedures for knowing. This empathic potential—the capacity for
what Weil calls "attentive love" (1951) and what Ruddick identifies with
"maternal thinking" (1980)—is particularly characteristic of constructivist
women. The ability to imagine and be sensitive to the interior life of others,
however, has its drawbacks as well as its gratifications. One woman told
us of the pull she felt into the lives of *all* women, recognizing parts of
herself in them. She described the problems this empathic pull created for
her. "I might be sitting in McDonald's or something. I would see a woman
come in who was like 100 pounds overweight, and she'd have four kids
with her and they'd all be fighting, and she'd look so unhappy, and I'd
just start crying and have to leave. I would just be so sensitive to that
woman."

For women at this position, attentive caring is important in understanding not only people but also the written word, ideas, even impersonal
objects. Constructivists establish a communion with what they are trying
to understand. They use the language of intimacy to describe the relationship between the knower and the known.

Jessica, a forty-two-year-old woman returning to college, said she had
let go of a host of "shoulds and oughts" that directed her learning for
years. She had begun to feel the freedom and renewal that came when
she could draw her own experience and affinities into her learning. She
realized that her way of reading had altered: "It's a sense of communicating
with an author and having rapport with the reading matter. And a lovely
feeling of 'Oh! I have somebody to communicate with. Somebody has had
this experience, too.' It's a nurturing reaction."

Barbara McClintock, whose important work on the genetics of corn
plants won her a Nobel prize, used the language of intimacy in describing

her way of doing science. She told her biographer, Evelyn Fox Keller, that you had to have the patience "to hear what [the corn] has to say to you" and the openness "to let it come to you." McClintock could write the biography of each of her corn plants. As she said, "I know them intimately, and I find it a great pleasure to know them" (1983, p. 198).

Real Talk

Constructivists make a distinction between "really talking" and what they consider to be didactic talk in which the speaker's intention is to hold forth rather than to share ideas. In didactic talk, each participant may report experience, but there is no attempt among participants to join together to arrive at some new understanding. "Really talking" requires careful listening; it implies a mutually shared agreement that together you are creating the optimum setting so that half-baked or emergent ideas can grow. "Real talk" reaches deep into the experience of each participant; it also draws on the analytical abilities of each. Conversation, as constructivists describe it, includes discourse and exploration, talking and listening, questions, argument, speculation, and sharing.

We saw that at the earlier positions women often felt that they had to choose between speaking and listening or that, at best, they might alternate. As a sophomore, Bridget described teetering between these two modes.

> I am very much of a listener instead of a talker. I will try to contribute things, but I find the moment I start thinking about what I want to say, I stop listening to what everybody else is saying. So I have a tendency to keep my mouth shut, to concentrate on what I am absorbing instead of what I want to throw back out.

Four years later, after having finished college and traveled abroad, Bridget was thinking as a constructivist and described the hard work entailed in bringing listening and speaking into balance.

> I always was the kind of person who felt I had to entertain people or keep the conversation going. I was brought up to be really wishy-

washy, at least by my mother anyway. To be the one who enter-
tains, who supports, who perhaps provides the forum for the
discussion, but is never a participant in that discussion herself.
I'm still finding it difficult in certain circumstances to truly express
what I feel or what I want. But I am trying—at least for my own
mental health—to be honest and forthright in my communication
with people. That is a big challenge—a big, big challenge!

Listening to others no longer diminishes women's capacity to hear
their own voices. The capacity for speaking with and listening to others
while simultaneously speaking with and listening to the self is an achievement that allows a conversation to open between constructivists and the
world.

The devotion of constructivists to "real talk" as a way of connecting
to others and acquiring and communicating new knowledge distinguishes
them in both their personal and professional lives.* With family and friends
they are eager to describe their own experience so that others can understand; they question and listen to others, urging them to speak, so that
they might better know the world from the other person's vantage point.
At work and in public forums, they believe that people have an obligation
to share with others how they know and what they learn when they "jump
outside of the given." Kay said, "Somebody can be an expert, but if they
do not articulate what they've learned, then that renders their knowledge
useless if they can't share it with other people." Alice Koller described the
task in other terms: "Once on the other side, [one] must look back and
throw down a footbridge . . . for followers to use" (1983, p. 95). In addition
to sharing what you know, having a willingness to describe how you got
there is important. Adele said, "I tend to trust people who share the process
of their thinking."

Political scientist Jean Bethke Elshtain describes a kind of "ideal speech
situation"—a term introduced by the philosopher Jurgen Habermas—that
is close to what constructivists mean when they refer to "really talking."
It is speech of a particular kind: "Speech that simultaneously taps and
touches our inner and outer worlds within a community of others with

* Carol Edelsky, based on her study of interactions in mixed-sex professional meetings,
distinguishes between two kinds of "floors": the *turn-taking floor* (F1), in which one speaker
at a time holds the floor and is center stage, and the *collaborative floor* (F2), which is less
formal and is developed by several people "operating on the same wave length." Characteristic
of the F1 is a "monologue . . . and hierarchical interaction in which floors are won or lost—
and which shares features with other contexts in which women have learned they had best
not assert themselves." Women come into their own in the F2 interaction, which results in
"high levels of communicative involvement and satisfaction" (1981, p. 416).

whom we share deeply felt, largely inarticulate, but daily renewed intersubjective reality" (1982, p. 620).

In "real talk" domination is absent, reciprocity and cooperation are prominent. Although doubting may still be used to test ideas and may even be described as invigorating or fun, constructivist women are much more likely to replace doubting with believing as the best way of getting the feel of a new idea or a new friend or colleague. At times, particularly in certain academic and work situations in which adversarial interactions are common, constructivist women may feel compelled to demonstrate that they can hold their own in a battle of ideas to prove to others that they, too, have the analytical powers and hard data to justify their claims. However, they usually resent the implicit pressure in male-dominated circles to toughen up and fight to get their ideas across.

Silence and Conflict

Even among women who feel they have found their voice, problems with voice abound. Some women told us, in anger and frustration, how frequently they felt unheard and unheeded—both at home and at work. In our society, which values the words of male authority, constructivist women are no more immune to the experience of feeling silenced than any other group of women.

Once a woman has a voice, she wants it to be heard. Some women told us that they had arrived at a point in their chosen work where they could "say what they mean and mean what they say," but then they often added that they longed for someone with whom they could genuinely share their visions and problems. They hoped to find understanding and communicative people—people who were invested in "really talking."

For Ruddick, finding her voice and life's work as a feminist philosopher taught her that her intellectual life could "satisfy a deep personal need *and* be intellectually challenging *and* still mean something to an attentive stranger" (1984, p. 148). Constructivist women need and value attentive strangers as well as understanding friends and colleagues. Learning that their ideas can be taken in and put to use—that their ideas can spark interest among unknown others—is an exhilarating and confirmatory experience.

However, many women told us of the anger they felt when no one listened or when their "womanly voice" was dismissed as soft or misguided, a particularly common complaint of women working in a setting where men predominated. One successful professional woman told us, "You know, the older I get the more I realize that I'm willing to talk about things I care about *only* if I know the other person is really listening. If I don't feel that, I find myself falling into a silence, even when I'm at work or in the middle of a professional meeting." She contemplated changing jobs, even changing her career, in the search for a more attentive response from her colleagues. Like many women, she suspected that her ideas might find a more receptive audience among other women. However, as another woman said, "In being a woman, you have to make men see things they haven't had to see. It's not their fault. It's just the way it is."

Most constructivist women feel that women have a special responsibility to try to communicate to both men and women how they view things and why they value what they do, even though they feel that their words may fall on deaf ears.

In addition to the accounts about problems in the workplace, we heard stories about the conflicts and silence between women and the men they cared for. Especially in talk between the sexes, dialogue can stumble on discrepant assumptions and edge toward silence or anger or both.

Donna, a married Hispanic woman in her forties who spent the last seven years finally obtaining her B.A. degree, recognized why she and her husband were heading for difficulties in their marriage. He had supported her in her wish to become "educated" even though he was not; however, she felt they now had very different ways of understanding and dealing with their children and domestic problems.

> We now view events that happen in our lives very differently. He reads them very straightforward, on a superficial kind of level. And I don't. I probe them. I read into them. He says he sees things in black and white and I see all kinds of shades of grays—all these gradations he doesn't see. That's been exacerbated by my education. I think it's a good thing. He thinks it's not so good.

Although she was not contemplating it for the moment, Donna feared an end to the marriage. She was not sure if she could cope with her differences with her husband or if she would have the strength to give up some of the things she only recently discovered she wanted for herself— more education, greater involvement in a career in government, aims that would take her far beyond the boundaries of the home as she and her

husband originally defined it. Optimistically, Donna foresaw the beginning
of a new phase of her marriage in which she and her husband perhaps
could "get to know each other in a different way."

We heard many women describe more negative outcomes in their
intimate relationships. Adele, the musician-turned-counselor, told us of
the difficulties she had with her ex-husband, difficulties that were beginning
to repeat themselves in her relationship with a new man.

> I'm saying as the woman, "I want more—more talk, more sharing,
> more feeling." And the man is saying, "You're too needy or too
> demanding" or whatever. I feel like what ends up happening,
> when the man does that enough, is that I begin not to want to
> even bother any more. I begin withdrawing a lot, begin feeling
> angry most of the time.

Adele observed that this was a problem she often came across in counseling
couples. As she was well aware, relationships sometimes do not survive
the stress of such seemingly unbreachable differences in perspective.

For some constructivist women, particularly those who do not shy
away from speaking their minds, enduring, intimate relationships may be
hard to establish. The women have difficulties finding companionable and
supportive men, and they experience loneliness and discouragement.

> I intimidate many men. It's hard. It means loneliness lots of times. It's
> necessary to learn to compromise to a certain extent—how much
> you have to shut up and how much you have to talk. And how
> to be effective by talking at the right moment.

Social expectations, which shape the behavior between the sexes, continue to exert pressure on constructivist women to accept the status quo.
Although persistent in their efforts to be heard and to hold on to their new
sense of voice, constructivist women can end up accommodating the needs
and ground rules of men out of the sad wisdom that change does not come
easily.

Moral Imperatives

When we asked these women what they "should" do in a moment of moral choice, they usually told us that it depended on the situation. Asked Kohlberg's classic hypothetical moral dilemma—"Should Heinz steal medicine from a druggist who is charging an outrageous price, in order to save his wife's life?"—they tended to respond with further questions: "What does Heinz wish?" "What is the condition of Mrs. Heinz's life?" "Why is the druggist behaving so?" "Does Heinz have children dependent on him for care?" "Who would care for the children if Heinz went to jail?" In contrast, the mature men whom Kohlberg describes invoke a general principle: The right to life must take precedence over the right to property.

Women's question posing when faced with moral conflict indicates a sensitivity to situation and context. Constructivist women resist premature generalization about what they would do or what should be done, particularly about matters of right and wrong. They insist on a respectful consideration of the particulars of everyone's needs and frailties, even if that means delaying making decisions or taking action. They do not want to neglect the "practicalities of everyday life" for the sake of abstract justice or for the illusory search for "some kind of end all, be all, cure all."

We have already noted that question posing is central to the constructivist way of knowing. It is also at the heart of the responsibility orientation that Gilligan (1982) heard in women's voices but that is rarely noted in the rights orientation to morality. In the responsibility orientation to morality, women resolve conflicts not by invoking a logical hierarchy of abstract principles but through trying to understand the conflict in the context of each person's perspective, needs, and goals—and doing the best possible for everyone that is involved. For constructivists, the moral response is a caring response. The theme of "caring for people" echoed throughout their interviews (although this was a major concern of many women at other positions). In the case of constructivists, this motive even affects the definition of a "good opinion": "The only good opinion is a humanistic one, one that shows an immense respect for the world and the people in it and for those you are going to affect." An opinion is more than an exercise of the intellect. It is a commitment; it is something to live by. "I don't take on an opinion as my own unless I have really thought about it and believe in it. Once I do, I really would fight for something I believe in." The constructivists' conviction that they *must* care and develop "an affinity for the world and the people in it" drives the formation of commitments and eventual action. As Sara Ruddick says, "I now care about my thinking and think about what I care about—about lives and what endangers them" (1984, p. 151).

Commitment and Action

Most constructivist women actively reflect on how their judgments, attitudes, and behavior coalesce into some internal experience of moral consistency. More than any other group, they are seriously preoccupied with the moral or spiritual dimension of their lives. Further, they strive to translate their moral commitments into action, both out of a conviction that "one must act" and out of a feeling of responsibility to the larger community in which they live.

The formation of commitments in women follows a different track than for men. In Perry's description of the evolution of commitments (1970), it is clear that the average Harvard student foresees a single clarifying and self-defining act before him. Usually that choice concerns a career. Less frequently do we find accounts of choices regarding moral values and relationships. Similarly, George Vaillant, in his longitudinal Grant Study of the male adult life cycle, notes that for men in their twenties and thirties, idealism and intimacy take a backseat in the quest for career consolidation. About the average man he studied who was caught up in "making the grade" in a career, Vaillant says: "Having achieved intimacy with a few fellow humans, he then tries to run faster and in a slightly different direction from all his classmates" (1977, p. 217).

Women also foresee that initial act of commitment. But as they go on to describe the context in which their decisions will occur, their descriptions ultimately emphasize the action less than the context. Constructivist women mitigate any single choice by considering the effects it will have on others. Further, all these women are careful to describe not only the commitment to career that they foresee but also the commitment to relationships. Whether they plan to work immediately after their education or delay work for home and a family, they assume they will live at least some part of their lives with another adult and usually as a parent as well. For these women, it is a *life* foreseen rather than a single commitment foreseen.

Beverly, a college graduate who recently married, reflected on her future. She said that it was important to her to think about what kind of friendships, work, and family she would have in her life. She forecast all the major arenas in which she would ultimately make decisions. Any commitment she made now was merely a part of a bigger story. "A lot of time now I spend thinking, 'What am I going to do with my future? Go back to school? What kind of job will I get if I don't? What do I think about having children?' And the whole thing of being married is almost an unknown land." Beverly also worried about constructing a meaningful life.

> I was reading Becker, and he talks a lot about heroic tasks and how we can find things important to us and other people, and by doing these tasks, we gain our own self-importance, self-meaning. And I think, "What is my heroic task?" If I don't have one, I don't really have anything to kind of center my life around.

She decided against business school for the moment, saying that she did not feel she had the energy for managing the hard work business school would entail and still have time for the marriage and "the people in my life." This decision did not protect her from resentment, though. She wondered if she was being "fair to herself" for "giving up something that is important to me so that I can spend more time with my husband." She said, "I certainly don't see him doing that for me."

For Beverly, as for all women constructivists, the process of shaping and acting on commitments is not a simple matter. It is not a clear-cut linear movement from "here to there," the orderly progression that characterizes the behavior of the many men and some women who set out to "make it" in a given career. She sought to balance and honor the needs of the self with the needs of others, even though at times this felt like an insurmountable task to her. She did not want to create compartments and place work in one and family in another. She tried to develop all aspects of her life simultaneously and adhered faithfully to her assertion that they are interrelated.

Many of the women told us, with a sigh and luckily a sense of humor, about their "juggling act" with the pieces of their life. These women were not necessarily high-achieving "superwomen" who aspired to perfection in everything they undertook. They were ordinary women, faced with what for them were average "womanly" tasks. And they could be, at times, overwhelmed as they tried to balance their commitments—work, children's schedule, groceries, political action, time with their husband or lover, the needs of friends and parents, reading, learning, time with nature. Inclusion ("doing it all") rather than exclusion ("turning the world off") was an ideal as well as a formidable problem.

Of course, these women cannot do it all, certainly not in a society that urges women to succeed but still assigns them primary domestic and child-care responsibilities (Chodorow 1978; Contratto 1984). They learn to live with compromise and to soften ideals that they find unworkable. Nevertheless, they set an example of a refreshing mixture of idealism and realism. Although they want to make a difference in the world, they realize, as Adele did, that "there are things that won't happen and that I can't do."

Constructivist women aspire to work that contributes to the empowerment and improvement in the quality of life of others. More than any other group of women in this study, the constructivists feel a part of the effort to address with others the burning issues of the day and to contribute as best they can. They speak of integrating feeling and care into their work—"using my mind to help people" (in careers in human services, psychotherapy, education, child and women's advocacy, antipoverty legislation), "cradling the environment" (through social action and work in environmental protection agencies and antinuclear movements), and "humanizing cities" (via city planning and community cooperatives).

What stands out most strongly in narratives of constructivist women, and particularly in the part of their story that pertains to the future they foresee for themselves, is their desire to have "a room of their own," as Virginia Woolf calls it, in a family and community and world that they helped make livable. They reveal in the way they speak and live their lives their moral conviction that ideas and values, like children, must be nurtured, cared for, placed in environments that help them grow.

PART II

DEVELOPMENT IN CONTEXT: FAMILIES AND SCHOOLS

8

Family Life and
the Politics of Talk

> I've begun to appreciate what a family
> means. I think that if I am committed to
> anything right now, it is to nourishing those
> bonds with my family, making them strong,
> getting them to understand me more, mak-
> ing an effort to understanding them more
> from the point of view of greater honesty.
> —Bridget
> Senior year of college

THE DESCRIPTIONS of family life that the women shared with us suggest that Tolstoy's observation that "happy families are all alike; every unhappy family is unhappy in its own way" is not quite right. The daughters from happy families told stories that seemed very much alike, but daughters from unhappy families also told stories that were very similar to one another. Indeed, the women who held each of the different ways of knowing we described tended to tell a common story of family life. Only a few—usually with the help of supportive friends, neighbors, and excellent schools—were able to move far beyond the epistemological atmospheres depicted in their family histories. In this chapter we will recapitulate our scheme and describe the shared family histories held by women who utilized each way of knowing.

Given that we have been describing frameworks for meaning-making that evolve and change rather than personality types that are relatively permanent, it is curious that people who share an epistemological position

would have so much family history in common. The following are among
the many ideas that may account for the phenomenon:

> The families as described accurately reflect the environments that give rise to
> each of these ways of knowing. Individuals are typically supported by their
> families to develop only to a certain point, lingering on at that level throughout
> much of their adult lives.

> The social forces that operate on a family during the daughter's formative
> years continue to shape her experience. Thus the families, schools, and jobs
> that involve poor women are likely to be very hierarchically arranged, de-
> manding conformity, passivity, and obedience—all unsupportive of continued
> intellectual growth. The same institutions that are provided for the privileged
> are more likely to encourage active, creative thinking and lifelong intellectual
> development. (See, for example, Kohn 1977, 1980.)

> Being a construction, family histories are rewritten from the perspective of
> each new epistemological era. Daughters at each position tell a similar family
> story because people who share common ways of knowing construe the world
> similarly. Thus, a person who believes that truth comes only from authorities
> may describe a parent in terms that can only be characterized as dictatorial.
> Later, this same woman, being more able to imagine an inner life, may become
> aware of her parents' deep interest in the truths that she herself might offer.
> (See, for example, Kegan 1982.)

> Both the story and the actualities of family life change because parents and
> children evolve in tandem, supporting and challenging each other to develop
> ever more complex ways of knowing as they play out their lives together.
> Children encourage the development of parents as much as parents encourage
> the development of children. (See, for example, Galinsky 1981; Gutmann
> 1975; Rossi 1980.)

The distinctive family patterns common to each epistemological position were revealed to us most clearly when we looked for themes that
focused on the "politics of talk." By this we mean those forms of discourse
that a family permits and encourages and those that they minimize and
prohibit. To lay bare these politics we asked ourselves the following kinds
of questions as we examined the family histories:

> What are the rules about speaking and listening that can be inferred
>   from a family story? Are children to be seen but not heard in the
>   day-to-day life of the family? Or do both parents and children
>   listen to one another with care?

> Do parents assume only the role of teacher? Or do they actively try
>   to learn from and with their children as well?

Do parents teach by asking as well as by telling? Are the questions asked genuine, rhetorical, or reproachful? Do the questions draw out and enlarge feelings, ideas, plans, and the possibilities for compromises? Or do the questions squelch and constrict?

Are feelings and intimacies permitted? Does the intellectual and the impersonal reign? Or are the two intertwined?

Are conversations seen as a means that collaborators have for sharing and building, block by block, on one another's ideas? Are conversations held for nurturing ideas and people? Or are debates staged for honing the individual's logic? For outdoing others?

Do the forms and content of conversations that daughters have with their mothers differ, in regular ways, from those that they hold with their fathers?

By considering these questions we hope to deepen our understanding of the kinds of environments that nurture and constrain the development of a sense of mind and voice in women. By focusing our attention on the family and the mothering role—an institution and relationship devoted to care, connection, and human development, we might help bring a different language into the study of psychology. This study, traditionally grounded in the premise of separation, has evolved a language Gilligan describes as unparalleled in its depersonalization, in which people are "objects" and relationships are "holding environments . . . creating an imagery of love that is indistinguishable from the imagery of war." The study of mothers, Gilligan holds,

> is of particular interest for the psychology of love, holding in it the promise of elucidating a love that combines intensity and wisdom, a love that is neither exclusive nor finite but at once constant and changing. In contrast to the image of women as either self-absorbed or self-effacing, the study of women may bring to psychology a language of love that encompasses both knowledge and feelings, a language that conveys a different way of imagining the self in relation to others. (1984, p. 91)

Stories of Family Life as Told by the Silent

Not imagining that they can understand and remember the words of others, silent women do not see themselves participating in the give-and-take of talk with others. They have little inkling of their intellectual powers or of the possibilities of an inner voice and dialogue.

These women essentially lived their lives in silence or din, looking for nourishment in the most barren soil. Their family histories suggest only the sparsest opportunity for dialogue. Bonnie's story captures the essence of the tales.

> If you just knew my parents. You couldn't talk to them. They weren't talking parents. They were parents that said, "You shut up to everyone. You don't tell nobody nothing." I couldn't go to dances. I couldn't do this or that. Nothing involved with other people. They were to themselves. They don't want nothing to do with other people. That was the way I was supposed to be. No friends, no phone calls, no nothing. Just to yourself. That's all that they wanted.

Talk had little value or was actively discouraged in the homes in which they grew up. When conversations did occur they were quite limited in nature. The way Cindy described conversing with her mother and sister since she became pregnant was characteristic of the fleeting mechanical images of "two-way talk" that we found in this first group of stories.

> We've grown closer in the last few months. We talk more than we did. My mother helps me a lot, telling me what she went through when she was that way [referring both to being raped and pregnant] and I tell her what I went through. And with my sister, we have got something in common now. My sister tells me how she felt when she was pregnant and I tell her how I feel being pregnant.

VIOLENCE INSTEAD OF DIALOGUE

Because the families of silent women see words as having an impact on others only when they are uttered with force and violence, they yell rather than talk when they wish to influence one another. They do little to help each other think through and articulate the problems of the moment, not to mention long-range plans and hopes for the future: "Whenever he would get mad at me about something, he could never come to me and tell me what he was mad about. He would just flare up, all out of proportion. He would not ever try to talk to me or anything." Without conversation, these families use violence—out of necessity—as the primary means for getting what they need and want from each other. Failing that (and in the long run, violence does fail to produce what they want), they withdraw or "exit," the remaining alternative to "voice" or dialogue for coping with conflict (Gilligan 1986).

Because silent women use either/or, dualistic thinking, they often liken the world to a zero-sum game in which all the players compete with one another for scarce resources, believing that if one wins the other will lose, because they think the pool of spoils is predetermined and limited (Boulding 1962; Rapapport 1960). Thus it is not surprising that the silent women we interviewed depicted the marriages of their parents—if they endured—as relationships of great inequality. One parent—usually, but not always, the father—lorded it over the other. As one woman put it, "Men dominate women. In my family there is a lot of that. They rules [sic] over the house. And woman submits and children obey. That's cut and dry. That's where it is at." The images of the powerful are stark, brutal—and wordless.

Silent women frequently described their parents as chaotic and unpredictable. Everyone in this small group of women experienced some form of gross neglect and physical and/or sexual abuse, by one or both of their parents. Some had essentially been abandoned by one or both parents; others experienced the death of parents or siblings at a very early age. Much more often than not, alcoholism fueled the parents' uncontrolled emotions. Many of the women described their parents as volatile, a few as extraordinarily violent. Undoubtedly, Bonnie provided the most horrifying example.

> My father used to do the weirdest things to me. I hate him. He was in the navy, back in the war and stuff like that. I guess he picked up weird things like that. He used to put me in a corner and put a bag over my head and every time he'd walk by he'd kick me— just like a dog. My mom told me once he put a tick on my stomach and let the tick suck my blood. Things like that—really gross, things that a father would never do to their daughter. He'd stick toothpicks up my fingernails until it would bleed. [*Did he sexually abuse you, too?*] Oh, yeah. When I was six. Had to get me to the hospital. I had twenty stitches. I just can't talk about it.

The ever-present fear of such volcanic eruptions and catastrophic events leaves children speechless and numbed, unwilling to develop their capacities for hearing and knowing. Children develop their intellectual capacities for finding order in the world only if they have some basis for trusting that order does, indeed, exist. It is no wonder that these women imagine a world where everyone is preoccupied with survival of their single, isolated selves, where everyone acquiesces to authority or runs for cover. (See Lifton 1976, on psychic numbing.)

Family psychiatrist Salvador Minuchin and colleagues (1967) depict a pattern of family life among the urban poor that is remarkably similar to the pattern we found in these families among the rural poor. They describe disorganized slum families unable to withstand the demoralizing and shattering effects of poverty. The children tend to be action-oriented, with little insight into their own behaviors or motivations. Since they do not expect to be heard, and if heard they expect no response, the volume of their voices is more important than the content. They lack verbal negotiating skills and do not expect conflicts to be resolved through nonviolent means.

Families that are relegated to the bottom of the social class structure are often shaken by the collapse of an outmoded way of life. Values, symbol systems, and patterns of communication are torn asunder. Parents feel they have lost their way and have nothing to teach. One generation no longer tells its stories to the next.

While violent families often suffer from the stresses of poverty, family violence occurs at all levels of the social class structure. Researchers have repeatedly found violent families, whether rich or poor, to be characterized by high levels of social isolation, rigid sex-role stereotyping, poor communication, and extreme inequalities in the distribution of power among family members. These characteristics are consistently noted, whether the studies are of wife battering, child abuse, or abuse of the elderly (Finkelhor 1983).

THE ALLOCATION OF LIFE CHANCES

Occasionally women of lower-class origins who grew up in families characterized by silence, hierarchy, and violence were able to find strengths elsewhere—from other relatives, neighbors, and excellent schools—that helped them transcend the epistemological atmospheres of their families. On the whole, however, when poor families fail their children, the society provides precious little help; while children of privilege are more likely to find rich sources of sustenance to promote their development elsewhere.

The stories of two women—Liz, born into privilege, and Mimi, born into poverty—illustrate the difference that social class can make in the distribution of life chances. Each woman described her father as tyrannical and her mother as unavailable. Each woman suffered sexual assaults from her father, which they believed began in the third or fourth year of life. Each sought help to end the incest in their thirteenth year. Each was disbelieved by her mother. From that point on the similarities stop.

The father from the poor home was jailed. The mother blamed the daughter. When Mimi ran away, the authorities caught her and placed her in a shelter home. "The shelter mother was really mean to me. I was afraid of the dark so she used to take the light bulbs out at night and lock me in my room." From there Mimi was moved through a series of foster homes and residential schools. While she occasionally met people who were kindly, she met no one who believed in her, drew her out, sponsored her, or educated her. At twenty-six she lives with her two babies and no husband. Having no skills she looks to welfare, not her own efforts, for maintenance.

Liz's father, "the biggest tyrant and the most indifferent man who ever lived," committed an identical crime but was not sent to jail. While Liz's mother was "like a loose limb, like an arm that is all shriveled up," there were many others to receive, encourage, counsel, and educate Liz. While the first daughter remained mired in silence, the second was, at the time of the interview, a constructivist who had a well-developed sense of voice and mind.

Among the many who helped Liz transcend her family, some were not even human. "When I was really feeling cast off I had my dog and me. That was my world. Then I started riding horses. That became my world. It was completely detached from my family. I didn't want anything from them. I just wanted my pony. I wanted to ride. I wanted to ride all day. And I'd do it." Her animals and the woods surrounding the family's vacation house offered her solace and escape. Her animals helped her develop capacities that are cultivated only in loving relationships.

> My relationship with my horse is amazing. He would save your life for you, if you needed it. He loves to do things for you. He loves to please. From him I learned reciprocity. I mean the reason that we were so great together was because we understood give-and-take with one another. How can you talk about a horse this way? He taught me a lot about responsibility, about what it would be like having a child.

Like a good teacher, her horse gave her confidence in herself and in her ability to learn. "I have a feeling that I'm good with horses, that I know horses pretty well, that I am sensitive and I am pigheaded—*but I can learn when I decide I want to learn*" (emphasis added).

She also found good teachers in the therapists and counselors she consulted, who were able to provide much of the information and the language that she needed to make sense of her family. She also found good teachers in the schools she attended. Some of her teachers even opened their homes to her, making themselves available as a "surrogate family." "They showed me what parents ought to be like. They taught me a lot about loving relationships that I don't think I would ever have learned otherwise. They have been great for me. They gave me confidence in myself. I have been using them as a model of what I want out of my own life."

The arts seemed particularly important in helping her develop the powers of her own voice and mind. In the schools that she attended she was helped to cultivate her abilities in almost all of the expressive arts, winning "a whole bunch of awards" and accolades as a dancer, actor, and singer. The arts, she said, "took care of me emotionally so well. It was something you could do, that you love, that you work at." Her schools and her home also had extensive libraries, so she could read and reread her favorite books—mostly about artists and the unfolding of their personhood and their gifts. But most of all, some of the schools she attended gave her "a love of learning." "Learning for learning's sake, not learning for an A or B. It helped me feel like there was a world out there that I could have and be interested in." Having cultivated her capacities as a knower, she could make sense of her experience, put it in perspective, and move on. "You can't really move on in your life until you've accepted certain things about your parents and have integrated them and then started moving on. It is the only way you can face the world and walk into it with an open heart and an open mind." The daughter from the poor family, having no inkling that hearts and minds could be opened, walks nowhere.

BREAKING THE CYCLE

Indeed, the women we interviewed who moved far beyond the epistemological atmospheres depicted in their histories had much in common with Liz. Each learned to immerse herself in at least one symbol system from a very early age. This might have been music or art, but most often they found another world through books and literature. Frequently they kept a diary. Whatever the medium, as children these women were producers as well as consumers in the medium that they chose to develop. The schools they attended supported such activities and helped them cultivate the life of the mind. They often had younger siblings who looked up to them and needed their care. Most found important, decent human relationships outside of the home—in their neighborhood, school, or among distant relatives. A few created such relationships for themselves through the sheer power of their imaginations, by endowing their pets and imaginary playmates with those attributes that nourish the human potential.

It has been the accepted wisdom that emotional problems are central causes of psychopathology and that only by alleviating emotional difficulties can intellectual deficits be ameliorated. Our stories and the works of Réuven Feuerstein (1980), Nicholas Hobbs (1982), and Myrna Shure and George Spivack (1978) all suggest the central importance of intellectual development if emotional difficulties are to be prevented or overcome. "Gaining a voice" and developing an awareness of their own minds are the tasks that these women must accomplish if they are to cease being either a perpetrator or a victim of family violence. It is also necessary if these women are to stop passing down these patterns from one generation to the next. Many of the young women who viewed the world from silence began raising families of their own. Unfortunately they were replicating the same patterns of family life that they themselves experienced. Cindy, pregnant at fifteen, tried to imagine herself as a teacher to her child. She was reminded of her sister's child who had a "rear end like leather." "We figured, you know, if you spanked him every time he did something wrong, he would straighten himself up as he gets bigger." Cindy could imagine wielding force but not words when teaching and influencing her child. Another adolescent mother, who was under investigation for child abuse, had similar views: "I try to make them mind the best I can without beating them to death. You know that they still don't understand it. They just blurt out what they want to blurt out." She also assumed that beatings would "straighten them up." She did not realize that it was hard for the children to understand what was wanted of them if they were not told. She could not imagine that what they might "blurt out" could have value.

Mothers who have so little sense of their own minds and voices are unable to imagine such capacities in their children. Not being fully aware of the power of words for communicating meaning, they expect their children to know what is on their minds without the benefit of words. These parents do not tell their children what they mean by "good"—much less why. Nor do they ask the children to explain themselves. (See also Bernstein 1964; Ward 1971.)

We observed these mothers "backhanding" their children whenever the child asked questions, even when the questions seemed to stem from genuine curiosity and desire for knowledge. It was as if the questions themselves were another example of the child's "talking back" and "disrespect."

Such a mother finds the curious, thinking child's questions stressful, since she does not yet see herself as an authority who has anything to say or teach.

The Families of Those Who Listen to
the Voices of Others

The women who sought ideas and ideals and listened to others in order to fill their storehouses full of truths told a different story.

ONE-WAY TALK

The parents of these women were certainly not uncommunicative. Typically, they told their children everything. These parents assumed that their daughters should and would listen to them, that they would understand them, and that they would obey. A student from a community college illustrates the point.

> Learning under my mother was—powerful. She could figure people out. She wasn't one to be beating you and knocking you all the time. She talked and talked and talked. Every time she opened her mouth she would be telling you something that would really do you some good. It wasn't a lot of frivolous talk. Me and my mother would sit down and she would talk. She taught me the facts of life. I would tell my mother everything and she would tell me what to do and what not to do, what was right and what wasn't right. I would go out on dates and come back and relate the whole story to her. She would go, "This is good and this was bad. Don't do this the next time."

Although these stories show more effective communication patterns than those of the silent women, these parents used only "one-way" conversations as the predominant mode of operating with their children. The parents did most of the talking, while the children did most of the listening. While some of the women described their parents as warm and supportive, others as cold and sometimes abusive, almost all of the women in this second group had at least one parent whom they depicted as being only "one way."

These parents said what was on their minds, but they did not strive to understand what was on their daughters' minds. They did all the active thinking and talking about the ins and outs and the rights and wrongs of the situation. The parents expected their daughters to absorb their ideas, but they seldom encouraged their daughters to think things through for themselves. Because they were children, they were expected to hear but not to be heard.

INEQUALITY

These daughters and their parents accepted the inherent inequality built into the parent-child relationship as a permanent condition. In comparison, the women who cultivated more elaborate modes of meaning-making assumed that the inequality between parent and child was only temporary. Indeed, as we shall see, the creation of a relationship of equality, collegiality, and intimacy between daughters and parents—especially mothers—becomes valued as a central achievement by most of those who come to understand that all knowledge is constructed.

The women who assumed that knowledge came from outside the self brought these same patterns of speaking and listening to their new families as they began to raise children of their own. One adolescent mother had begun lecturing her infant. She said, "I am going to teach Nellie right from wrong. I am going to tell her what I think is best. Then I am going to hope and pray that she will listen."

The marriages created by these women and those of their parents conformed to the sex-role stereotypes the culture upheld. The women almost always depicted them as being very hierarchical, with talking and listening being unevenly divided between the partners. It was typically the husband who did the speaking and the wife who listened. As one woman recounted, "Women were more or less to be seen and not heard. The men were supposed to be the ones with the voice of the family, the go-getter, the breadwinner. I think a man feels he is superior to women—most women." Only rarely were these roles reversed, with the wife being dominant and the husband subordinate. As one woman said of her father, "He recedes into a vast degree of silence." The widespread tendency for men to do the talking and for women and children to do the listening has been repeatedly documented in the studies of social scientists, who have only recently begun to focus attention on the politics of discourse in family life

(Bernard 1981; Engle 1980; Fishman 1978, 1983; Gleason and Greif 1983; Greif 1980; West and Zimmerman 1983).

When these women described their mothers as wives, they seldom depicted them as speaking up and speaking out. If their mothers departed from the conventional pattern of quietness and submissiveness, the daughters almost always described them as being shrill and destructive. One adolescent illustrated how upsetting it could be to have a mother who was "gaining a voice": "When others told her off my mother used to take it and just walk off. Now she will just tell them where to put it. She's just different since she and my father got a divorce. I don't understand her at all."

REBELLIONS—ADOLESCENT AND OTHERWISE

In the stories the received knowers told, there were no images of rebellion against adult authority. These daughters took it and just walked off quietly, exactly as they wanted their mothers to do. Although a few of these women, like most of the silent women, lived socially deviant lives guided primarily by impulse, none described themselves as ever questioning parental authority. None spoke of efforts to overrule their parents and to become self-directed. There were no accounts of adolescent rebellions. Even though many of them told of beatings, incest, abandonment, and foster placements, none protested. Such things just happened. These women did not try to explain why. They did not sit in judgment of their parents. They never mentioned being angry.*

Only one of these women ever spoke of fighting back. At the age of fifty she recalled her stepfather trying to rape her when she was thirteen. She had bit him and he never tried again. Almost four decades later she recounted only shame and confusion that she had become an aggressor in that long-ago incident: "I've never been that type of person that wants to hurt other people. I'd rather take the hurt myself than to hurt other people." This woman, as is characteristic of others in this group, extended care and protection to others but not to herself. She might be hurt, but she would not inflict hurt—whatever the cost. She was still ashamed that she stood up for herself. She recalled no images of pride for having been brave and victorious. She expressed no sense of outrage at what her stepfather attempted, at a trust violated.

In denying her own selfhood this woman provided a classic example

---

* In their studies of the authoritarian personality, Adorno et al. (1950) found that inmates in San Quentin prison espoused more deference to parental and other authorities than did any other population they studied.

of the conventional feminine voice that Gilligan (1982) was able to hear in women's moral judgments. In actuality, these women do not speak in a different voice. They have no voice at all. Conventional feminine goodness means being voiceless as well as selfless.

MEN AS SPEAKERS, WOMEN AS LISTENERS

The continued injunction against articulating needs, feelings, and experiences must constrain the development of hearts and minds, because it is through speaking and listening that we develop our capacities to talk and to think things through. The fact that women are expected to curtail their voice may account for the greater prevalence of clinical depression and learned helplessness among women than among men (Al-Issa 1980; Weissman and Paykel 1974).

The tendency to allocate speaking to men and listening to women impairs the development of men as well. The frequent failure of men to cultivate their capacity for listening has a profound impact on their capacity for parenting, for it is mothers more than fathers who are most likely to still their own voices so they may hear and draw out the voices of their children. Fathers and daughters more often stand at a great distance, literally, because many, many of these fathers are absent, and figuratively, because fathers and daughters seldom try to understand each other or to stand in each other's shoes. One teenager described how it was with many fathers. "My father is all right to talk to—but he's got to realize where everybody else stands, too. Like every now and then he thinks that where he stands is the only place to be, and nobody else is supposed to stand where they want to be."

As dialogue is the primary means for preventing or resolving conflicts, not listening and imagining the other invites coercion or withdrawal. Indeed, if our interviews are an index of current trends, it appears that fathers are having great difficulty fulfilling their parental roles at this point in history. To a degree that surprised and disturbed us, we found women describing their fathers as unable to see others in their own terms, as dictatorial and sometimes violent, and as fleeing from family life and their children.

Family Histories of Those with an Inner Voice

The subjectivists, finding an inner source for truth, turned from their parents' words and sought self-direction by listening to their own "infallible gut." "I didn't seem to get along with my parents at all. I just did not want to hear their side of the story—or what they had to say about anything." Realizing that there were as many sides to a story as there were storytellers, these women often ignored the stories that their parents told so that they might concentrate on creating their own.

Those who focused on cultivating their own intuitive voice admired their parents only to the extent that the parents listened to them. The parents had to still their own voices and listen with a nonjudgmental, unconditionally accepting ear if these women were to feel heard. What their parents had to say in return was the least of their concerns. Proper talk as envisioned by them was still one-way talk. Any advance over the previous position was that it was the daughter who talked and the parent who listened. Again, mothers more than fathers were likely to be available as listeners.

QUESTIONING PARENTAL AUTHORITY

Unlike the more passive listeners, these women tried to wrest control for their own lives out of the hands of their parents or other authorities. "I was very rebellious—not wanting to be told what to do. I thought I was old enough to know right from wrong." If the subjectivists' parents did not support their efforts to become self-directed, the daughters often began an educational campaign to bring the parents around to their way of thinking. A college student, who went through childhood "never disagreeing," remembered a confrontation with her mother that stood out for her as a major turning point. "I sat her down and told her, 'Look, the only way I am going to learn is for me to experience it for me. Let me find out. God knows, you found out. So let me find out. I will even let you say, "I told you so." Please!' "

If their parents did not yield power willingly, the subjectivist daughters grabbed the reins for themselves. Some even imagined taking them by force.

My mother used to hit me. She doesn't hit me anymore. I think it is because I've outgrown her and I'll hit her back. Before I was very trapped. I never went out. I was too scared to go out. Now my horizons have broadened. I have seen that there is more than just being at home, being scared of everything, being the baby of the family with someone always hovering over me—always telling me what to do.

In sharp contrast to the numbness and muteness inherent in the previous positions, the subjectivists see themselves finding and venting their inner feelings—even rage. While the others remain resigned and remarkably uncomplaining in the face of even great injustices, the subjectivists are overtaken by fury if wronged by their parents. For the most part, these stories were told in the present tense and with the heat of the battle still in the air. One of the women who held this perspective imagined that some day—far in the future—she would likely forgive her parents and put her anger aside. Another spoke of the anger that persisted beyond her mother's death and prayed that she might be able to find room in her heart to forgive her father before he, too, passed away.

Sometimes the women remembered experiencing an outpouring of rage over an ongoing injustice they had previously accepted. A college student described her earlier passivity and how she had acquiesced to her father's incestuous demands throughout her childhood. Then things changed about the time she reached early adolescence. Most likely she, too, was recounting a time when she began to find inner sources of knowing.

> So when he tried to have sex with me when I was thirteen, *I did know the difference.* After that I remember being really furious with him. I remember just fury running through my veins. I remember wanting to run out and scream to him, "Don't you ever touch my sister like this or I will kill you!" He betrayed one of the most precious things a human being has—a sense of faith in the people who brought you up (emphasis added).

Why are subjectivists able to revolt and rebel against their parents, while the women who see themselves only as receivers of knowledge remain so acquiescent? The subjectivists' ability to imagine an "infallible gut" provides guidance and standards independent of parents. With an "inner gut" subjectivists can imagine themselves having some sort of a voice and a right to speak out—even against authorities.

The subjectivists are advantaged in still another important way. They imagine the world and themselves in a state of constant flux. They can even imagine themselves initiating some of the changes. The silent and received knowers, however, see everything as static and stationary—including themselves. They understand the world as arbitrary, unamenable to analysis, and unalterable. If their parents are unjust, that is how it is. To protest would only increase their own difficulties.

Many of the subjectivists we interviewed were fortunate enough to have parents who supported their efforts to become independent. These women frequently reported that their parents became less dictatorial as they grew older. While it might have been that these daughters constructed their view of their parents differently as they themselves grew more mature, it was also likely that their parents had actually undergone change. Jane Loevinger (1962, 1976) found a decline in authoritarian family attitudes in parents as they aged and raised more children (even after having considered the parents' age). Many children reported that their parents became more flexible with each succeeding child.

Adult development regularly proceeds in the direction that supports the developmental progress of children. Indeed, the process of promoting the growth and development of children is an important source of growth and development for parents (Bell and Harper 1977, Galinsky 1981, Loevinger 1976). Furthermore, there is some historical evidence of a broad, current trend away from authoritarianism and dualism toward relativism; an increased awareness of inner emotional and intellectual capacities; and a prolonged capacity for change and adaptation occurring during the adult years (Hagen 1962, Perry 1970, Riesman, Denny, and Glazer 1961; Veroff, Douvan, and Kulka 1981). Indeed, two major shifts in the study of psychology suggest an accommodation to such a trend. Adult development as a field of study has become a rapidly growing area of concentration, although in the past it was assumed that development was confined to the childhood and adolescent years. Cognitive psychology has increasingly attracted attention away from the behaviorist perspective where the individual is seen as a passive agent reacting only to external stimulus. Concern with the memorization process is being replaced by studies of how knowledge is constructed all along the life span (Gardner 1985). Educational practice—at least for the privileged—appears to be following the trend.

The subjectivists who struggle to overcome parental authority are often successful. When parents do actively support their daughters' efforts to become self-directed, a renewed sense of connection often occurs between the generations. Some subjectivists described how they started talking with their parents—most often their mothers—as if they were peers. It is just this kind of shift that regularly moves the daughter to begin another revision of the family history. "I always thought of her more as an authority. She was my mother and I was a kid. Now it's more like friends. We are on a friendship level instead of two generations. (Laughs.) Now I listen a lot better to my mother than I used to. I find out later, she was right all along! (Laughs.)" These daughters, feeling more heard, more in control of their own destinies, and more able to maintain an equal footing, could once again afford to listen to their parents.

However, it is a different story if subjectivists' parents remain dictatorial and unable to appreciate their daughters' unique points of view. These daughters are likely to dismiss their parents as narrow-minded and look elsewhere for support and conversation.

> When I was little I thought my father was the smartest person on the
> planet. I thought he knew everything. That has changed dra-
> matically. Now I get real frustrated with his narrow-minded view
> of the world; with his demands that I live up to his preconceived
> notions. I think he views the world through a real small scope.

Another woman echoed,

> I once saw my mother as a woman who was very good. A woman
> who drew a very fine line between what was right and what was
> wrong. And she lived on the right side of the line. Then I began
> to see my mother as a very narrow-minded woman. I began to
> see my mother as a bigot.

Subjectivists love their parents if they perceive them as responsive, open, and flexible; they reject their parents if they see them as doctrinaire and rigid.

Unlike any of the women who held the previous perspectives, some of the subjectivists depicted parents as having inner sources of knowing, such as intellect or intuition. A community college student said of her father,

> I have always thought of my father as a man who was very wise. I
> did then and I do now. He was a lover of humanity. He would
> watch and think about people—why they do the things that they
> do. He was a lover of porches and rocking chairs. Even though
> he was barely literate, he had a quick mind. He could separate
> out the trivial.

Another woman described her mother: "My mother is very strong-minded.

She knows what she is talking about." There are several reasons why subjectivists are more likely to notice such capacities in their parents. It is possible that their parents involve themselves more in utilizing their inner resources for constructing knowledge than do the parents of the women from the previous perspectives. It is also possible that the daughter herself has to adopt the subjectivists' perspective before she can begin to conceptualize and describe the inner life that her parents may have been drawing on all along.

As images of parents' cultivating and utilizing their inner sources of knowing increased, we see a corresponding decrease in images of impulsive, chaotic, and violent behavior on the parents' part—at least in the descriptions the daughters offered. The parents' behavior is either becoming more subordinated to the parents' own symbolic processes or the daughter is becoming more capable of conceptualizing such a possibility, or both. Taking the stories at face value, it seems as if both the subjectivist women and their parents were more able to replace anarchy and despotism with self-government than were the more voiceless women and their parents.

FATHERS AND MOTHERS AS KNOWERS

When we examined the subjectivists' stories to see if they attributed different capacities to fathers than to mothers, a pattern did emerge. If, for instance, a subjectivist described her father as being intelligent, she left it at that; but if she depicted her mother as being intelligent, she would, as likely as not, add a qualifier suggesting that the mother's intellectual gifts came to naught. For example,

> My mother is a smart, creative, beautiful woman who is wasting away.

> You'd never know that my mother is so intelligent as she was always hiding it.

> My mother is smart. She never finished grade school but I always sensed a real common sense about her. But she refuses to face the truth about my dad. Whenever there was any sort of problem [that is, incest], she always blamed me.

SUPERMOMS

When daughters strove to stand on their own two feet—as they often did in the subjectivist period—they scrutinized their mothers for signs of independence and self-sufficiency. They frequently described their mothers as powerful, even if they did not specifically attribute intelligence to them. Many of these mothers "pulled themselves up from the bottom" and, with fathers unavailable or inadequate, became the primary or sole supporters of their children. One woman, whose mother supported eight people, suggested the admiration that these women could have for such power-houses—and how cherished such mothers made them feel. "She really raised herself up. She works for us. She is very, very pushy and ambitious for us."

Admiration for powerful mothers is a theme that recurs again and again in the fiction that depicts the lives of American blacks. Such images appeared in the stories of the black women we interviewed as well. The theme, however, is prominent in many of the interviews of women, black or white, whose mothers raised their children without the help of fathers—if their mothers were not broken by the burden. As the phenomenon of fathers abandoning responsibility for the raising of children becomes more widespread, so does the image of mothers as saviors and superwomen.

That the images of uncompromised power in women are so often associated with being abandoned by men lends some credence to Barbara Ehrenreich's argument in *The Hearts of Men* (1983) that the current wave of feminism is a response of women to the withdrawal of men from family life. Women are becoming so strong and independent because their survival and the survival of their children depend on it.

Images of mothers in intact families reflect a different pattern. Subjectivists whose parents never divorced also depicted their mothers as being powerful. However, the images of the power held by mothers with husbands often involved discomfort and subterfuge: "My mother is a very fierce woman. She is very strong. She yields and yields—just until she gets what she wants. She goes after things. I like that about her. When she sets herself a goal she reaches it by any means possible." Another woman described her mother trying to contain her own power while bolstering that of her husband. "She tries her best to let my father be the man of the house. Sometimes it doesn't work. Sometimes she is the man of the house—so to speak. Sometimes she needs to be—in my opinion." While the women from the previous positions criticized their mothers if they became strong, independent, and outspoken, the subjectivists criticized their mothers if they did not. One woman expressed her disdain by saying, "Her whole life was molded around my dad and making him happy."

SELFLESSNESS QUESTIONED

For the first time criticism of conventional feminine goodness entered the stories. At this juncture, mothers who exhibited selflessness, dependence, and avoidance of speaking out were held in contempt. Mothers who rejected this mode of relating to others were increasingly described with images of pleasure and pride. As we will show, the image of the "little woman" disappeared by the time we reached the stories told by constructivists.

Essentially, the subjectivists began to question the traditional role women played in the zero-sum game. They were no longer willing to lose or to curtail their own chances so that the fortunes of others might be enhanced. A woman spoke of the conflict she experienced between the demands of her family and the demands of her career: "There is always an emergency when something I am doing is important to me. I resent giving that time to anybody else. Every time there is something that is important to me, somebody wants part of me. I resent it a lot." For the subjectivists, however, the win/lose model still prevailed. The only advance over the previous positions was that the subjectivists now claimed the right to be one of the winners.

SUBJECTIVISTS AS PARENTS

Not only did the view of subjectivists' parents evolve and change with epistemological development, but their relationships with their own child went through similar transformations. Only as a mother begins to find in herself sources of knowledge is she likely to look for such resources in her child. The woman we called Inez provided us with an example. It was she who gave us the "infallible gut" metaphor that we have used to suggest the essence of the subjectivist's inner voice. Inez, like many who were delayed in development, grew up in a family where the father was dictatorial and abusive. The mother, concerned about community opinion, continually denied his incestuous behavior and failed to protect her daughters. Inez, like others raised by parents who fail to acknowledge the truths of what is going on and of what the children are thinking and feeling— or even that the children can think and feel—grew up believing that she was "dumb," good only as a "doormat," and "that I am not worth anything. That my opinion ain't worth shit. Until recently I didn't realize that I could think and be smart and still be a woman. I had no faith in myself. I didn't trust my judgment at all." This woman who saw no interior strengths began to find within herself an "infallible gut." This discovery was followed by changes in the way she was able to perceive her children as well. As we shall see, however, such changes take time. This is how she began the first of two interviews: "What stands out for me is that I'm learning how to make a good home. . . . I care a lot about my kids and the people close to me. When I care, I really care. Before I didn't think I could be loved or that anybody would care."

"To make a good home" can mean many things. When we first talked, Inez was trying to become less passive with her children, to become more comfortable with her authority as a parent. She was pleased to learn that she could make her kids obey by using a variety of punishments: confining them to their rooms, denying meals, and washing their mouths out with soap. She said,

> My impression of power was what my father was—abusive, destructive, and unloving. Everything was win or lose. Either you were on top or you're the dummy on the bottom. I had to become the boss of the family. Now I see that I'm the mother and I have some knowledge that my kids don't have. I've lived longer than they. I've got more information than they do. Now, if they look at me cross-eyes, I stick a bar of soap in their mouths. I learned that I can be the authority figure in my kids' lives and still be loved. I can set down the rules because I love them.

After a year of much hard work with therapists, college courses, and several self-help groups, Inez's second interview had a new focus. Although she was still very concerned about exercising her authority as a parent, Inez now showed some concern for helping the children "be smart," "to think things through themselves," and "to make their own decisions." To do that she saw that she had to curtail her lectures to them and let them find their own voices. Inez then said, "I still don't talk with my kids enough. I still dictate." The previous year she mentioned only the use of force in influencing her children. Then she began to see the difference between discourse and dictation. Inez's own voice appeared in their relationship and she began to understand that she could and should tell them what she wanted and why. Inez was also beginning to see the importance of drawing forth the children's own voices. It is likely that the time lag we observed between the development of Inez's ability to conceptualize her own mind and power of voice and being able to imagine such capacities in her children is a regularly occurring phenomenon: that you must first begin to hear your own inner voice in order to understand the importance of drawing out the voices of others, whether the other is your child, spouse, student, client, or friend.

Family Life and Integrating the Voices of Reason and Feeling

The women who questioned the infallibility of the gut and who were consciously cultivating and integrating the voices of reason and emotion wove still another pattern in the family story. While not all these women came from happy homes, they were much more likely than the women who held other perspectives to describe family relationships characterized by images of connection, care, mutuality, and reciprocity. Because the themes in the family histories told by the procedural and the constructivist knowers were so similar, we combined their stories, noting the exceptions when they occur.

MOTHERS AND DIALOGUE

Daughters who integrated the voices of reason and feelings were likely to be interested in the quality of the voices of their mothers. Many noted with admiration that their mothers developed strong, clear voices of their own. As one young woman said, "My mother is only five feet tall, but if you heard her over the phone, why you would think that she is at least five feet and seven inches."

Again we see that it is important to daughters that parents have a voice. Those who receive knowledge from others look to their parents for truth and direction and often feel helped when their voices are loud and clear. At this new juncture daughters wish their parents to have voices of their own so that they might be full participants in an ongoing conversation. A twenty-three-year-old college alumna described such talk. "I was her confidante. She would tell me things about herself. It was sort of a relationship of equals." It was only in this last collection of stories that family conversations routinely involved two-way talk. In these stories both parents and daughters were given a voice, each spoke and listened, each had an equal say.

These daughters were disappointed if their mothers did not have the courage to speak their minds straight out, or if their mothers only provided others "with a forum for discussion, but is never a participant in that discussion herself."

Some noticed their fathers listening with care. When that occurred it was highly valued. However, none of these daughters particularly admired their fathers for speaking out. For fathers to have a voice was a given—not an achievement. For fathers to develop a listening ear and for mothers to "gain a voice" were the feats that those who were integrating the voices of reason and feeling noted and appreciated.

CONNECTEDNESS BETWEEN MOTHERS AND DAUGHTERS

Although the basic themes of attachment and autonomy were interwoven, a greater sense of connection and of commonalities pervaded the daughters' portraits of mothers, while the sense of distance and difference continued to predominate in the descriptions of life with father. This pattern was also observed by James Youniss and Jacqueline Smoller (1985) in their extensive study of adolescents' perceptions of mothers and fathers. This pattern was also reflected in the descriptions of family life Lillian Rubin heard in the interviews she conducted with husbands and wives in her study of lower-class family life, *Worlds of Pain* (1976). Chodorow (1978) argued that the basic sense of living connected or separated from others—different conceptions of self and of the self-world relationship—is deeply rooted in the experience of the infant's earliest relationships with his or her caregiver. Universally, mothers and/or other women attend to the care of the young, with fathers and other men remaining on the periphery. Chodorow maintains that when caregivers primarily from only one sex nurture infants, the stage is set for two distinctive developmental consequences, depending on the match or mismatch of the caregiver's and the infant's gender. The female infant nurtured by her mother has only to affirm her connectedness and sense of sameness as she begins to develop an understanding of gender and of her own identity as a person in the world. The male baby, on the other hand, has to declare his separateness from his mother, his primary caregiver and first source of identification, in order to build a conception of his gender and identity.

Chodorow's argument is compelling and helps explain the differing sense of connectedness and separateness that can readily be observed in well-developing boys and girls from the earliest ages on. However, as we reexamined these stories of family life, two considerations emerged that threw Chodorow's argument into a different light. With an increasing awareness of how much the sense of connectedness to others deepens with maturity, we believe that important causal factors that occur later in the life cycle must also be considered. For many women being a mother as well as having a woman as a mother provides a profound experience of human connection. That adult experiences as well as childhood experiences contribute to the evolution of a sense of connection is consistent with our observations that connectedness with others is one of the most complicated human achievements, requiring a high level of development. As Jerome Kagan (1984) suggests, there is a general tendency to attribute characteristics to the infant that are opposite to those that are prized in adults in the culture. Thus, he argues, Americans valuing independence and individuality in adults tend to see the baby as being dependent and undifferentiated from others. In contrast, the Japanese, valuing a close interdependence between people, see the infant as too autonomous and needing to be coaxed into a dependent role in order to encourage the mutual bonding necessary for adult life. The more we come to understand and value attachment and connectedness in adults, the more likely we will conceptualize autonomy and independence as part of the infant's nature and act to encourage the development of the capacity for connection with others.

GUIDING METAPHORS

Whatever the roots of connectedness, communal and family life is threatened whenever members fail to see the interdependence of all. As Gilligan and her colleagues suggest, the individual who conceptualizes the self as basically connected to others sees the bonds that knit human relationships together as bonds of attachment. They spin visions of the ties between persons, which can best be suggested by the metaphors of webs and nets. Webs and nets imply opposing capacities for snaring or entrapment and for rescuing or safety. They also suggest a complexity of relationships and the delicate interrelatedness of all so that tension and movement in one part of the system will grow to be felt in all parts of the whole. In the complexity of a web, no one position dominates over the rest. Each person—no matter how small—has some potential for power; each is always subject to the actions of others. It is hard to imagine other ways of visioning the world that offer as much potential for protection to the immature and the infirm.

In contrast, the self premised in autonomy sees individuals relating through bonds of agreements, such as contracts, laws, and the like. Their metaphors for suggesting the world are more often images of pyramids and mountains. On the metaphorical mountain the few at the top dominate the many on the bottom. Those near the base must move the whole mountain to affect those near the apex; in the image of the net, even the least can affect all others by the slightest pull on the gossamer thread.

Those on a mountain find it easier to maintain the view that some must lead and others must follow, that some will win while the rest will lose. In the hierarchical world that the players with these limited epistemologies construct, the game is rigged. Typically, it is the men who dominate the women and the parents who hold sway over the children. Mothers taking this either/or stance believe that they must choose to lose in order for their children to succeed. Thus mothers try to remain voiceless, powerless, and selfless so that their children will prosper (Miller 1976).

Carole Klein (1984), in *Mothers and Sons*, tells us that the mothers of sons feel more guilt and receive more condemnation from others when they pursue their own interests than do the mothers of daughters. Because women are expected to subordinate themselves to males, it may take longer for mothers and sons to realize that the win/lose model is not the best model for most human relationships than it takes mother and daughters. It is the relationship between mothers and daughters in which the possibility of common interests and a win/win game is most likely to become apparent. Because mothers and daughters can affirm and enjoy their commonalities more readily, they are more likely to see how they might advance their individual interests in tandem, without one having to be sacrificed for the other—an understanding that most of the constructivist women and their mothers have achieved.

HEALING THE SPLIT BETWEEN INTELLECT AND EMOTION

When the procedural knowers first began to cultivate the voice of reason, they were more likely to see intrapsychic powers being allocated to their parents according to the conventional pattern. They saw their fathers as imbued with intelligence, while they portrayed their mothers as warm and sensitive. While they saw each of their parents as having developed one aspect of their powers rather fully, they portrayed them as denying other aspects of their selfhood.

Occasionally when this bifurcation was sharply drawn, the volcanic eruptions that were so typical of the earlier stories remained a theme, albeit the theme was now largely muted and the level of violence greatly diminished. While these mothers were depicted as hot-tempered and hysterical, it was the cold, unemotional fathers who erupted with volcanic force. The fathers relied on their wives to mediate and interpret their feelings to others. Such fathers were unemotional only in the sense that they did not articulate feelings. Indeed, it often appeared that it was the mother who was actually the thinker and the father who was the feeler—at least in terms of dealing with the personal and the interpersonal. A smooth relationship between such fathers and their daughters was often dependent on the mediation services provided by sensitive, feeling mothers. Such mothers tried to imagine, understand, and articulate each person's feelings. The conversations of these fathers and daughters could enter into the personal only when the mother became an interpreter and supplied them with the language of emotions.

It may be that the father's unmet need for the absent mother to intercede as an intermediary and translator explains why marital separation is so often followed by the abandonment of children by fathers. When a separation or divorce occurs, a father has to face his children directly, without the services of a mediator. Some fathers may feel so uncomfortable without an intermediary that they withdraw altogether. Teaching children and fathers to talk with each other directly might go a long way toward reducing the amount and intensity of such estrangements.

The descriptions of volcanic activity, alcoholism, violence, and abandonment were markedly diminished in the stories of family life told by procedural and constructivist knowers—in terms of both prevalence and virulence—when compared with the stories told by women who held the earlier perspectives. While fully 75 percent of the silent and the received knowers depicted one or both of their parents as alcoholic, only two (6 percent) of the reflective and constructivist knowers combined gave a parent this label. A third woman had a mother she proudly called a "sober alcoholic." "I really respect her for her progress in stopping drinking and being successful at it. That's one of the great accomplishments of her life. Being able to accept that she had a problem and that she could be doing something about it and being successful in it."

While a few of these women had parents who were separated or divorced, none of the fathers abandoned the father-daughter relationship altogether—an event that occurred with remarkable frequency in the previous collection of stories. When all family members were encouraged to draw on their whole range of capacities to deal with both the personal and the impersonal, they no longer needed to rely on the use of either power or abandonment for the resolution of conflicts. Instead, talking things through—however heatedly—became the preferred alternative. As Patti, the adolescent mother who helped us understand procedural knowing, said, "My mother and I can fight, argue, and scream about different points of things and yet end up saying, 'Well, thank you!' You know, appreciating each other no matter how much we disagree."

MOTHERS AND DEVELOPING THE VOICE OF REASON

The tendency to allocate intellectual capacities to fathers and emotional ones to mothers was largely overcome in the stories told by women who were integrating the voices of reason and emotions themselves. These women were much more likely to see mothers and fathers as endowed with both intellectual and emotional capacities. Almost all of them portrayed their mothers as having good minds and many of their fathers as having some capacity to acknowledge and articulate their feelings.

While subjectivists' mothers had the ability to speak from the gut and say what they felt, it was only in this last group of stories that the daughters consistently depicted their mothers as also having the ability to speak from the mind and to say what they thought. As Patti said,

> My mother is a wonderful person to talk to. I can talk to her about anything now. She is the type that can draw stuff out of a person. *She stands up for what she thinks* (emphasis added).

Another elaborated,

> My mother is very independent, very strong—a very verbal kind of person. She has got her opinions and she is not the least bit afraid to express them. When she gets into arguments there is a lot of love—but there is that independence of thought.

Mildred illustrates the pleasure that constructivist women and their mothers often take in each other's intellectual powers.

> My mother is a liberated woman who has a wonderful mind. After getting a Ph.D. in philosophy, she produced nine children and became the perfect housewife. About the age of forty she realized that she spent her whole life making other people happy and there are a lot of other things for women out there. She has gotten a second degree and now she teaches. She is very successful. Her students adore her and her children adore her.

Another college student saw her mother in similar terms.

> My mother is a wonderful person! She is really a miracle. Very creative, very political, very involved with life. She is complicated. I was always her friend. She included me in her life. She always comes to something with understanding.

These women portrayed their intelligent mothers as being very active learners.

> My mother always wants to be on top of the news. She is always questioning, investigating, and looking for something else, making challenges and demands on herself, in her job and with her children.

Like their daughters, these mothers had two inner voices at their command: a voice for expressing emotions and a voice for sharing reasons. Both could be heard. The use of one did not drown out the other.

FATHERS AND DEVELOPING THE VOICE OF EMOTIONS

As these women came to value their mothers for their good minds, many also began to find in their fathers emotional capacities that they never knew existed. As Patti said, "My father is trying to be more under-standing, which makes it easier for me to express myself. He realizes now that emotions play a much larger part than logical thinking." While Patti saw her father changing, others saw that it was their own view of their fathers that was undergoing change. As one college student said, "My father is an emotional man who doesn't let you know that he is emotional. He is very intelligent, very logical, and very accepting. I can see now that he really has a depth of emotions that I've never really seen before."

The shift that these women noticed—where fathers became more tolerant of their nurturant and affiliative responses and mothers became more active and agentic—has been documented in many studies of adult men and women approaching mid-life (Cumming and Henry 1961; Gurin, Veroff, and Feld 1960; Gutmann 1964, 1975; Lowenthal, Thurnher, and Chiriboga 1975; Neugarten 1969; Rossi 1980). Again, it appears that when all goes well parents and children develop in tandem, that in the natural course of things the different generations can provide each other with the mutual supports that each requires for continued growth and development.

THE MOTHER-DAUGHTER RELATIONSHIP AND
THE DEVELOPMENT OF CONNECTED KNOWING

However much the parents of these women moved toward developing and integrating their intellectual and emotional capacities, distinctive differences remained between the ways the women depicted their mothers and fathers and related to them as knowers. While fathers served as models of separate knowing, it was in the relationships with mothers that these daughters found the most developed models of and opportunities for connected knowing. Connected knowing arises out of the experience of relationships; it requires intimacy and equality between self and object, not distance and impersonality; its goal is understanding, not proof.

Most of the procedural knowers reported that they talked with their mothers about personal things and they talked to their fathers—if they talked at all—about relatively impersonal topics. (In no case did this pattern reverse.) For example, a woman in her mid-twenties said,

> My mother is the one that I have more intimate discussions with. I can talk with her about stuff that I don't discuss with my father. . . . My mother deals more with that part of me which is able to deal with people, and sympathize with people, and communicate with people. My father has more to do with my intellectual development and my appreciation of literature.

And Faith said, "My dad has this dislike of what he calls 'idle chitchat,' but that's sort of necessary for a person." Faith's father liked to talk about "world affairs and crossword puzzles."

When fathers do talk to their daughters about matters of personal importance to the daughters, they tell them what they ought to do. One senior told us that her father was "still in the advice-giving mode." The father offered his advice out of loving concern. He wanted his daughter to major in economics in order to get a good job in business and become financially secure. But to the daughter, who was interested in painting and taking care of animals, the father's advice felt cold and controlling. When she failed to pursue her father's goals, she was aware that she had disappointed him. "My father categorizes me, and he always finds me wanting."

The intelligent mothers these women depicted were more like students, trying to understand; and they spoke of their intelligent fathers as being more like conventional teachers, bent on passing out truths. Linda's description of her parents provided an outstanding example. Both of her parents were psychiatrists involved as researchers and practitioners with adolescents and young adults (Linda's age group). Linda's mother looked to Linda as an expert she could consult. "She asks me—We talk a lot about her cases and her work. I kind of help her see the point of view of my generation—or whatever." Linda's mother asked, she did not tell. To her father, Linda was not an expert but a case that proved his points. She believed that her father was not interested in her as a unique person but as a general case for fitting into his "little classifications." She believed that he had little interest in the classifications that she might offer. "He makes me a case study. I'm just a little piece of evidence. . . . He is not interested in what goes on in my head." As Linda saw it, her father did not look to her for help to expand his understanding of her age group. Instead of asking her about her experience, he told her what she was experiencing. "Since I'm in this position, I must feel this way, this way, and this way. He has all of these little classifications which he fits everything into." She also believed that he was only interested in proving his old theories, not in generating new ones. She tested out this hunch: "I said, 'Dad, are you still learning new things?' And he goes, 'Well, not particularly.' " To her mother, Linda was a colleague or a teacher; to her father, Linda was a research subject, a student, or a child.

That such differences between mothers and fathers are so common may be accounted for by the fact that many men are used to being the expert, while many women are used to consulting others; many men are interested in how experience is generalized and universalized, while many women are interested in what can be learned from the particular; and the work of men frequently involves maintaining or increasing the status differential between persons, while the life work of many women focuses on maternal practice, where the main goal is to bring the smallest, least members up into relations of equality. While mothers and daughters slip into chairs around the kitchen table with ease, only occasionally do fathers abdicate their platforms without pressure from below.

To see themselves as equals, daughters often had to cut their fathers down to size. As one college alumna recounted,

> I am awed by my father. He is very smart, very intelligent, and very articulate. He can really pop the bubble. I can pop his bubble now and then! (Both laugh.) I never knew it before, but I can throw it right back to him—and he can be devastating!

By being devastating herself, she could meet him on equal ground. She continued,

Eventually I began to realize that my father wasn't perfect. That he was a human being—with frailties and problems of his own. If my father said something, that was that. You never argued with him. I began to realize that he could be wrong about stuff and that he did have deficiencies as a person. I think that helped our relationship in the sense that I could be a little more equal to him and able to communicate with him more. I think that's when we really started being very good friends.

Another woman definitely had seen her father, the professor, as God. She had once called him "Zeus" and said he was "a magnificent sight to look at." She agreed with one of his students that if her father "was running for God," she, too, would have voted for him. This father seemed to have campaigned for such a role. "He tends to have the approach that he is better than anyone else. He really has an overinflated ego. I think that any person will admit that early on in life parents are God—the authority. Later on they don't know a damn thing. And then after a while, you realize that they are reasonable people after all." In saying this, she paraphrased the words that Mark Twain put in the mouth of a young man: "My parents were so dumb when I was seventeen and so much smarter when I was twenty-one; I can't believe how much they learned in just four years."

While fathers of the constructivists occasionally still required dethroning, such images were largely absent from their stories of mothers. Indeed, the women in this group characterized the relationship between mothers and daughters as one of great intimacy, equality, and collegiality. While one might worry that such close, personal ties might hamper the individuation and development of these women, it was rare for women in this group to express such concerns. Indeed, Bertram Cohler and Henry Grunebaum (1981), in their study of daughters, mothers, and grandmothers, were also surprised at the intimate relationships they observed between different generations of women and revised their opinions about the difficulties such closeness might necessarily entail.

Not only did these women tend to cultivate relationships with their mothers that were very close and collegial, such relationships served as models for guiding and assessing many other relationships. As such, most of the constructivists were able to turn at least one of their professors into a colleague/friend of the highest order. Whenever such relationships took place, the sense of pleasure and accomplishment was unmistakable. Bridget shared her delight in the changes that even she and her father were able to bring about. "I tease him about the fact that I am finally getting myself established in life and that now he can start learning things from me.

(Laughs.) I am going to love it! (Laughs.) It makes me feel great! He laughs! He agrees!" These women, along with many of their mothers, some of their professors, and a few of their fathers, became perpetual students *and* perpetual teachers. In trading these roles back and forth, they made colleagues of one another.

MATERNAL CONVERSATION

"Gossip," Spacks says, "proceeds by a rhetoric of inquiry rather than of authority" (1982, pp. 33–34). The same is true of maternal conversation. Mothers interview their daughters. Mothers try to enter into their daughters' heads. Patti, for example, said of her mother, "She's the type of person that can draw stuff out of a person." A college student also described how her mother interviewed her. "She makes me question. I think that is intelligence. She is always asking me, 'Why?' She sees what I am doing." These mothers posed questions and took care to hear their daughters' answers. They valued the answers that their daughters gave. The parents— particularly the mothers—of these women even brought their own questions to the daughters for answers. "My parents are always telling me about dilemmas where they don't know what to do. They never know what to do!" The daughters, having developed the capacity for problem posing, interviewed their mothers as well. As one said, "My mother probably gets tired of me asking her hard questions. I suppose that I challenge her morals sometimes. That might annoy her about me." This daughter might like to know that such interviews, unlike lectures, are often appreciated.

Some of the women at the previous epistemological positions undoubtedly had parents who were also adept at question posing, but they did not describe such behavior. There may be a regular unfolding of the abilities to conceptualize and to articulate the processes involved in dialogue. "Telling" is understood long before the complexities of "asking" are comprehended (Arlin 1975). We feel that in most cases, mothers are no more caring than fathers, but their caring is more likely to take place in the connected mode. They try to help their daughters on the daughters' own terms, while fathers try to help in the fathers' terms. The effort to see others in their own terms is typical of the people Gilligan (1982) and her colleagues (Attanucci 1984; Lyons 1983) describe—mostly women—who are grounded in the responsibility mode of moral reasoning. Those who operate out of response strive to understand others in their own terms, while those oriented to a morality of rights see others in terms of social roles, norms, standards, and principles. Linda provided a good example when describing her mother.

> She trusts me. Any decision that I make. . . . We have a constant understanding of one another, a constant trust of each other's judgment. I could do just about anything, and if I sat down and explained it to her she would see my point of view and trust that I was doing it right—as I would for her. If I felt uncomfortable about something that she was doing, she would explain it to me and I'd feel comfortable. I'd trust her.

Both suspended judgment, listened to one another, and found their trust rewarded. Another woman could even trust her mother with the trouble that she was only anticipating. "She is interested in what I am doing. I can talk to her about the trouble that I have gotten into and the trouble I am getting into. She is able to receive what I have to say."

These daughters often felt that their mothers heard and valued them in their own terms, even when they were in disagreement. Many talked about a father who basically wanted his daughter to fit into his categories, that her own terms had no value unless they were congruent with his.

> My father assumed all sorts of things about me. He evaluated me in five minutes, just like any old surgeon. "Hip bones, this and that and the next thing." He judged me and then he categorized me. Sort of slotted me away nicely into the little mesh grid system he had for his little children. He never knew what was going on in my mind, but he was certain that he did. He never asked. I despise being categorized.

Linda assumed that her father just talked and never asked questions because he could not tolerate her point of view if it were to disagree with his. "He won't listen, 'cause it's like he refuses to trust us. It's like he refuses to believe that anything we would do is right, if it is different from what he would do." Really listening and suspending one's own judgment is necessary in order to understand other people in their own terms. As we have noted, this is a process that requires trust and builds trust.

Just as these daughters are seen in their own terms by their mothers, the daughters strove to see their mothers in their mothers' terms. Their success suggested that these daughters rejected the conventional expectation that mothers should remain selfless in their dedication to others. Indeed, almost all the mothers of these women were deeply committed to work outside the family, suggesting that the mothers also rejected the notion of selflessness and made a considerable investment in their own self-development as well as the development of others. The fact that these daughters showed only pride in the mothers' achievements, while other daughters often felt slighted by the mothers' outside commitments, suggests that these mothers were relatively successful in taking their own needs into consideration without sacrificing those of their families.

Just as it takes a long while to develop the capacity to pose questions for yourself, it takes a good deal of time before you can imagine and appreciate the questions that others pose for you; and it takes even longer to understand the importance of posing questions to others.

Patti was one of the few adolescent mothers we interviewed who acknowledged the importance of drawing out and listening as well as speaking to her child. About helping her child in trouble, Patti said that she would inquire and argue but that she would not dictate.

> I hope that we will sit down and argue about everything until we can finally understand each other. I will try to understand why she did it, but I don't ever want to dictate to her. It is very important that you look at things in all aspects. To understand your daughter, you have to have a broad view over everything, an overlook of every possible aspect. Sometimes it is hard to understand what your kid is going through. That is where it is really difficult being a parent.

Patti saw talk—not rewards and punishments—as the most important teaching tool that she had at her disposal. She strove to understand what her child was thinking and why she did what she did. She realized that understanding another person—especially a small child—is an awesome and important responsibility. She asked the child questions so that the child could explain herself. Her questions encouraged the child to consider the consequences of her actions and to evaluate her choices of behavior. She wished that her child would be guided by her own understanding and choices, not by parental dictates. Patti was not simply child-centered, however. While she strove to understand her child and to meet her needs, she continued to request the child also to consider the needs and honor the perspective of others.

Women pose questions more than men, they listen to others, and they refrain from speaking out—these have long been considered signs of the powerlessness, subjugation, and inadequacy of women. When women's talk is assessed against standards established by men's behavior, it is seen as tentative, vacillating, and diminutive (Lakoff 1975).

The pattern of discourse that women have developed, however, may best be considered as an appropriate response to women's work. The care of children, or maternal practice, gives rise to maternal thought and particular modes of relating to the world (Ruddick 1980). Any speaker appreciates listeners who will still their own voices and pose good questions. To the small child, just beginning to frame ideas with words, such help is indispensable. Even Socrates abstained from sharing his thoughts with the educated men of Athens for fear that his ideas might prevent the men from working out ideas of their own. In "talking cures," therapists listen and refrain from speaking as they, too, understand the value of drawing out the human voice.

Many mothers interview their children, rather than lecture, possibly because they are genuinely fascinated by the child's thoughts and feelings and enjoy drawing the child out. Also, mothers may intuit that drawing out the child's ideas helps him or her articulate and develop emotions and thoughts. Ultimately, it is the receiving of the child and hearing what he or she has to say that develops the child's mind and personhood. There is now considerable evidence that this is the case. Parents who enter into a dialogue with their children, who draw out and respect their opinions, are more likely to have children whose intellectual and ethical development proceeds rapidly and surely (Baumrind 1971; Bayley and Schaefer 1964; Haan, Smith, and Block 1968; Hauser et al. 1984; Hess and Shipman 1965; Hoffman 1975; Holstein 1968; Kohlberg 1984; Lickona 1983; Parikh 1975; Shure and Spivack 1978).

Question posing, as we have seen, is central to maternal practice in its most evolved form. Question posing is at the heart of connected knowing. We argue that women's mode of talk, rather than being denigrated, should become a model for all who are interested in promoting human development. It is through attentive love, the ability to ask "What are you going through?" and the ability to hear the answer that the reality of the child is both created and respected.

9

Toward an Education
for Women

A better understanding of women's experience would permit, even force, a far-
reaching revision of the broader fields of
higher education and intellectual life in the
United States.
—PATRICIA PALMIERI, 1979

MOST of the institutions of higher education in this country were designed by men, and most continue to be run by men. In recent years feminist
teachers and scholars have begun to question the structure, the curriculum,
and the pedagogical practices of these institutions; and they have put forth
useful proposals for change (for example, Bowles and Duelli-Klein 1983;
Martin 1985; Nicholson 1980; Rich 1979; Spanier, Bloom, and Boroviak
1984; Tarule 1980). But, as the scholar Patricia Palmieri (1979, p. 541)
suggests, in order to design an education appropriate for women we must
learn about the academic experiences of ordinary women.

All of the individuals we interviewed were ordinary women. Most of
them were neither teachers nor scholars nor even feminists but simply
students. We asked each woman what she thought would stay with her
about her experiences in the school or program she attended. We asked
her to tell us about specific academic and nonacademic experiences, about
good and bad teachers, good and bad assignments, good and bad programs
or courses. We asked her whether she thought that her participation in the
program changed the way she thought about herself or the world. We
asked, "In your learning here, have you come across an idea that made

you see things differently? What has been most helpful to you about this place? Are there things it doesn't provide that are important to you? Things you would like to learn that you can't learn here?" Finally, we asked, "Looking back over your whole life, can you tell us about a really powerful learning experience that you've had, in or out of school?"

The women responded, of course, in diverse ways; but as we examined their accounts of what they learned and failed to learn, of how they liked to learn and how they were forced to learn, some common themes emerged, themes that are distinctively, although surely not exclusively, feminine.

Reminiscences of College

We begin with the reminiscences of two ordinary women, each recalling an hour during her first year at college. One of them, now middle aged, remembered the first meeting of an introductory science course. The professor marched into the lecture hall, placed upon his desk a large jar filled with dried beans, and invited the students to guess how many beans the jar contained. After listening to an enthusiastic chorus of wildly inaccurate estimates the professor smiled a thin, dry smile, revealed the correct answer, and announced, "You have just learned an important lesson about science. Never trust the evidence of your own senses."

Thirty years later, the woman could guess what the professor had in mind. He saw himself, perhaps, as inviting his students to embark upon an exciting voyage into a mysterious underworld invisible to the naked eye, accessible only through scientific method and scientific instruments. But the seventeen-year-old girl could not accept or even hear the invitation. Her sense of herself as a knower was shaky, and it was based on the belief that she could use her own firsthand experience as a source of truth. This man was saying that this belief was fallacious. He was taking away her only tool for knowing and providing her with no substitute. "I remember feeling small and scared," the woman says, "and I did the only thing I could do. I dropped the course that afternoon, and I haven't gone near science since."

The second woman, in her first year at college, told a superficially similar but profoundly different story about a philosophy class she had attended just a month or two before the interview. The teacher came into class carrying a large cardboard cube. She placed it on the desk in front of her and asked the class what it was. They said it was a cube. She asked what a cube was, and they said a cube contained six equal square sides. She asked how they knew that this object contained six equal square sides. By looking at it, they said. "But how do you know?" the teacher asked again. She pointed to the side facing her and, therefore, invisible to the students; then she lifted the cube and pointed to the side that had been face down on the desk, and, therefore, also invisible. "We can't look at all six sides of a cube at once, can we? So we can't exactly *see* a cube. And yet, you're right. You know it's a cube. But you know it not just because you have eyes but because you have intelligence. You invent the sides you cannot see. You use your intelligence to create the 'truth' about cubes."

The student said to the interviewer,

> It blew my mind. You'll think I'm nuts, but I ran back to the dorm and I called my boyfriend and I said, "Listen, this is just incredible," and I told him all about it. I'm not sure he could see why I was so excited. I'm not sure I understand it myself. But I really felt, for the first time, like I was really in college, like I was—I don't know—sort of *grown up.*

Both stories are about the limitations of firsthand experience as a source of knowledge—we cannot simply see the truth about either the jar of beans or the cube—but there is a difference. We can know the truth about cubes. Indeed, the students did know it. As the science professor pointed out, the students were wrong about the beans; their senses had deceived them. But, as the philosophy teacher pointed out, the students were right about the cube; their minds had served them well.

The science professor was the only person in the room who knew how many beans were in that jar. Theoretically, the knowledge was available to the students; they could have counted the beans. But faced with that tedious prospect, most would doubtless take the professor's word for it. He is authority. They had to rely upon his knowledge rather than their own. On the other hand, every member of the philosophy class knew that the cube had six sides. They were all colleagues.

The science professor exercised his authority in a benign fashion, promising the students that he would provide them with the tools they needed to excavate invisible truths. Similarly, the philosophy teacher planned to teach her students the skills of philosophical analysis, but she was at pains to assure them that they already possessed the tools to construct some powerful truths. They had built cubes on their own, using only their own powers of inference, without the aid of elaborate procedures or fancy apparatus or even a teacher. Although a teacher might have told them once that a cube contained six equal square sides, they did not have to take the teacher's word for it; they could have easily verified it for themselves.

The lesson the science professor wanted to teach is that experience is a source of error. Taught in isolation, this lesson diminished the student, rendering her dumb and dependent. The philosophy teacher's lesson was that although raw experience is insufficient, by reflecting upon it the student could arrive at truth. It was a lesson that made the student feel more powerful ("sort of grown up").

No doubt it is true that, as the professor in May Sarton's novel *The Small Room* says, the "art" of being a student requires humility. But the woman we interviewed did not find the science lesson humbling; she found it humiliating. Arrogance was not then and is not now her natural habitat. Like most of the women in our sample she lacked confidence in herself as a thinker; and the kind of learning the science teacher demanded was not only painful but crippling.

In thinking about the education of women, Adrienne Rich writes, "Suppose we were to ask ourselves, simply: What does a woman need to know?" (1979, p. 240). A woman, like any other human being, does need to know that the mind makes mistakes; but our interviews have convinced us that every woman, regardless of age, social class, ethnicity, and academic achievement, needs to know that she is capable of intelligent thought, and she needs to know it right away. Perhaps men learn this lesson before going to college, or perhaps they can wait until they have proved themselves to hear it; we do not know. We do know that many of the women we interviewed had not yet learned it.

Confirmation of the Self as Knower

In the masculine myth, confirmation comes not at the beginning of education but at the end. "Welcome to the community of scholars," the president announces at the Harvard commencement. ("That sure sounded weird to me," said a woman graduate. "He says 'Welcome.' Then he shows us the door.") Confirmation as a thinker and membership in a community of thinkers come as the climax of Perry's story of intellectual development in the college years. The student learns, according to Perry, that "we must all stand judgment" and that he must earn "the privilege of having [his] ideas respected" (1970, p. 33). Having proved beyond reasonable doubt that he has learned to think in complex, contextual ways, the young man is admitted to the fraternity of powerful knowers. Certified as a thinker, he becomes one of "them" (now dethroned to lower-case "them"). Doubt precedes belief; separation leads to connection. The weak become powerful, and the inferiors join their superiors. This scenario may capture the "natural" course of men's development in traditional, hierarchical institutions, but it does not work for women. For women, confirmation and community are prerequisites rather than consequences of development.

Most of the women reported that they had often been treated as if they were stupid. This was especially (although by no means exclusively) true of the less privileged. Consider, for example, the case of Lillian, a student at one of the "invisible colleges." When Lillian's infant son suffered an attack of projectile vomiting, she called her pediatrician. "Don't worry about it," he said. Instead of respecting her concern, he dismissed it. Lillian wanted respect, and she wanted information.

> I wasn't asking for the complete history of projectile vomiting. I just really wanted an explanation, simple, something like you would give a child if they asked you a question like where do babies come from. You don't give them a whole routine, just a piece of it, and let them deal with that. You don't say, "Never mind." You don't patronize them. I don't do that with my own child, so I don't like to be treated like that. I really wanted to be dealt with as a person, not just a hysterical mother, not even as a mother, as just another person who was halfway intelligent.

Lillian's encounters with authority (teachers, bosses, doctors, priests, bureaucrats, and policemen) taught her that "experts" usually tried to assert dominance over less knowledgeable people either by assaulting them with information or by withholding information. But her experience as a mother provided her with a different model, a model we call "connected teaching," in which the expert (parent) examines the needs and capacities of the learner (child) and composes a message that is, in the psychologist Jerome Bruner's felicitous term, "courteous" to the learner (1963, p. 52). Although Lillian knew more than her son knew, she did not think she was better than he. She did not want to exert power over him. She wanted to help him on his own terms, and she needed experts who would do the same for her.

Fortunately a public health clinic for children, run on the connected teaching model, opened up in Lillian's area. The director of the clinic defined the clinic's job not as "teaching mothers how to raise children" but as "trying to help mothers do what they need to do." Lillian, having placed her child under the clinic's care, exclaimed, "What a difference!" Members of the clinic staff never patronized her, nor did they patronize her son. "They've always seemed to deal with me and, now that Shaun's older, with him on equal levels." To allay Shaun's fears of examinations, the nurse practitioner carried out an entire examination on the little boy's teddy bear, explaining "very sincerely," in terms the child could understand, what she was doing and why. Lillian marveled at the staff's patience, as did Ann, another client whom we met in earlier chapters of this book. Ann's private pediatrician always made her feel rushed. Embarrassed to ask for clarification, she pretended she understood his directions. Afraid of "wasting his time," she hesitated to raise issues that were bothering her. At the clinic, on the other hand, they "take time to explain things"; they "spell it all out."

Having been subjected to the usual view of health care professionals that parents are incompetent, mothers who used the clinic were astonished to discover that members of the staff, nearly all of them women, believed in them. As Lillian said, "They seemed to have trust in me. I hadn't had that in a long time, that feeling like my parents gave me, that I was—no questions asked—trusted."

What these women needed and what the clinic provided, perhaps more clearly, consistently, and sincerely than any other institution we sampled, was confirmation that they could be trusted to know and to learn. Given confirmation, they felt they could "just do anything." Lacking it, as one woman said, they were "crippled" and "just can't function." Most of the women we interviewed made it clear that they did not wish to be told merely that they had the capacity or the potential to *become* knowledgeable or wise. They needed to know that they already knew something (although by no means everything), that there was something good inside them. They worried that there was not. "Suppose one woke and found oneself a fraud?" wrote Virginia Woolf. "It was part of my madness that horror" (1980, p. 138).

The worry was especially acute among older women returning to college or entering it for the first time. Some of these women found the confirmation they needed in an adult education program. A fifty-four-year-old widow, having raised six children, said, "I had reached a point in my life where I wasn't sure I had any worth as a human being. As the kids grew up and left, that kicked out any props I had. If I had any worth at all it was as their mother. What was I going to be for the rest of my life? A shell of what I had been?" But in the program, she found, "I'm accepted for what I am, the ability to be me. I came here and discovered I'm not a shell. I've got a lot of stuff in me."

A younger adult in the same program said that her teachers and fellow students made her realize that the knowledge she gained through her life experiences "is important and real and valuable." At the urging of a teacher, she wrote a paper about her escape to the Arctic in search of self. The paper was accepted for credit and circulated among members of the community. The woman said, "It validated who I was, that something that was real personal to me, that I carried around alone—that I could share that in writing and get credit for it. That I was recognized and respected." And a twenty-seven-year-old single parent, who "needed people to believe me," found them in the same program: "The people just accepted that of course I was a person, that I had something to say. They didn't look down on me at all. It was a whole different environment than I was used to. There was no oppression."

Even the most privileged women in our sample expressed the need to be accepted as a "person," as opposed to being oppressed or patronized. Privilege does not ensure freedom from oppression—incest, for instance, occurs in the "best" of families—and achievement does not guarantee self-esteem. Indeed, highly competent girls and women are especially likely to underestimate their abilities.* Most of the women who attended the more prestigious colleges in the sample had a history of privilege and achievement, but most felt uncertain about their abilities. Several suspected that they had been admitted through a fluke.

Some women found the confirmation they needed in these colleges. Faith, for example, said that although she had always done well in school, no one had ever told her that she was intelligent until she came to college. There, Faith said, "people say, 'Well, you know, you're a pretty smart person.' If people say that to you enough you have to figure that they know at least a little of what they're talking about."

A classmate, however, interviewed toward the end of her first year, told a different story. Although she had entered college with SAT scores in the high 600s, she felt that she was "the dumbest girl here." Her high school teachers doled out constant praise but in college the teachers were silent.

* For research showing that girls with higher scores on intelligence tests than other girls express unrealistically low expectations of success, see Crandall (1969) and Stipek and Hoffman (1980).

> You need a little bit of praise to keep you going. If you get an idea
> that the teacher likes what you're doing, it helps you go on more,
> whereas most of my courses the teachers are kind of—They don't
> say "bad," they don't say "good," so you start having doubts and
> thinking, "Well, if he doesn't say something nice, he must not
> like it." And you just get into such a rut where you can't do
> anything. There's just an extreme lack of praise around here.

In high school she and her friends had been stars; in this highly competitive college they were just average.

> We all had a lot of self-esteem, and we didn't really think about it,
> we just knew we could do it. Whereas now, it's totally different.
> If I could just think to myself that I've done something really
> exceptionally good, 'cause sometimes I feel like I'm getting lost
> in the crowd. If I could just write maybe one paper and have a
> teacher say, "Hey, that was really, really good," I think that would
> help a lot.

We asked her if the approval had to come from a teacher. Could it not
come from within her? "Not at this point," she said. "It's been so far
pushed down it couldn't come back up by itself."

Some women were so consumed with self-doubt that they found it
difficult to believe a teacher's praise, especially when the teacher was a
man. One young woman told us that she never felt sure a male professor
would take her seriously. The women worried that professors who praised
their minds really desired their bodies. Elizabeth "got suspicious" of a male
professor because he praised her so much.

> I got to know him personally, and it then became hard for me. I learned
> that evaluation is subjective, that there's not such a thing as an
> objective evaluation of things like work. I realized the guy liked
> me, so he's going to like my papers. Then I said, "This is really
> screwed up."

Elizabeth went on to describe a woman teacher who encouraged and helped
her with her writing without babying her. "She was the only one who
said, 'Yeah, that's good,' " "But," said the interviewer, "I thought you said
[the male professor] was encouraging." "He was encouraging," Elizabeth
replied, "but I think I felt that there were strings attached."

Several women spoke of the ambiguity inherent in male professors' praise for women students, of the "games" that male professors and female students fell into. Stella, an artist, said, "That's something every woman deals with, going to college: Am I a student or a flirtation? Why is the teacher giving them attention? Why does he draw on your pad and not hers?" The teacher may have to draw the lines very carefully in order to avoid ambiguity.

The problem was exacerbated—and the need for clear boundaries especially acute—for the many women who arrived at college having already suffered sexual abuse at the hands of a male in a position of authority, such as Elizabeth, whose father had repeatedly molested her. Whenever powerful men praised relatively powerless women, the women started looking for "the strings," especially when, as many admitted, they knew that they, themselves, had used their sexuality in the past to elicit praise.

Knowing the Realities: The Voice of Experience

In considering how to design an education appropriate for women, suppose we were to begin by simply asking: What does a woman know? Traditional courses do not begin there. They begin not with the student's knowledge but with the teacher's knowledge. The courses are about the culture's questions, questions fished out of the "mainstream" of the disciplines. If the student is female, her questions may differ from the culture's questions, since women, paddling in the bywaters of the culture, have had little to do with positing the questions or designing the agendas of the disciplines. (See, for example, Harding and Hintikka 1983; Reinharz 1984; Sherman and Beck 1979; Smith 1974.) Indeed, as writer Mary Jacobus points out, although nineteenth- and twentieth-century feminists have sought access to education as a means of liberation, "this access to a male dominated culture may equally be felt to bring with it alienation, repression, division— a silencing of the 'feminine,' a loss of women's inheritance" (1979, p. 10).

Most women students do not expect colleges to honor their concerns. One young woman who had always relied heavily on authorities as the source of truth told us that she hesitated before signing up for a women's studies course at her university, fearing that the course would not be respected; but it turned out to be the best course she'd ever taken. For the first time, she said, she was really interested in what she was studying. Two women team-taught the course, and it fascinated her that two people thought it was important enough to teach. The authorities' sanction enabled her to respect her own interests.

Cynthia, the alumna whose mother digested her experiences for her during college and told her what she felt, said that although she enjoyed the "austerity" of the college curriculum and did well, she felt lonely and sad throughout the four years. At the time, she thought her problems were "just personal," but lately she had begun to wonder if the curriculum contributed to her depression. She had been reading an essay by E. B. White about a battle between an old gander and a younger, stronger gander.

> They have this heroic battle. And the older goose at the end of the story is seen leaping off to lick his wounds somewhere in a patch of sun in a field. And it struck me that E. B. White saw everything in terms of great struggles—these great clashes between opposing forces—and that's what life was like, this—uh—sort of larger-than-life thing.

The larger-than-life knowledge contained in the college curriculum seemed to her at the time the only respectable form of knowledge; but now that she had more sense of herself as a woman, it struck her as a distinctively masculine perspective.

> You know, it's not a battle between the gods that concerns women. Women are concerned with how you get through life from minute to minute. What each little teeny tiny incident—how it can affect everything else you do. Women see things close at hand and are more concerned with minutiae.

This feminine mode seemed "realer, somehow," to Cynthia. It was a real way of knowing, an embryonic form, perhaps, of the close-up mothering eye that won for Barbara McClintock, belatedly, a Nobel prize (Keller 1983). Although Cynthia's grades in college suggest that she mastered the masculine mode, she felt that it really never quite "took." Someday she hopes to master it. "I guess ultimately I would like to balance them. I would like to have a larger picture, too. I would like to be able to study history the way men can study history and see patterns in the development of the world and of civilization." But not right now. Right now she wants to put her ear to the ground, listen to the squirrel's heart beat, as George Eliot put it, and prowl among the webs of little things.

> At this point I want to explore those things that are more womanlike, the kinds of sensations and responses that I have to things on a very day-to-day small scale. I like playing with my impressions of the silliest things. I think I haven't ever seen things in quite this way, been quite as aware of the fun I could have with introspection and observation of daily life.*

Most of the women we interviewed were drawn to the sort of knowledge that emerges from firsthand observation, and most of the educational institutions they attended emphasized abstract "out-of-context learning" (Cole, Gay, Glick, and Sharp 1971). We asked a young woman from such an institution to tell us about a good paper that she had written. She said she had not written many good papers, but there was one that she really liked.

> It was for a writing course. We were allowed to write about whatever we wanted. And I just described a place where I had worked— the social structure and all the cattiness—and I really enjoyed that. I was just so excited about what I was writing, and I thought it was just the greatest thing to read, and I sent copies to friends I had worked with, and they just loved it. [But the teacher] didn't think it was an important issue. He said it was well written but lacked content, whatever that means. [Laughs.] (*"How about a bad paper?" the interviewer asked.*) There was one I wrote analyzing a book that I hadn't finished. That wasn't too good. You know, it's really easy, though, to read part of a book and then pick up a few sources and annotate everything. I just thought it was horrible. I just knew that I didn't know what I was talking about, and I think it showed.

But apparently it did not; the teacher liked the paper. The student's standards were in conflict with the teacher's. When she wrote out of her own experience, she felt she knew what she was talking about, but the teacher felt the paper was not about anything. When she pasted together a mess of undigested, secondhand information, he was satisfied.

The women we interviewed nearly always named out-of-school experiences as their most powerful learning experiences. The mothers usually named childbearing or child rearing. The kind of knowledge that is used

---

* We must beg to differ with Cynthia. The late E. B. White taught us quite a lot about how to hear the squirrel's heart beat.

in child rearing is typical of the kind of knowledge women value and schools do not. Much of it comes not from words but from action and observation, and much of it has never been translated into words, only into actions. As a single parent of nine children said, "There are things I have up here [taps her temple] that I can't put down on paper. I know I use a lot of it in my daily life, like in trying to help my children."

This kind of knowledge does not necessarily lead to general propositions. Good mothering requires adaptive responding to constantly changing phenomena; it is tuned to the concrete and particular. A response that works with a particular child at a particular moment may not work with a different child or with the same child at a different moment. Mothers expect change, Ruddick says, and "change requires a kind of learning in which what one learns cannot be applied exactly, and often not even by analogy, to a new situation" (1980, p. 111). In this sense "maternal thinking" differs from scientific thinking, which considers an experimental result to be real— a fact—only if it can be replicated. As the philosopher Carol McMillan says, mothers are understandably "extremely hesitant about concocting theories about how other people should bring up their children and are sceptical about the advice thrust upon them by the 'experts'" (1982, p. 54).

Many of the women we interviewed—mothers or not—remarked upon the discrepancy between the kind of thinking required in school and the kind required in dealing with people. A college junior, for example, said she found academics much easier than personal life.

> I'm very good at doing tasks. You know, you just compartmentalize something. It's time to sit down and write a paper and think about what someone said. And you do it. But when you're dealing with people you can't always compartmentalize—you know, sort of wrap them up in little packets and put them on the shelf and then you know how to deal with them from then on. Because everyone is always in an amorphous state. And they're all changing so much all the time. What may have worked with one person five days ago isn't going to work with them tomorrow.

Most of these women were not opposed to abstraction as such. They found concepts useful in making sense of their experiences, but they balked when the abstractions preceded the experiences or pushed them out entirely. Even the women who were extraordinarily adept at abstract reasoning preferred to start from personal experience.* Mary Lou was one of them.

> I think women care about things that relate to their lives personally.
> I think the more involvement they have in something that affects
> them personally, the more they're going to explore it and the
> more they're going to be able to give and to get out of it. I think
> that men—because they're male they haven't been put down all
> the time for their sex, so they can go into any subject with con-
> fidence, saying, "I can learn about this" or "I have the intellect
> to understand this." Whereas I think women don't deal with things
> that way. I think they break down an issue and pick out what it
> is about it that has happened to them or they can relate to in
> some way, and that's how they start to explore it.

After graduating from high school Mary Lou took an entry-level job
in day care, and worked her way up to be director of a center, designing
and administering a program for children with minimal brain damage.
Entering college at thirty-three, she did not regret the years spent in the
field.

> I think the way I've learned in the past it's always been a very expe-
> riential kind of thing. That's how I learned about day care and
> about children to begin with. It was doing it. It was having to do
> it every single day for eight hours a day. I think that's where I
> got the wealth of my knowledge. I feel more comfortable knowing
> that. I like to know the realities. I like to know what's going on,
> so it's hard for me to explore something on the theory aspect and
> then go out and get the practical. I like to have the practical first,
> so I know what's going on and what it's really like, and then look
> at the theories that way.

Mary Lou was driven to reenter college by the need to organize the
observations of women and children she had accumulated over the years.

> Things weren't sinking in. They were just all there, and there was no
> connection. Then when I came here and lived in the women's
> dorm and started having discussions about feminist theory and

---

* Shulamit Reinharz writes, "If we *start* with labels, we have excluded experience altogether." She urges researchers to "describe and analyze with as few assumptions, presuppositions, or definitions beforehand as possible.... Try to see things as they are without
blinders, labels, or intermediaries" (1984, pp. 359, 363).

philosophy, everything just kind of fell into place. There was a
lot that I had seen going on and I had observed, but I didn't have
anything really to relate it to. I feel much more knowledgeable
now. I have words. I know reasons.

Judith, a staff member at the children's health clinic and one of our
most highly educated and cerebral informants, said, "I don't like getting
things totally out of a book. I really like having some real experience of it
myself." Judith felt that much of what people thought they knew, they
knew only in the form of "general concepts"; they did not really know it.
"In the most exciting kind of learning, people are allowed to go right down
to rock bottom and really look at these concepts and find out what their
experience has been with it, what they know about it." Judith has had this
sort of intense conversation in informal meetings with friends but never
in school. In school, she said, people are "supposed to learn it the way
somebody else sees it."

Usually, we are supposed to learn it the way men see it. Men move
quickly to impose their own conceptual schemes on the experience of
women, says French feminist writer Marguerite Duras. These schemes do
not help women make sense of their experience; they extinguish the experience. Women must find their own words to make meaning of their
experiences, and this will take time. Meanwhile, "men must renounce their
theoretical rattle" (1973, p. 111).

Duras says that men have all the old words on the tips of their tongues,
and so they can speak right out, while

> Women have been in darkness for centuries. They don't know themselves.
> Or only poorly. And when women write, they translate this darkness. Men
> don't translate. They begin from a theoretical platform that is already in place,
> already elaborated. The writing of women is really translated from the un-
> known, like a new way of communicating, rather than an already formed
> language. (1975, p. 174)

It should come as no surprise that the courses most often mentioned
as powerful learning experiences were, as with Mary Lou, courses in feminist theory, which helped the women translate their ideas from the darkness
of private experience into a shared public language.

Women also described as "powerful" the opportunities for experiential
learning provided by their institutions. Mary Lou, studying to be a midwife,
said that she and her classmates were "terrified" before giving their first
pelvic exams. The teacher prepared them by taking them through a fantasy

exercise in which they imagined performing the exam. "She guided us through it and told us exactly what we would be feeling for and how it would feel. We had our eyes closed and were moving our hands along with her directions, like 'Now you move four inches this way.' " Initially cynical about the value of the exercise, Mary Lou found that it worked. When she performed her first real exam she found herself "saying the same things the teacher did. 'Okay, now we move over to the spine and then we go up and feel for the sacriatic curve.' That was something that was concrete, and it was there."

Freedom, Structure, and the Tyranny of Expectation

Probably the most pervasive theme we found in our interviews with women of all sorts was one we called "inner-outer," encompassing issues women raised concerning the source and types of control and validation they had experienced in their lives. In analyzing each woman's interview, we asked ourselves, Who or what, in this woman's eyes, defines the goals, sets the pace, and evaluates the outcomes of her behavior? In terms of education, we asked, To what degree does she perceive the tasks, the timetable, and the standards as imposed by the institution, to what degree by herself, and with what consequences?

THE NEED FOR STRUCTURE

All of the women we interviewed, even the most rebellious, wanted some structure in their educational environments. Those who relied most heavily upon received knowledge favored the most clear-cut externally imposed pattern. Some of the students at the community college, for example, appreciated the college's precisely articulated curriculum. "I need to follow something structured," said one of them. "I like to know what I have to do." Overburdened by responsibilities at home and at work, she had neither the energy nor the time to map out her own structure. She was irritated when teachers and students departed from the structure of the lesson. "I'm not good in math, and I need to listen to an instructor from the beginning of the session through to the end. I don't want to hear about his kids or his wife or his problems, right? Or the students who come in late. I don't want to hear that. I just want to listen to the instructor."

Some of the women at purportedly progressive institutions complained that the absence of structure served as an excuse for self-indulgence and led to a lack of seriousness among both students and faculty. A first-year student complained that in most of her seminars, although the material was excellent, both teachers and students were unprepared. Instead of helping the students focus their attention upon the material, the teacher drew attention to himself: "My experience with free-form classes has been the professor free-forming it. He does all the talking." In general, the student said,

> This place has no expectations as an institution. None. It's almost impossible to flunk out. Anything socially that you do is probably acceptable. There are no social guidelines. Some very basic expectations should be set up so that people have an obligation to their peers and to the faculty and to the administration.

Other students at this college and at the early college also complained that their classmates' irresponsibility corroded both academic and social life; but still others believed that the very absence of rules conveyed the message, as one early college student said, that "you're respected until proven irresponsible." She and several classmates appreciated the fact that the college, instead of pointing them in a particular direction and insisting that they stay on a prescribed path, allowed them "freedom to go through changes," floundering down blind alleys and into dead ends and changing course without penalty.

THE TYRANNY OF EXPECTATION

In general, we heard more complaints about excessive control than about lack of structure. Students from the most prestigious and academically "demanding" institutions were most eloquent in their complaints. Some alumnae of the women's college, for instance, said that they had never learned to make choices; the college made the choices for them. Cheryl, an alumna who majored in chemistry, was happy that she had attended this college but found it a painful experience also. It was hard, but in another sense, it was easy. To "keep up" was "a never-ending struggle," but the structure was clear-cut. If you did the assignments, you made the grade. But when she graduated, Cheryl encountered a more ambiguous world. "You don't know quite what to do to succeed in your job. It's not clear-cut. You have to make sense of a lot of things that are not well organized. You have to find out what's important. You have to establish priorities. And I didn't know how to do that."

Cheryl's first job was with a physician who asked her to set up a research project. Having no idea how to do it, she looked to him for direction, but he was as ignorant as she. Ultimately, she organized and executed the project, experiencing a depth of satisfaction she never felt in completing her assigned tasks in college.

Bridget's story illustrates what can happen when "good" girls go to good colleges. Like most girls in our society, Bridget was raised to be "nice." Two years out of college, niceness remained a problem.

> I'm constantly having to fight this natural tendency I have to be "a nice person." I've been mad at myself for being too nice for a long time, and yet, at the same time, I know I can get away with murder sometimes, because I'm so nice. I'm still very afraid of not being nice, very afraid.

Nice girls fulfill other people's expectations. Bridget thought that the women's college was wrong for her because it expected too much: "It was too competitive and too demanding. I'm a very conscientious person, and I found myself always trying to do the work."

In high school Bridget consistently achieved top marks without working very hard. At college she continued to take it easy, and her grades at the end of the first semester were terrible. In the second semester she tried a new approach.

> I worked my butt off. I have never been so intense and disciplined working before. I ended up getting the second highest grade in the economics final, coming up from the bottom of the class. I memorized every goddamn picture there was in art history. I spent three hours every day going over those pictures. For three hours every day I studied French; for three hours every day I studied art; and for three hours every day I ground myself through economics.

At the end of each day she went swimming to loosen her constipated brain.

> I swam a mile every day, and it wasn't until the end of that mile that I finally felt my muscles begin to loosen up, and my head was finally clear of all this crap that I was stuffing it full of. That was

probably the peak of my career at the college in terms of beating the system.

Bridget portrayed herself during the next three terms as a drudge, motivated by duty rather than desire (Weil 1951), slogging through dull courses in order to fulfill various "distribution requirements" and prepare herself for a successful career. But, although she worked constantly, she was always "behind" and she got mediocre grades.

In her third year she moved off campus and enrolled for two terms at an Ivy League college, where, she found, "You don't have to do that much work to keep up." She found time to carry a part-time job, to study dance, and to maintain a communal household. Returning to the women's college for her final semester, although continuing to live off campus, Bridget felt that everything had changed. She no longer worried about "getting caught up with things."

> I hardly did any of the reading I was supposed to do in most of my classes and still did very well. I don't know how it happened. I did loads of extra reading for the Women in American History course and loved it. I was so into the subject. I promised I would give myself the gift of no economics classes as a senior. I promised myself I'd only take classes that interested me. I did, and my grade point average just soared. It was incredible. I was so detached from the campus. It's as though I was walking through that place and felt no reality. I felt as though I was looking through a glass window at the whole thing. I was totally out of touch with that school. That was my overriding impression of the last semester, besides enjoying my work for the first time. Finally feeling as though I was making that school work for me, extracting from it what I wanted, no longer feeling pressured that I must be career-oriented and any number of the other things I felt.

Bridget and other women who attended the women's college and other equally "demanding" institutions felt in retrospect that their intellectual development was stunted rather than nourished by the incessant academic pressure. "Ever since leaving college," Bridget says, "my joy in reading and my desire to read has increased incredibly. I'm absolutely thrilled to be learning what I want to learn. It's been like a renaissance."

The teachers in these colleges do not intend, of course, to inhibit their students' intellectual development. Some are especially kind and concerned and accessible, but this only makes it worse. It is especially difficult for good girls to disobey good parents. Teachers, as well as students, yearn for an atmosphere less academic and more intellectual, but the teachers are unable to reduce the pressure and the students are unable to resist it, except on rare occasions. One undergraduate blushed as if about to confess to a crime and said,

> Last weekend—I don't know why I did it—I decided to read a book, a fun book. This is the first time since I've come here I've read a fun book from cover to cover—no worries if it was read with complete comprehension. I read it perfectly. It was mine.

Both teachers and students are proud of the institution's "high standards," and many see the standards as luring the students into performing at the top of their capacities. These standards play a major role in Perry's (1970) account of development. It is in attempting to discern the standards and to meet them that the student is propelled into independent contextual thinking. But for nice girls like Bridget, the standards act more as impediments than as goads to independent thinking, distracting their attention from the intellectual substance of the work and transforming their efforts to learn into efforts to please.

Women may benefit especially from systems in which the teaching function and the assessing function are separated. Teaching and certification of competence, at least as usually practiced, are quite different and often opposing functions; and, where certification is deemed necessary, it should be detached from teaching by, for example, using external examiners to evaluate the students' performance.

Some educators (for example, Elbow 1979) advocate competency-based programs in which the student must exhibit mastery of a set of clearly articulated objectives. Traditional professors, Elbow says, because they "contain the thing to be learned inside them . . . stand up in front of students and say, in effect, 'Get what is inside me inside you. Look at me; listen to me; be like me. I am important' " (p. 107). In competency-based programs the teacher no longer acts as the embodiment of knowledge or the container of secret criteria and so becomes less "important," less the authority, more a "coach" or an "ally" in Elbow's terms, more a "partner" in the language of Paulo Freire (1971). The teacher's attempts to "believe" the student, to confirm her as a knower, are not undermined by the inevitable "doubt" expressed in impersonal assessment.

It is not evaluation per se that subverts the aims of instruction but evaluation in the separate (impersonal, objective) mode. Evaluation in the connected mode requires that the standards of evaluation be constructed in collaboration with the students. Where impersonal standards are used, the students are turned into objects, and the connection between teacher and student is broken. The "feminine world of subjectness" is abandoned in favor of the "masculine world of objectness" (Noddings 1984, p. 196). As Noddings says, "Many of the practices embedded in the masculine curriculum masquerade as essential to the maintenance of standards," but in fact "they accomplish quite a different purpose: the systematic dehumanization of both female and male children through the loss of the feminine" (pp. 192–93). In an educational institution that placed care and understanding of persons rather than impersonal standards at its center, human development might take a different course, and women's development, in particular, might proceed with less pain.

But at traditional, hierarchically organized institutions run by powerful judges charged with enforcing the high standards of their disciplines and administering justice through blind evaluation of the students' work without respect for the students' persons, images of being watched ("God with His movie camera," as Bridget put it) flood the minds of women students. The women search the eyes that watch them for reflections of themselves. They cannot get back behind their own eyes. "Turn a pair of eyes on me," Alice Koller writes, "and instantly I begin looking into them for myself" (1983, p. 94). Ironically, Bridget managed to meet the standards only when she became able to ignore them. She produced what They wanted only when she became able to do what she wanted.

BEING BAD AND BREAKING OUT

Several women described moments of rebellion that produced turning points in their education. The moment often occurred late at night when an unwritten paper was due the next day. Saying, "Oh, the hell with it," the student wrote a "bad" paper, using her own voice, that broke the rules. Sometimes, she was punished. But sometimes she was rewarded with an "A," indicating that the teacher preferred the student's private voice to her public voice. The problem of "standards" for women, then, is a double problem. Nice women cannot help trying to produce what They want, but sometimes they are wrong about what They want.

The student's discovery that teachers respect her authentic voice is gratifying, of course, but for many of the women we interviewed, it came late. Much time had been wasted being good; and for many women the relentless effort to be good had prevented the development of a more authentic voice.

Women like Bridget, still struggling to formulate their own purposes and their own standards, although eager for formal graduate training in order to pursue professional careers, are fearful of entering another institution that may try and may succeed in shaping them according to its standards. Deborah had decided in high school that she would become a clinical psychologist, but after graduating from college she worked for three years before applying to graduate school.

> One of the reasons I took the years in between was so that I would be very certain that when I went I'd be able to do what I wanted to do there, and that I wouldn't feel I had to follow what they were setting up for me to do.

But, on the eve of entering graduate school, she did not sound so certain.

> I'm afraid of some clashes between what I want to do and what they want me to do, and I'm not sure how those will be resolved, not understanding the system. It may take me a semester to find out how you don't do what they're asking you to do.

Deborah was determined not to repeat the experience of her first year in college during her first year in graduate school. Instead of being good—doing everything she was supposed to do—she would figure out how to be bad and do what she wanted to do.

When we interviewed Gretchen in her senior year, she had already been accepted at a prestigious medical school but had decided to defer enrollment for a year.

> I have to find myself absolutely alone for a while. I don't feel as if I'm gonna *last* through another five years of school unless I sit back and find for myself or remind myself that I am an independent person and I am defined by my own standards and not by these external standards. Right now I feel sort of very wishy-washy about myself, and that's because I've been getting different sorts of signals from different people or institutions which have been evaluating me. And I've been letting these things sort of cloud over my own feelings about myself. Sort of refractional crystallization. Sort of getting rid of the dirt and the garbage and just sort of crystallizing out what is me. I want to spend a year not letting myself be evaluated by other people's standards.

Judith was eager to improve her skills as a therapist, but she dreaded a repetition of her graduate school experience.

> I worry about getting further analytic training, 'cause you're supposed to learn it the way that somebody else sees it. It would be different if I could find something—a program—where I was helped to see things in my own way. That would be gold.

THE NEED FOR FREEDOM

Some of the women we interviewed discovered "gold" in their institutions. We asked a twenty-seven-year-old mother of two what was most helpful to her about the adult program she was attending.

> The faculty not being above us, not being the boss. Making our own decisions and writing our own curriculum. And it's real hard at first, when you're not used to it. You expect, "Well, what do we do next?" It developed me a lot more in thinking, "What is it that I want?" instead of listening to what people tell me.

Another student described the program as operating according to a model like the one physician Mary Howell calls "housewifery," with the teacher respecting the student's own rhythms rather than imposing an arbitrary timetable.

> When I would get stuck in the middle of my studies—as I always did—I never got any silly notes from the teacher saying, "Now, now, you must produce your stuff on time, otherwise blah blah blah." He would just say, "Well, I guess you're stuck. You'll get over it." He gave me a lot of space and a lot of guidance.

For Stella, the progressive college, seen by some as lacking in standards, was Utopia.

> It was this plot of land where I could talk to these teachers or hear them lecture and read and write and really grow. It was this time for me to be away from my family, some place I felt safe, and just sort of feel out different things.

The freedom and support the college offered helped Stella feel her way toward becoming a painter and developing her "own sort of natural working habit."

> I choke under pressure, but I do very well under pressures that I've created, goals that I establish, so the college is perfect for me, because there's not a lot of pressure, and there's a tremendous amount of time to work on your own.

The college exempted her from formal classes during her senior year and provided her with a studio: "I'm able to work all day and all night on my own. If I was meeting with classes all the time, and if there was a different attitude about work and grades and competition, I'd hate painting." The college put little emphasis on grades.

> When something really attracts you, you can really get obsessive about it. There's a lot of freedom, trusting that people are going to want to work, that people have instincts and will find out what they want to do and how they're going to go about doing it. But with teachers that are knowledgeable and can give you guidance and support and believe in you.

A student at one of the more highly structured, high-pressure colleges gave a dramatically different account. "How much time do you really have," she asked, "to think about the material you're studying?"

> I remember last semester getting *really* almost terrified when I was studying for finals, because all of a sudden I got so wrapped up in the material. I hadn't put it down for a while. And I just realized, you know, that it was really exciting to do all this stuff. But if you did that all semester long, you'd go crazy. It seems that they require a lot more automated responses from you. Just turn in this paper now. It seems that you don't have a chance to reflect. I don't try and figure out anything while I'm at school. As soon as I get away from my books, then everything gets complex; but as long as I'm looking at a book, then I tend to open it up and read it and just do what's required of me.

Some of the students at this women's college feared that without the pressure they would "go bad," as one put it, or "go dead," as another said. They would sleep late, cut classes, and stop working. Bridget and others who moved temporarily into less pressured environments did indeed go bad. They cut more classes and they spent less time on assigned work. But they did not go dead; they emerged as more active agents in their own learning. The late psychologist Jeanne Block (1984) argued that because girls in our society are raised to accommodate to existing structures, they need colleges that will help set them free. But, for the same reason, women also need strong support in moving toward freedom.

We once heard a professor from a women's college remark that the students were passive because the teachers were "too nurturant" and that a more impersonal approach might produce more independent, responsible, and active learners. Presumably she meant that in "taking care" of students we rob them of responsibility; and there may be some truth in this. But surely there are forms of taking care that make the ones we care for stronger rather than weaker. Taking care need not mean taking over. The children's health clinic, the most nurturant institution in our sample, empowers its clients by fostering their expertise. Remember the client who said, "I feel like they could hire me. That's how much knowledge they've given me." And, indeed, it is the clinic's policy to make use of its clients' wisdom and even on occasion to invite them to join the staff.

The more traditional, formal educational institutions we sampled operated more in terms of bureaucracy than housewifery. Although teachers and staff in these colleges paid close personal attention to individual students, the system itself was relatively impersonal. All students were expected to perform certain tasks and deliver certain products at specified uniform dates to be evaluated according to objective criteria. Their work was compared not with their own past work but with other students' work. Students had duties and obligations; they had little choice and less responsibility than is required in the institutions that allow or insist that students participate in these decisions. At the other end of the continuum, institutions that do none of the defining clearly abdicate their own responsibility for helping students formulate their own agendas for learning; they rob women students of the support most of them need in order to break free.

10

Connected Teaching

It is time for the voice of the mother to be
heard in education.
— Nel Noddings
Caring

Sharing the Process

PAULO FREIRE describes traditional education as "banking": The teacher's
role is "to 'fill' the students by making deposits of information which the
teacher considers to constitute true knowledge" (1971, p. 63). The student's
job is merely to "store the deposits."

> The banking concept distinguishes two stages in the action of the educator.
> During the first, he cognizes a cognizable object while he prepares his lessons
> in his study or his laboratory; during the second, he expounds to his students
> about that object. The students are not called upon to know, but to memorize
> the contents narrated by the teacher. Nor do the students practice any act of
> cognition, since the object towards which that act should be directed is the
> property of the teacher. (Pp. 67–68)

Although none of the institutions in our sample adhered closely to
the banking model, our interviews contain poignant accounts of occasions
on which teachers seemed trapped against their will into the banker role.
The teacher who invited Faith and her classmates to "rip into" his interpretation of *The Turn of the Screw* is a case in point. It is easy to feel com-
passion for this beleaguered man. He has probably toiled much of the
previous night over his interpretation. He is excited about it and imagines
that the students, too, will get excited. He imagines hands waving, voices

raised in passionate debate. Instead, he sees rows of bowed heads, hears only the scratching of twenty-five pencils. The teacher does not wish to deposit his words in the students' notebooks, but the students insist upon storing them there. They treat his words as sacrosanct. He cannot understand why they will not risk a response.

But the teacher himself takes few risks. True to the banking concept, he composes his thoughts in private. The students are permitted to see the product of his thinking, but the process of gestation is hidden from view. The lecture appears as if by magic. The teacher asks his students to take risks he is unwilling—although presumably more able—to take himself. He invites the students to find holes in his argument, but he has taken pains to make it airtight. He would regard as scandalous a suggestion that he make the argument more permeable. He has, after all, his "standards," the standards of his discipline, to uphold, and he is proud of the rigor of his interpretation. The students admire it, too. It would seem to them an act of vandalism to "rip into" an object that is, as Freire might say, so clearly the teacher's private property.

A woman needs to know, one alumna said, that her own ideas can be "very good" and "thoroughly reliable," that a theory is "something that somebody thought up, and that's all that a theory is. It's not this mysterious thing only Einstein could figure out." Because they are in positions of power, teachers who speak in their own voices risk turning their students' voices into echoes of their own. On the other hand, the utterly objective, "disembodied" voice carries its own dangers. Rich quotes a university teacher of psychology:

> It seems to me that the form of many communications in academia, both written and verbal, is such as to not only obscure the influence of the personal or subjective but also to give the impression of divine origin—a mystification composed of syballine statements—from beings supposedly emptied of the "dross" of the self. (1979, p. 144)

So long as teachers hide the imperfect processes of their thinking, allowing their students to glimpse only the polished products, students will remain convinced that only Einstein—or a professor—could think up a theory.

The problem is especially acute with respect to science. Science is usually taught by males and is regarded as the quintessentially masculine intellectual activity. And science is taught—or, at least, it is heard by students in most introductory courses—as a series of syballine statements. The professor is not indulging in conjecture; he is telling the truth. And, in one of the most shocking statements in all our hundreds of pages of transcripts, a student concluded that "science is not a creation of the human mind."

Simone, one of our most sophisticated science students, said in an interview during her first year at college that you had to "accept at face value" anything a chemistry professor said. By her senior year Simone had come to realize that the professors had been talking not about facts but about models, although they presented the information as if it were fact. "Why do they do that?" we asked. "I don't know," Simone replied. "Maybe they think you wouldn't believe them otherwise. Maybe they do tell you that it's a model, and you just say, 'Oh, well, it must be true,' because a professor is telling you. I mean, he has a Ph.D. Who am I to argue?"

Simone was wise enough to wonder if she might have misheard the professors, but her story suggests that it is especially critical that teachers of science do all that they can to avoid the appearance of omniscience. Between the scientific expert and the layman, says the feminist scholar Elizabeth Fee, there is rarely any dialogue: "The voice of the scientific authority is like the male voice-over in commercials, a disembodied knowledge that cannot be questioned, whose author is inaccessible" (1983, p. 19).

The revelation that professors are not omnipotent, that "they're groping too" comes to Perry's hero at the end of the developmental story. After years of struggling to compose term papers worthy of his professors' praise, the student realizes that the process the professor goes through in writing his books—and even, perhaps, his lectures—resembles closely the process he himself undergoes in writing a term paper. The path that Perry traces, laid out by Harvard, is a tortuous one: Our teachers appear to us first in the guise of gods and are later revealed to be human. We think the revelation might occur sooner if those of us who teach could find the courage—and the institutional support—to think out loud with our students.

It can be argued, of course, that students need models of impeccable reasoning, that it is through imitating such models that students learn to reason. But none of the women we interviewed named this sort of learning as a powerful experience in their own lives. They did mention the deflation of authority as a powerful learning experience. Recall Faith, who learned, through catching her high school teacher in an error about Mount Everest, that teachers' words should not be accepted at "face value." Another student said she felt emancipated when she told her teacher she could not understand a book she was reading and the teacher replied, "Oh, yeah, I know the guy who wrote it. He's an asshole." The student had not realized that authors could be people, let alone assholes, and she was pleased to be disillusioned.

Women have been taught by generations of men that males have greater powers of rationality than females have. When a male professor presents only the impeccable products of his thinking, it is especially difficult for a woman student to believe that she can produce such a thought. And remember that in the groves of academe, in spite of the women's movement, most of the teachers are still male, although more than half of the students are now female. Women students need opportunities to watch women professors solve (and fail to solve) problems and male professors fail to solve (and succeed in solving) problems. They need models of thinking as a human, imperfect, and attainable activity.

The Teacher as Midwife

None of the women we interviewed wanted a system in which knowledge flowed in only one direction, from teacher to student. Even those who were most respectful of authority wished to be treated at least as containers of knowledge rather than empty receptacles. The community college student who said she "needed to listen to an instructor from the beginning right through to the end" added in the next breath, "I don't really think that anybody can really put something into someone that isn't there. It has to be there."

Many women expressed—some firmly, some shakily—a belief that they possessed latent knowledge. The kind of teacher they praised and the kind for which they yearned was one who would help them articulate and expand their latent knowledge: a midwife-teacher. Midwife-teachers are the opposite of banker-teachers. While the bankers deposit knowledge in the learner's head, the midwives draw it out. They assist the students in giving birth to their own ideas, in making their own tacit knowledge explicit and elaborating it.

"Banking education anesthetizes," Freire says; it "attempts to maintain the *submersion* of consciousness" (1971, p. 68). When anesthesia is administered to a woman in childbirth, the woman becomes, as McMillan says, "a passive spectator" of the birth of her child. She cannot participate actively because she cannot feel the contractions in the uterus. The physician "usurps the woman's natural role during childbirth as *he* now 'gives birth' to the baby with the aid of an array of technological devices" (1982, p. 135). Midwife-teachers do not administer anesthesia. They support their students' thinking, but they do not do the students' thinking for them or expect the students to think as they do.

Like Freire's partner-teachers, midwife-teachers assist in the emergence of consciousness. They encourage the students to speak in their own active voices.

> She helped me to be able to say what I wanted to say and not worry about whether it was getting too personal. Last semester I started having troubles with being too vague in my papers and using the passive voice a lot, and she hit it right on the head that I was being afraid to come out and say it, say "I believe that this and this and this happened in 1692," or whatever.

In "maternal thinking" Ruddick (1980) says the primary concern is preservation of the vulnerable child. The midwife-teacher's first concern is to preserve the student's fragile newborn thoughts, to see that they are born with their truth intact, that they do not turn into acceptable lies.

The second concern in maternal thinking is to foster the child's growth. Connected teachers support the evolution of their students' thinking.* A strikingly high proportion of the women's accounts of teachers who had helped took this form. The teacher said to the student something like Faith's teacher said to her: "What you're thinking is fine, but think more." The teacher did not tell Faith to replace her thought with a different thought but only to "think more," to let the thought grow.

Deborah's high-school English teacher praised her poetry. "She just let me do what I wanted to do and helped me do it, and pushed it further." Deborah's teacher helped her make her private words public; she put her in connection with the culture. She urged Deborah also to "send it someplace, see what they'll do with it. 'Will they give you a prize for it? Will they publish it?' That was when I first began to realize that what I was writing was worth something, that it wasn't just something I did to stay sane."

Midwife-teachers focus not on their own knowledge (as the lecturer does) but on the students' knowledge. They contribute when needed, but it is always clear that the baby is not theirs but the student's. A senior at one of the experimental colleges told us about her thesis adviser, who, she said, "epitomizes the school." The adviser never told her what to do. She read what the student wrote, discussed the writing with her, and suggested

---

* Freire writes, "Problem-posing education affirms men as beings in the process of *becoming*—as unfinished, uncompleted beings" (1971, p. 72).

something she might want to read. "It's sort of worked back and forth like that. I've followed up her suggestions, which have given me new ideas, but it's been mostly my own work which has been generated in each step." The cycle is one of confirmation-evocation-confirmation. Midwife-teachers help students deliver their words to the world, and they use their own knowledge to put the students into conversation with other voices—past and present—in the culture.

Midwife-teachers encourage students to use their knowledge in everyday life. Women spoke often of their need for "practical" information, ranging from the most obviously and immediately useful (facts on child rearing, how to dress for a job interview) to seemingly remote matters. A Greek drama read and only dimly understood in college rested in one woman's memory for years, rising to offer her solace upon the death of her child. A community college student, veteran of the streets of Spanish Harlem, credited a philosophy course with saving her from being mugged. "There was this teenager ready to mug me. I remember thinking so fast. I could do one of three things. I could scream, which is no good; no one's going to hear me. I could run away, but he'd catch me in a minute. Or I can face up to him. That's exactly what I did." She pretended she had a weapon, talked a fast line of street talk, and convinced the boy to let her alone. "If I hadn't been taking philosophy at that time I wouldn't even have said I had three choices. The whole course was about choices."

Connected Classes

In Freire's "problem-posing" method, the object of knowledge is not the private property of the teacher. Rather, it is "a medium evoking the critical reflection of both teacher and students." Instead of the teacher thinking about the object privately and talking about it publicly so that the students may store it, both teacher and students engage in the process of thinking, and they talk out what they are thinking in a public dialogue. As they think and talk together, their roles merge. "Through dialogue, the teacher-of-the-students and the students-of-the-teacher cease to exist and a new term emerges: teacher-student with students-teachers" (1971, p. 67).

Several women cherished memories of classes in which such dialogue had occurred. Bess described an English course that the teacher usually

conducted in the banking mode: "He just hands you his thoughts." On
one memorable occasion, however, he allowed a discussion to erupt.

> We were all raising our hands and talking about I forget what book,
> and some of the students brought up things that he hadn't thought
> about that made him see it in a whole different way, and he was
> really excited, and we all came to a conclusion that none of us
> had started out with. We came up with an answer to a question
> we thought was unanswerable in the beginning, and it just made
> you all feel really good when you walked out of class. You felt
> you had accomplished something and that you understood the
> book. And he was pleased, too.

Rushing eagerly into the classroom at the next meeting, Bess found to her
dismay that the professor had returned to his podium. "I guess he doesn't
like that method," she said.

At this traditional, elite institution the students had to adapt to whatever method the teacher chose. Another, older sophomore in an experimental adult program told us quite a different story about a "stern" new
teacher who tried to lecture. The students soon set him straight. "We really
wanted to be very involved and we wanted to talk as much as he did, and
it took him a while to understand that. He kind of rebelled at that because
he felt that the other way would be better. He was good after that, but it
took a while."

Once the midwife draws a woman's knowledge out into the world,
the third concern of maternal thinking becomes central. Ruddick writes,
"The mother must shape natural growth in such a way that her child
becomes the sort of adult that she can appreciate and others can accept."
Typically, the mother "takes as the criterion of her success the production
of a young adult acceptable to her group" (1980, p. 107). If a woman is to
consider herself a real knower she must find acceptance for her ideas in
the public world. Bridget's bleak praise of her college comes to mind.

> In a very unusual way, perhaps it was the right place for me to go.
> The first time I ever was not a wonder child, a superachiever, the
> apple of everybody's eye, the blue-ribbon kid, was when I got
> there. I never realized until I got there how I had based my own
> sense of worthiness on everybody else's estimation of what I was.
> Suddenly it was like that support that I had used was whisked
> out. I didn't have everybody else's approval, so it had to come
> from some other source. Myself. So in a way, it was probably the

most valuable place I could ever have gone to, because it forced that kind of individual growth. But it's not a goal of the school.

The connected class provides a culture for growth—as Elbow (1973) says, a "yoghurt" class, as opposed to a "movie" class (in which students are spectators). The connected teacher tries to create groups in which members can nurture each other's thoughts to maturity. A college senior told us about an art seminar in which each student was to arrive at approaches to art that seemed most useful to her. The senior tried to define the atmosphere the teacher had established that made the seminar so special. "It's allowing everyone to voice things that they think are uncertain. It's allowing people to realize that they're not stupid for questioning things. It's okay to say 'Why?' or 'How?' or 'What?' I think it's important to let everybody voice their uncertainties."

In a connected class no one apologizes for uncertainty. It is assumed that evolving thought will be tentative. Spacks, writing about feminist criticism, argues that women can mimic a masculine authority rooted in "a universal systematic methodology" and therefore speak with certainty, but we can also try to construct a different sort of authority, based on personal individual experience and acknowledging "the uncertainties implicit in an approach which values the personal" (1981, p. 16).*

The discussion that erupted in Bess's English class was not a debate between finished interpretations. It was a conversation in which teacher and students collaborated in constructing a new interpretation. It is this sort of class that women remember with pleasure. Marylyn Rands, who teaches at a women's college, encourages students in her innovative social psychology course to use a variety of formats in making their presentations. Not one student has ever chosen the debate.† In a "woman-centered university," Adrienne Rich says, more courses would be conducted in the style of community, fewer in the "masculine adversary style of discourse," which has dominated much of Western education (1979, p. 138).

In a community, unlike a hierarchy, people get to know each other. They do not act as representatives of positions or as occupants of roles but as individuals with particular styles of thinking. A first-year undergraduate remarked that her editing group composed of three classmates in a writing course was not working.

---

* Catherine Stimpson, a pioneer in the development of women's studies, writes, "We need to find a judicious balance between the claims of personal authority and the waste of reinventing the wheel that occurs when non-personal authority is rejected" (1978, p. 17).

† Personal communication, October 1984.

> We just talk about commas and junk like that. I had a peer editing
> group in high school, and it was terrific. But we all knew each
> other inside out, so you knew what each person was trying to do
> in her writing and you knew what kinds of criticisms helped her
> and what kind hurt her feelings. You can't really help if you don't
> know people.

Unless she knew the critic personally and the critic knew her personally,
she found criticism of her work "hurtful but not helpful"; and she found
the concept of "blind grading" simply incomprehensible.

Our vision of a connected class follows directly from our conception
of connected epistemology. Norman Holland, a teacher of literature who
shares our epistemological assumptions, describes the epistemological
assumptions underlying many literature courses.

> People often speak as though the literary work or, in general, some other
> existed in all its fullness, while I perceive that fullness imperfectly, subtracting
> out certain aspects. It is as though my perception of the other equaled the
> other *minus* something. . . . Thinking this way leads to images like the *prison*
> of the self or the *limits* of what I can see, or the *risk*, even the *peril* of interpreting
> wrongly. All such discomfort proceeds from the debilitating assumption that
> each of us experiences something imperfectly and someone else knows just
> how imperfectly. (1975, pp. 281–82)

Given such a model, students in such a class must inevitably "measure
their words" in an attempt to avoid disgrace. The model is, as Holland
says, both "confusing and discouraging," because "we cannot suddenly
know more" (p. 282). We cannot stop being ourselves or step out of ourselves. As one woman told us, "I live within myself. I know only through
myself."

"All this confusion and sense of limitation and loss," Holland says,
"comes from positing a literary work or, in general, an other which is full
and complete and from which we subtract" (p. 282). Suppose that instead
of asking what readers fail to see (what they subtract from the text in
constructing their own experience of it), we start not with the text but with
the students and ask, as Holland suggests, what they are adding to themselves by the act of reading. When teachers and students learn to ask this
question of each other, to respect and to enter into each other's unique
perspectives, the connected class comes into being.

The connected class recognizes the core of truth in the subjectivist
view that each of us has a unique perspective that is in some sense irre-
futably "right" by virtue of its existence. But the connected class transforms

these private truths into "objects," publicly available to the members of the class who, through "stretching and sharing," add to themselves as knowers by absorbing in their own fashion their classmates' ideas.

The connected class constructs truth not through conflict but through "consensus," whose original meaning, Holland reminds us, was "feeling or sensing together," implying not agreement, necessarily, but a "crossing of the barrier between ego and ego," bridging private and shared experience (p. 291).

Objectivity in Connected Teaching

Connected teachers try to discern the truth inside the students. It is essential that the search be disinterested. A fifty-four-year-old mother of six in her second term at an adult program said,

> I keep discovering things inside myself. I see myself for the first time through the eyes of others. In the past, whenever I've seen myself through the eyes of others it's been another that I cared a great deal about, who had the power to destroy me, and usually did. Now I see myself through the eyes of others who matter, but not that closely. I'm not entwined with them emotionally. I feel that it's a truer thing that I'm getting back from these people.

Several women spontaneously remarked that in this adult program they were able for the first time since childhood to initiate a conversation, because they knew that they would be listened to in their own terms. "Everyone wants what's best for me," said one.

Connected teachers welcome diversity of opinion in class discussion. Many of the women we interviewed spoke with appreciation of teachers who refrained from "inflicting" (a common term) their own opinions on the students. Elizabeth remembered a Bible course as "just great."

> We had Baptists and we had Jews in there and we had atheists in there. We had people with just absolute disregard for humanity in there. And all of us could contribute and learn something and gain something because he could tolerate so many different views.

I think that's a mark of excellence, the ability to accept dissent from your own opinion.

Objectivity in connected teaching, as in connected knowing, means seeing the other, the student, in the student's own terms. Noddings contrasts separate and connected (in her terms, "caring") approaches to teaching.

> Suppose, for example, that I am a teacher who loves mathematics. I encounter a student who is doing poorly, and I decide to have a talk with him. He tells me that he hates mathematics. I do not begin with dazzling performances designed to intrigue him or to change his attitude. I begin, as nearly as I can, with the view from his eyes: Mathematics is bleak, jumbled, scary, boring, boring, boring. From that point on, we struggle together with it. (1984, pp. 15–16)

In traditional separate education, the student tries to look at the material through the teacher's eyes. In contrast, the caring teacher "receives and accepts the student's feeling toward the subject matter; she looks at it and listens to it through his eyes and ears." She acts "as if for herself," but in the interests of the student's projects, realizing that the student is "independent, a subject" (Noddings 1984, p. 177). In the developmental story Perry tells, the student becomes an independent thinker through executing the teacher's projects in the teacher's own terms. Connected education follows a straighter path: The student is treated from the start not as subordinate or as object but as "independent, a subject."

Teaching can be simultaneously objective and personal. There is no inherent contradiction, so long as objectivity is not defined as self-extrication. Connected teachers use a technique similar to the "participant-observation" method anthropologists use. Participant-observers maintain "a dynamic tension" between the separate stance of an observer and the connected, "subjective" stance of a participant, being "neither one entirely" (Wilson 1977, p. 250).* Reinharz (1984) found the participant-observation method uncomfortable for precisely this reason; investigating friendships among patients in a mental hospital she felt herself to be in an anomalous position, neither truly attached nor truly detached from her subjects, a stranger in their midst. In a subsequent field project

---

* Those who believe that the social sciences should mimic the natural science stance of "objective outsider" criticize participant-observation for its subjectivity. But in a sense the participant-observer is less subjectivist than is the traditional empiricist. The sociologist Sylvaner Bruyn points out that "the traditional empiricist considers himself (as a scientist) to be the primary source of knowledge, and trusts his own senses and logic more than he would trust that of his subjects. The participant observer, on the other hand, considers the interpretations of his subjects to have first importance" (1966, p. 12).

in an Israeli town she and her colleagues on the research team coined the phrase "temporary affiliation" to describe their modification of the participant-observation method. This term, Reinharz thinks, better captures the "human mutuality" that should characterize the relationship between researchers and their informants. The researchers act as "short-term partners" who give the informants a chance to be heard and provide feedback to them. For a brief period, researcher and subject meet on common turf, each "truly being with the other."

Noddings describes the relation between caring teachers and their students in similar terms. "I do not need to establish a lasting, time-consuming personal relationship with every student. What I must do is to be totally and nonselectively present to the student—to each student—as he addresses me. The time interval may be brief but the encounter is total" (p. 180).

Portrait of a Connected Teacher

Candace remembered an English professor at the women's college who could serve as an ideal prototype of a connected teacher. Candace was "moved" by this woman's "rigorous" approach to teaching. "You had to assume that there was a purpose to everything the writer did. And if something seemed odd, you couldn't overlook it or ignore it or throw it out." This teacher was throroughly "objective" in treating the students' responses as real and independent of her own.

> She was intensely, genuinely interested in everybody's feelings about things. She asked a question and wanted to know what your response was. She wanted to know because she wanted to see what sort of effect this writing was having. She wasn't using us as a sounding board for her own feelings about things. She really wanted to know.

She was careful not to use the students to "develop her own argument." Candace recalled with special vividness an occasion when the teacher became embroiled in a real argument with a student and stubbornly refused to hear the student's point.

And she came in the next day and said, "You know, my response to this student was being governed by my own biases." And she learned from that, she said, how she really did feel about something, and then she related it actually to the work we were studying. And it was just so wonderful, so amazing that somebody would really—in this theater of the classroom—that she was fully engaged in what was going on.

This teacher managed not only to present herself as a person while retaining her objectivity but to present objectivity as a personal issue. By her actions as well as her words she made it clear that to overlook or ignore or throw out a piece of data or another person's words was a violation of her own person. And the violation itself became another piece of data not to be overlooked or ignored or thrown out. Instead, it had to be acknowledged in full view of the class, understood, and even used to illuminate the material the class was studying. The personal became the professional; the professional became the personal. And subjectivity and objectivity became one. The anthropologist Mary Catherine Bateson, attempting to define the method of participant-observation, writes,

> These resonances between the personal and the professional are the source of both insight and error. You avoid mistakes and distortions not so much by trying to build a wall between the observer and the observed as by observing the observer—observing yourself—as well, and bringing the personal issues into consciousness. (1984, p. 161)

Investigators who use this sort of method, whether they label it "participant-observation" as Bateson does or "experiential analysis" as Reinharz (1984) does, practice a sophisticated form of connected knowing, a "technique of *disciplined* subjectivity" (Erikson 1964) requiring that they "systematically empathize with the participants" (Wilson 1977, p. 259). They participate in the enterprise they are studying in order to undergo experiences similar to those of the other participants, placing themselves in a better position to understand the experiences of the other participants. They use their own reactions to formulate hypotheses about the other participants' reactions.

Candace's English teacher behaved in a similar way. She did not treat her own experience of the material under study as primary, and she did not assume that her students experienced the material as she did; this would be undisciplined subjectivity or, in Elbow's words, "projection in the bad sense" (1973, p. 171). She really wanted to know how the students were experiencing the material. As a teacher, she believed she had to trust each student's experience, although as a person or a critic she might not agree with it. To trust means not just to tolerate a variety of viewpoints, acting as an impartial referee, assuring equal air time to all. It means to try to *connect*, to enter into each student's perspective.

But, again, subjectivity is disciplined. Like the participant-observer, the connected teacher is careful not to "abandon" herself to these perspectives (Wilson 1977, p. 259). A connected teacher is not just another student; the role carries special responsibilities. It does not entail power over the students; however, it does carry authority, an authority based not on subordination but on cooperation.

Belief, Doubt, and Development

Connected teachers are believers. They trust their students' thinking and encourage them to expand it. But in the psychological literature concerning the factors promoting cognitive development, doubt has played a more prominent role than belief. People are said to be precipitated into states of cognitive conflict when, for example, some external event challenges their ideas and the effort to resolve the conflict leads to cognitive growth.* We do not deny that cognitive conflict can act as an impetus to growth; all of us can attest to such experiences in our own lives. But in our interviews only a handful of women described a powerful and positive learning experience in which a teacher aggressively challenged their notions. The midwife model was much more prominent.

This could be interpreted to mean that the midwife model was more prominent than the conflict model in the institutions we sampled, but we do not think so. Women did tell of occasions when teachers challenged their ideas—and we have retold some in this book—but they did not describe them as occasions for cognitive growth. On the whole, women found the experience of being doubted debilitating rather than energizing. Several women said that they and their friends left school as soon as they legally

* On the role of cognitive conflict in learning see Cantor (1983), Langer (1969), Moessinger (1978), Murray (1983a, 1983b), Zimmerman and Blom (1983a, 1983b). For critical commentary on the "disequilibration studies" of moral development, see Rest (1983). For recent theory and research on the effect of conflict among peers on psychological growth, see Berkowitz (1985).

could, married, and got pregnant (not necessarily in that order) "so that we wouldn't have to put up with being put down every day."

Because so many women are already consumed with self-doubt, doubts imposed from outside seem at best redundant and at worst destructive, confirming the women's own sense of themselves as inadequate knowers. The doubting model, then, may be peculiarly inappropriate for women, although we are not convinced that it is appropriate for men, either.

Both the authoritarian banking model and the adversarial doubting model of education are, we believe, wrong for women. Freire says that if we abandon the banking model in favor of the problem-posing model, we will "undermine the power of oppression" (1971, p. 62). If we replace the separate with the connected model, we can spare women the "alienation, repression, and division" their schooling currently confers upon them (Jacobus 1979, p. 10). Education conducted on the connected model would help women toward community, power, and integrity. Such an education could facilitate the development of women's minds and spirits rather than, as in so many cases reported in this book, retarding, arresting, or even reversing their growth.

Women's Development as the Aim of Education

Some years ago, in a now classic paper called "Development as the Aim of Education," Kohlberg and Mayer suggested that the proper purpose of education was to assist students in moving toward more mature stages of intellectual, epistemological, and ethical development. They argued that this sort of education did not entail indoctrination, because it merely stimulated children in the "natural directions" of development (1972, p. 475).

We found this argument compelling at the time, and we still believe in development as the aim of education; but parts of the Kohlberg-Mayer argument now make us uneasy. It turns out, of course, that those "natural directions" in which all human beings supposedly head are toward principled moral judgment and an epistemology based on standard (and separate) "principles of scientific method" serving "as the basis of rational reflection" (p. 475).

Along with many of our colleagues, we believed at the time that psychologists such as Piaget and Kohlberg had established through empirical investigation that these were the universal and natural trajectories in human development. And we believed that they had discovered effective strategies for "moving" students to more advanced levels, such as instigating moral arguments among students at varying stages (the adversarial model) and exposing students to real or fictional people making statements at a slightly more sophisticated stage ("plus-one-model"). Most of the research on these matters had, of course, been done by and "on" males.

Since the publication of Kohlberg's paper, research by, with, and for women has increased. (We like to think less work is being done "on" women.) This research suggests that the directions then assumed to be natural do not come naturally to many women. Gilligan (1982) and Lyons (1983) have demonstrated that an ethic of responsibility may be more "natural" to most women than an ethic of rights. We believe that connected knowing comes more easily to many women than does separate knowing.

We have argued in this book that educators can help women develop their own authentic voices if they emphasize connection over separation, understanding and acceptance over assessment, and collaboration over debate; if they accord respect to and allow time for the knowledge that emerges from firsthand experience; if instead of imposing their own expectations and arbitrary requirements, they encourage students to evolve their own patterns of work based on the problems they are pursuing. These are the lessons we have learned in listening to women's voices.

Appendix A

Interview Schedule

Section A—Background

A1.   What stands out for you in your life over the past few years?
      What kinds of things have been important?
      What stays with you?

A2.   Tell me something about what your life is like right now.
      What do you care about, think about?

Section B—Self-Descriptions (Gilligan)

Having talked a bit about your life, now I would like you to think about yourself.

B1.   How would you describe yourself to yourself?
      If you were to tell yourself who you really are, how would you do that?

B2.   Is the way you see yourself now different from the way you saw yourself in the past?
      What led to the changes?

Have there been any other turning points?

B3.   How do you see yourself changing in the future?

Section C—Gender

C1.   What does being a woman mean to you?

Do you think there are any important differences between women and men?

How has your sense of yourself as a woman been changing?

Section D—Relationships

D1.   Looking back over your life, what relationships have been really important to you? Why?

How would you describe those relationships?

How do you think the other person would describe the relationship?

How has the relationship changed, and how do you account for the change?

Have you had a relationship with someone who helped you shape the person you have become?

Have you had a really important relationship where you were responsible for taking care of another person?

How would you describe that?

How important was that in your life?

D2.   How would you describe your mother (or primary caregiver)? Your father?

Has your view of your parents been changing?

And how would you describe each of your children (if any)?

D3.   One of the things that we have been finding is that many women were sexually abused at some time in their lives, even as children. Studies have shown that a large percentage of women have been victims of sexual or physical abuse. Has this ever happened to you?

Section E—Real Life Moral Dilemma (Gilligan)

Everyone has had the experience of being in situations where they had to make a decision but weren't sure what was the right thing to do. Could you describe to me a situation where you weren't sure what was the right thing to do?

E1.   What was the situation? What was the conflict for you in the situation?
E2.   In thinking about what to do, what did you consider? Why? Were there other things that you thought of in trying to decide what to do? How did you weigh each alternative?
E3.   What did you decide to do? Why? What happened?
E4.   Looking back on it now, did you make the best choice? Why or why not?
E5.   Thinking back over the whole thing, what did you learn from it?

Section F—Education

As I said earlier, this project is concerned with women and learning and the role of learning and education in women's lives . . . and I'd like to ask you to think about that now.

F1.   What do you think will stay with you about your experiences here [in this school, in this program]?
(Probe for specific academic and nonacedemic experiences; good and bad teachers; good and bad assignments; good and bad programs or courses; residential or off-campus arrangements.)
F2.   Has being here [being in this program] changed the way you think about yourself or the world?
F3.   In your learning here, have you come across an idea that made you see things differently . . . or think about things differently?
F4.   What has been most helpful to you about this place?
F5.   Are there things this [school, program, environment] doesn't provide

that are important to you?

Are there things you would like to learn that you don't think you
can learn here?

F6. Looking back over your whole life, can you tell me about a really
powerful learning experience that you've had, in or out of school?

Section G—Ways of Knowing*

(If woman is in out-of-school program, go to Section G–1. If woman is in
school setting, go to Section G–2.)

SECTION G–1 (OUT-OF-SCHOOL WOMEN)

G1. When learning about something you want to know (for example,
how to bring up children, deciding who to vote for, and so on),
do you rely on experts?

G2. If not, who or what do you rely on?
If so, what do you do when the experts disagree?

G3. How do you know someone is an expert?

G4. If experts disagree on something today, do you think that someday
they will be able to come to some agreement?

G5. How do you know what is right/true?

SECTION G–2 (WOMEN IN SCHOOL, OR ALUMNAE)

(The interviewer should have comments A, B, C, and D typed on
separate cards.) Now I'd like to do something a little different. This is a
comment that was made by somebody else. (Hand the woman the card
with Comment A typed on it.) I'd like you to read this aloud and then
comment on it.

A.   "In areas where the right answers are known, I think the experts
should tell us what is right. But in areas where there is no right
answer, I think anybody's opinion is as good as another."
Probe extensively on this item. For example:

---

* A revised version of the Ways of Knowing interview, integrating the current findings,
is available from B. Clinchy, Department of Psychology, Wellesley College, Wellesley, Mass.
02181.

G1. In learning about something you really want to know, can you rely on experts?

G2. How do you know someone is an expert?

G3. What do you do when experts disagree?

G4. If experts disagree on something today, do you think that someday they will come to some agreement? Why or why not?

G5. How do you know what is right/true?

G6. Do you agree with this person who says that where there are no right answers anybody's opinion is as good as another's?

G7. Can you think of an opinion that you think is wrong?

G8. I know this wouldn't happen, but what if someone said they thought that all blue-eyed babies should be drowned at birth? Would you say that opinion was wrong? Why or why not?

G9. What if 100 people saw a movie (read a book, etc.) and all 100 people said it was good? Does that mean it is good?

G10. Are some movies (books, ideas) better than others? (If yes) What makes them better?

G11. Sometimes people talk about "searching for truth." I'm not sure what they're talking about. What do you think people mean when they say that?

Is that what scientists are doing, do you think? Searching for truth? Will they find it?

How about artists (painters, writers, and so on)? Are they searching for truth?

(Ask the woman to comment on one or more of the following cards only if you feel you need more information about her conception of knowledge, truth, rightness, etc.)

B. "Sometimes I read something that someone has written or I hear somebody say something, and it really impresses me. I think to myself, 'I'll never have an idea as good as that.' I just don't know how people ever get to the point where they have something so important to say."

C. "If the people in one country say, 'We believe such and such is the right way to think about something,' and people in another country say just the opposite, and the opposite is so or the right way to think, then time will usually tell which country is right."

D. "Sometimes I really get bored with school, because it is just so much sitting around listening to other people or the teacher talk about things that aren't important."

Section H—Hypothetical Moral Judgments (Kohlberg)

Now I would like to read you a little story and ask you some questions about it.

The Heinz Dilemma: In Europe, a woman was near death from a rare disease. There was one drug the doctors thought might save her. It was a drug that a druggist in the town had recently discovered. The drug was expensive to make, and the druggist was charging ten times what the drug had cost him to make. He paid $200 for the materials and was charging $2,000 for the prescription. The sick woman's husband, Heinz, went to everyone he knew to borrow the money, but he could only get together about $1,000, which was half of what he needed. He told the druggist that his wife was dying and asked him to sell it cheaper or to let him pay later. But the druggist said, "No, I discovered the drug and I'm going to make money from it."

H1. What do you think the problem is here?
     What should be done about it?
H2. Should Heinz steal the drug?
H3. If Heinz doesn't love his wife any more, should he still steal the drug for her? Why or why not?
H4. Suppose the person dying is not his wife but a stranger. Should he steal the drug for a stranger? Why or why not?
H5. Suppose Heinz does steal the drug. He is caught and brought to trial. The jury finds him guilty and the judge has to decide on the sentence. Should the judge sentence him or let him go free? Why?

Section I—Conclusion

Okay, thanks. Now before we stop I have just one or two more questions.

I1. What will you and your life be like fifteen years from now?
I2. Are there any other questions that I should have asked you, that would have thrown some light on these issues we are interested in . . . that is, women's lives and women's learnings?

Appendix B

Educational Dialectics

A. **Process Oriented** ....**Goal Oriented**
   Means   Ends
     What are the aims of education?

B. **Discovery**..............................**Didacticism**
   Constructed knowledge   Received knowledge
     How is knowledge viewed? How is the act of becoming a
     "knower" explained?

C. **Rational** ....**Intuitive**
   Logical, analytical, objective   Gut feeling,
                                        subjective, ESP
     What method(s) are used for analysis? What method(s) are
     valued?

D. **Discrete** ....**Related**
   Compartmentalization   Synthesis
     What is the relationship between learning and "life"?

E. **Being with Others** ....**Being Alone or
                                        on Own**

   Collaborative   Solitary
   Cooperative   Competitive
     What arrangements for learning are preferred? Have been
     experienced?

F. **Breadth**................................**Concentration**
   Generalist   Specialist
   Dilettantism   Narrowness, blinders
     What is the range of interests in learning?

G. **Support** . . . . **Challenge**

What are the optimal conditions for learning?

Who and what are experienced as supportive/nonsupportive? Challenging/nonchallenging?

H. **Personal** . . . . **Impersonal**

What is the relationship between self and the content of one's learning?

How are these relationships structured in terms of the curriculum, relationship with peers, relationship with faculty and staff?

I. **Self-Concern** . . . . **Responsibility and Caring for Others**

Is concern for self vs. concern for others an issue in educational decision making?

J. **Inner** . . . . **Outer**

What factors control goal setting, pacing, decision making, and evaluation?

Who and what is experienced as validating/nonvalidating?

K. **Listening** . . . . **Speaking**

What are the experiences of voice?

References

Adorno, T. W., Frenkel-Brunswik, E., Levinson, D. J., & Sanford, R. N. (1950). *The authoritarian personality.* New York: Harper & Row.

Al-Issa, I. (1980). *The psychopathology of women.* Englewood Cliffs, NJ: Prentice-Hall.

Argyle, M., Mansur, L., & Cook, M. (1968). The effects of visibility on interactions in a dyad. *Human Relations, 21,* 3–17.

Aries, E. (1976). Interaction patterns and themes of male, female, and mixed groups. *Small Group Behavior, 7,* 7–14.

Arlin, P. (1975). Cognitive development in adulthood. *Developmental Psychology, 11,* 602–606.

Asch, S. (1952). *Social psychology.* New York: Prentice-Hall.

Attanucci, J. S. (1984). *Mothers in their own terms: A developmental perspective on self and role.* Unpublished doctoral dissertation, Harvard University.

Bakan, D. (1966). *The duality of human existence.* Boston: Beacon Press.

Bateson, M. C. (1984). *With a daughter's eye.* New York: William Morrow.

Baumrind, D. (1971). Current patterns and parental authority. *Developmental Psychology Monographs, 4*(1, Pt. 2).

Bayley, N., & Schaefer, E. S. (1964). Correlations of maternal and child behaviors with the development of mental abilities: Data from the Berkeley Growth Studies. *Monograph of the Society for Research in Child Development, 29* (6, Serial No. 97).

Belenky, M. F. (1978). *Conflict and development: A longitudinal study of the impact of abortion decisions on adolescent and adult women.* Doctoral dissertation, Harvard University.

Belenky, M. F. (1983). *The role of dialogue in human development and in the reduction of family violence.* Paper presented at Teachers' College, Columbia University.

Belenky, M. F. (1984). The role of deafness and education in the moral development of hearing impaired children and adolescents. In A. Areson & J. DeCaro (Eds.), *Teaching, learning and development* (pp. 155–184). Rochester, NY: National Technical Institute of the Deaf (Eric File #248 646).

Bell, R. Q., & Harper, L. V. (1977). *Child effects on adults.* Hillsdale, NJ: Lawrence Erlbaum.

Berkowitz, M. S. (Ed.). (1985). *Peer conflict and psychological growth.* San Francisco: Jossey-Bass.

Bernard, J. (1972). *The sex game: Communication between the sexes.* New York: Atheneum.

Bernard, J. (1973). My four revolutions: An autobiographical history of the American Sociological Society. *American Journal of Sociology, 78,* 773–791.

Bernard, J. (1981). *The female world.* New York: The Free Press.

Bernstein, B. (1964). Elaborated and restricted codes: Their social origins and consequences. In J. Gumperz & D. Hymes (Eds.), *The ethnography of communication. American Anthropologist,* special publication, *66*(6, Pt. 2), 55–69.

Block, J. (1984). Gender differences and implications for educational policy. In J. Block (Ed.), *Sex role identity and ego development* (pp. 207–252). San Francisco: Jossey-Bass.

Blos, P. (1979). *The adolescent passage*. New York: International Universities Press.

Bolker, J. (1979, April). Teaching Griselda to write. *College English*, pp. 906–908.

Boulding, K. (1962). *Conflict and defense: A general theory*. New York: Harper & Row.

Bowlds, M. K. (1985). Pre-school toy preferences as a function of age and sex. Unpublished manuscript, Wellesley College, MA.

Bowles, G., & Duelli-Klein, R. (1983). *Theories of women's studies*. London: Routledge & Kegan Paul.

Bruner, J. S. (1963). *The process of education*. Cambridge, MA: Harvard University Press.

Bruner, J. S. (1985). Narrative and paradigmatic modes of thought. In *Learning and teaching the ways of knowing. 84th Yearbook of the National Society for the Study of Education*. Chicago: University of Chicago Press, pp. 97–115.

Bruyn, S. (1966). *Human perspective in sociology*. Englewood Cliffs, NJ: Prentice-Hall.

Butler, S. (1978). *Conspiracy of silence: The trauma of incest*. San Francisco: New Glide.

Cantor, G. (1983). Conflict, learning, and Piaget: Comments on Zimmerman and Blom's "Toward an empirical test of the role of cognitive conflict in learning." *Developmental Review*, 3, 39–53.

Chodorow, N. (1978). *The reproduction of mothering*. Berkeley: University of California Press.

Clance, P. R., & Imes, S. A. (1978). The imposter phenomenon in high achieving women: Dynamics and therapeutic intervention. *Psychotherapy: Theory, Research, and Practice, 15*, 241–247.

Clinchy, B., & Zimmerman, C. (1975). Cognitive development in college. Unpublished manuscript, Wellesley College, Wellesley, MA.

Clinchy, B., & Zimmerman, C. (1982). Epistemology and agency in the development of undergraduate women. In P. Perun (Ed.), *The undergraduate woman: Issues in educational equity*. Lexington MA: D.C. Heath.

Cohler, B., & Grunnebaum, H. (1981). *Mothers, grandmothers, and daughters*. New York: Wiley & Sons.

Cole, M., Gay, J., Glick, J., & Sharp, D. (1971). *The cultural context of learning and thinking*. New York: Basic Books.

Connor, J. M., & Serbin, L. A. (1977). Behaviorally based masculine—and feminine—activity-preference scales for preschoolers. *Child Development, 48*, 1411–1416.

Contratto, S. (1984). Mother: Social sculptor and trustee of the faith. In M. Lewin (Ed.), *In the shadow of the past: Psychology portrays the sexes* (pp. 226–255). New York: Columbia University Press.

Costanzo, P. R., & Shaw, M. E. (1966). Conformity as a function of age level. *Child Development, 37*, 967–975.

Crandall, V. C. (1969). Sex differences in expectancy of intellectual and academic reinforcement. In C. T. Smith (Ed.), *Achievement-related motives in children* (pp. 11–46). New York: Russell Sage.

Cross, P. (1968). College women: A research description. *Journal of the National Association of Women Deans and Counselors, 32*, 12–21.

Cuming, E., & Henry, W. H. (1961). *Growing old: The process of disengagement*. New York: Basic Books.

Daly, M. (1973). *Beyond God the Father*. Boston: Beacon Press.

de Beauvoir, S. (1976, October). Interview by Alice Schwarzer in *Marie-Claire*. Reprinted in E. Marks & I. de Courtivron (Eds.), *New French feminisms*. New York: Schocken Books, 1981, pp. 151–153.

Du Bois, B. (1983). *Passionate scholarship: Notes on values, knowing, and method in feminist social science*. In G. Bowles & R. Duelli-Klein (Eds.), *Theories of women's studies*. Boston: Routledge & Kegan Paul, pp. 105–116.

Dubois, B. L., & Crouch, I. (Eds.). (1976). *The sociology of the languages of American women*. San Antonio, TX: Trinity University.

Duras, M. (1973). Smothered creativity. Reprinted in E. Marks & I. de Courtivron (Eds.), *New French feminisms* (pp. 174–176). New York: Schocken Books.

Duras, M. (1975). Interview by Susan Husserl-Kapit. *Signs: Journal of Women in Culture and Society, 1*(2), 423–434.

Dzeich, B. W., & Weiner, L. (1984). *The lecherous professor: Sexual harassment on campus.* Boston: Beacon Press.

Eakins, B., & Eakins, G. (1976). Verbal turn-taking and exchanges in faculty dialogue. In B. L. Dubois & I. Crouch (Eds.), *The sociology of the language of American women* (pp. 53–62). San Antonio, TX: Trinity University.

Edelsky, C. (1981). Who's got the floor? *Language in Society, 10,* 383–421.

Ehrenreich, B. (1983). *The hearts of men: American dreams and the flight from commitment.* New York: Doubleday.

Elbow, P. (1973). *Writing without teachers.* London: Oxford University Press.

Elbow, P. (1979). Trying to teach while thinking about the end. In G. Grant, P. Elbow, T. Ewens, Z. Gamson, W. Kohli, V. Olesen, & D. Riesman, *On competence* (pp. 95–137). San Francisco: Jossey-Bass.

Eliot, G. (1985). *Middlemarch.* New York: Penguin Books. Originally published 1871–72.

Elshtain, J. B. (1982). Feminist discourse and its discontents: Language, power and meaning. *Signs, 7,* 603–621.

Engle, M. (1980). Language and play: A comparative analysis of parental initiatives. In H. Giles, W. P. Robinson, & P. M. Smith (Eds.), *Language: Social psychological perspectives.* Oxford: Pergamon Press.

Epstein, A. (1982). Teen parents: What they need to know. *High/Scope Resource, 1*(2), 6–7.

Erikson, E. H. (1964). The nature of clinical evidence. In *Insight and responsibility* (pp. 47–80). New York: Norton.

Erikson, E. H. (1968). *Identity: Youth and crisis.* New York: Norton.

Fee, E. (1983). Women's nature and scientific objectivity. In M. Loew & R. Hubbard (Eds.), *Woman's nature: Rationalizations of inequality* (pp. 9–27). New York: Pergamon Press.

Feuerstein, R. (1980). *Instrumental enrichment: An intervention program for cognitive modifiability.* Baltimore: University of Maryland Press.

Finkelhor, D. (1979). *Sexually victimized children.* New York: Free Press.

Finkelhor, D. (1983). Common features of family abuse. In D. Finkelhor, R. J. Gelles, G. T. Hotaling, & M. A. Strauss (Eds.), *The dark side of families: Current family violence research* (pp. 17–28). New York: Sage.

Fishman, P. (1978). What do couples talk about when they're alone? In D. Butturff & E. L. Epstein (Eds.), *Women's language and style* (pp. 11–22). Akron, OH: L & S Books.

Fishman, P. (1983). Interaction: The work women do. In B. Thorne, C. Kramarea & N. Henley (Eds.), *Language, gender and society* (pp. 89–102). Rowley, MA: Newbury House.

Freedman, A. M., Kaplan, H. I., & Sadock, B. J. (Eds.). (1975). *Comprehensive textbook of psychiatry* (2nd ed.). Baltimore: Williams & Wilkins.

Freire, P. (1971). *Pedagogy of the oppressed.* New York: Seaview.

Freud, S. (1952). *Totem and taboo.* New York: W. W. Norton.

Furth, H. G. (1973). *Deafness and learning: A psychological approach.* Belmont, CA: Wadsworth.

Gagnon, J. (1965). Female child victims of sex offenders. *Social Problems, 13,* 176–192.

Galinsky, E. (1981). *Between generations: Stages of parenthood.* New York: Berkley.

Gallese, L. R. (1985). *Women like us.* New York: William Morrow.

Gardner, H. (1982). *Art, mind, and brain: A cognitive approach to creativity.* New York: Basic Books.

Gardner, H. (1985). *The mind's new science: A history of the cognitive revolution.* New York: Basic Books.

Gaskell, E. (1894). *Cranford.* London: Macmillan.

Gilligan, C. (1977). In a different voice: Women's conceptions of self and of morality. *Harvard Educational Review, 47,* 481–517.

Gilligan, C. (1979). Woman's place in man's life cycle. *Harvard Educational Review, 49,* 431–446.

Gilligan, C. (1982). *In a different voice: Psychological theory and women's development.* Cambridge, MA: Harvard University Press.

Gilligan, C. (1984). The conquistador and the dark continent: Reflections on the psychology of love. *Daedalus, 113,* 75–95.

Gilligan, C. (1986). Exit-voice dilemmas in adolescent development. In A. Foxley, M. McPherson, & G. O'Donnell (Eds.), *Development, democracy, and the art of trespassing: Essays in honor of Albert O. Hirschman.* Notre Dame, IN: University of Notre Dame Press.

Gleason, J. B., & Greif, E. B. (1983). Men's speech to young children. In B. Thorne, C. Kramarae, & N. Henley (Eds.), *Language, gender and society* (pp. 140–150). Rowley, MA: Newbury House.

Goldberger, N. (1978). Breaking the educational lockstep: The Simon's Rock experience. In P. E. Kaylor (Ed.), *The early college in theory and practice* (pp. 62–87). Great Barrington, MA: Simon's Rock Early College.

Goldberger, N. (1981). *Meeting the developmental needs of college students.* Final report presented to The Fund for the Improvement of Post Secondary Education (FIPSE), Simon's Rock of Bard College, Great Barrington, MA.

Gornick, V. (1983). *Women and science: Portraits from a world of transition.* New York: Simon & Schuster.

Greenfield, P. M. (1972). Oral or written language: The consequences for cognitive development in Africa, USA and England. *Language and Speech, 15,* 169–178.

Greenfield, P. M., & Lave, J. (1982). Cognitive aspects of informal education. In D. Wagner & H. Stevenson (Eds.), *Cultural perspectives on child development* (pp. 181–270). San Francisco: Freeman & Co.

Greif, E. B. (1980). Sex differences in parent-child conversations. In C. Kramarae (Ed.), *The voices and words of men and women* (pp. 253–258). New York: Pergamon Press.

Griffith, J., & Chapman, D. (1982). *Learning context questionnaire.* Davidson, NC: Davidson College.

Gurin, G., Veroff, J., & Feld, S. (1960). *Americans view their mental health.* New York: Basic Books.

Gutmann, D. (1964). An exploration of ego configurations in middle and later life. In B. L. Neugarten (Ed.), *Personality in middle and later life* (pp. 114–148). New York: Atherton.

Gutmann, D. (1975). Parenthood: A key to the comparative study of the life cycle. In N. Datan & L. Ginsberg (Eds.), *Life-span developmental psychology: Normative crisis* (pp. 167–184). New York: Academic Press.

Haan, N., Smith, M. B., & Block, J. H. (1968). The moral reasoning of young adults: Political-social behavior, family background, and personality correlates. *Journal of Personality and Social Psychology, 10,* 183–201.

Habermas, J. (1973). *Legitimation crisis.* Boston: Beacon Press.

Hagen, E. V. (1962). *On the theory of social change: How economic growth begins.* Homewood, IL: Dorsey Press.

Hagen, R. I., & Kahn, A. (1975). Discrimination against competent women. *Journal of Applied Social Psychology, 5,* 362–376.

Hall, R., & Sandler, B. R. (1982). *The classroom climate: A chilly one for women?* Washington, DC: Project on the Status and Education of Women, Association of American Colleges.

Hall, R., & Sandler, B. R. (1983). *Academic mentoring for women students and faculty: A new look at an old way to get ahead.* Washington, DC: Project on the Status and Education of Women, Association of American Colleges.

Harding, S., & Hintikka, M. B. (Eds.). (1983). *Discovering reality: Feminist perspectives on epistemology, metaphysics, methodology, and philosophy of science.* Dordrecht, Holland: Reidel.

Hauser, S., Powers, S. I., Noam, G., Jacobson, A. M., Weiss, B., & Follansbee, D. J. (1984). Familial contexts of adolescent ego development. *Child Development, 55,* 195–213.

Hayakawa, S. I. (1964). *Language in thought and action.* New York: Harcourt Brace and World.

Herman, J. (1981). *Father-daughter incest.* Cambridge, MA: Harvard University Press.

Hess, R. D., & Shipman, V. C. (1965). Early experience and the socialization of cognitive modes in children. *Child Development, 36,* 869–886.

Hobbs, N. (1982). *The troubled and troubling child: Reeducation in mental health, education and human service programs for children and youth.* San Francisco: Jossey-Bass.

Hoffman, M. L. (1975). Moral internalization, parental power, and the nature of parent-child interaction. *Developmental Psychology, 11,* 228–239.

Holland, N. N. (1975). *Five readers reading.* New Haven: Yale University Press.

Holstein, C. (1968). *Parental determinants of the development of moral judgement.* Doctoral dissertation, University of California, Berkeley.

Horner, M. S. (1972). Toward an understanding of achievement-related conflicts in women. *Journal of Social Issues, 28,* 157–176.

Howe, F., & Lauter, P. (1980, February). The impact of women's studies on the campus and the disciplines. *Women's Studies Monograph Series,* Washington, DC: Department of Health, Education & Welfare, National Institute of Education.

Howell, M. (1977, December). Just like a housewife: Delivering human services. *Radcliffe Alumnae Magazine,* 5–7.

Jacobus, M. (Ed.). (1979). *Women writing and writing about women.* New York: Harper & Row.

Janssen-Jurreit, M. (1980). *Sexism: The male monopoly on history and thought.* New York: Farrar, Straus, & Giroux.

Jaynes, J. (1977). *The origin of consciousness in the breakdown of the bicameral mind.* Boston: Houghton Mifflin.

Kagan, J. (1984). *The nature of the child.* New York: Basic Books.

Kanter, R. M. (1977). *Men and women of the corporation.* New York: Basic Books.

Kegan, R. (1982). *The evolving self.* Cambridge, MA: Harvard University Press.

Keller, E. F. (1978). Gender and science. *Psychoanalysis and Contemporary Thought, 1,* 409–433.

Keller, E. F. (1982). Feminism and science. *Signs: Journal of Women in Culture and Society, 7,* 589–601.

Keller, E. F. (1983). *A feeling for the organism: The life and work of Barbara McClintock.* New York: W. H. Freeman.

Keller, E. F. (1985). *Reflections on gender and science.* New Haven, CT: Yale University Press.

Keller, E. F., & Grontkowski, C. R. (1983). The mind's eye. In S. Harding & M. Hintikka (Eds.), *Discovering reality* (pp. 207–224). Dordrecht, Holland: Reidel.

Kinsey, A. C., Pomeroy, W. B., Martin, C. E., & Gebhard, P. H. (1953). *Sexual behavior in the human female.* Philadelphia: Saunders.

Kitchener, K. (1983). Cognition, metacognition, and epistemic cognition: A three-level model of cognitive processing. *Human Development, 26,* 222–232.

Klein, C. (1984). *Mothers and sons.* Boston: Houghton Mifflin.

Knefelkamp, L. L. (1978). Training manual for Perry raters and rater training cue sheets. Unpublished manuscript, University of Maryland.

Kohlberg, L. (1969). Stage and sequence: The cognitive-developmental approach to socialization. In D. A. Goslin (Ed.), *Handbook of socialization theory and research* (pp. 347–480). Chicago: Rand McNally.

Kohlberg, L. (1981). *The philosophy of moral development.* New York: Harper & Row.

Kohlberg, L. (1984). *The psychology of moral development.* New York: Harper & Row.

Kohlberg, L., & Gilligan, C. (1971). The adolescent as a philosopher: The discovery of the self in a postconventional world. *Daedalus, 100,* 1051–1056.

Kohlberg, L., & Mayer, R. (1972). Development as the aim of education. *Harvard Educational Review, 42,* 449–496.

Kohn, M. L. (1977). *Class and conformity: A study in values* (2nd ed.). Chicago: University of Chicago Press.

Kohn, M. L. (1980). Job complexity and adult personality. In N. J. Smelser & E. H. Erikson (Eds.), *Themes of work and love in adulthood* (pp. 193–212). Cambridge, MA: Harvard University Press.

Koller, A. (1983). *An unknown woman.* New York: Bantam.

Labouvie-Vief, G. (1980). Beyond formal operations: Uses and limits of pure logic in life-span development. *Human Development, 3,* 141–161.

Lakoff, R. (1975). *Language and woman's place.* New York: Harper & Row.

Lakoff, G., & Johnson, M. (1980). *Metaphors we live by.* Chicago: University of Chicago Press.

Landis, C. (1940). *Sex development.* New York: Harper & Brothers.

Landis, J. (1956). Experiences of 500 children with adult sexual deviance. *Psychiatric Quarterly Supplement, 30,* Part 1, 91–109.

Langer, J. (1969). Disequilibrium as a source of development. In P. Mussen, J. Langer, & M. Covington (Eds.), *Trends and issues in developmental psychology.* New York: Holt, Rinehart & Winston.

Langland, E., & Gove, W. (Eds.). (1981). *A feminist perspective in the academy.* Chicago: University of Chicago Press.

Lasch, C. (1979). *The culture of narcissism: American life in an age of diminishing expectations.* New York: Warner Books.

Lever, J. (1976). Sex differences in the games children play. *Social Problems, 23,* 478–487.

Levinson, D. (1978). *The seasons of a man's life.* New York: Alfred A. Knopf.

Lewis, M. (1983). Newton, Einstein, Piaget, and concept of self: The role of the self in the process of knowing. In L. S. Liben (Ed.), *Piaget and the foundations of knowledge* (pp. 141–178). Hillsdale, NJ: Lawrence Erlbaum.

Lickona, T. (1976). *Moral development and behavior: Theory, research, and social issues.* New York: Holt, Rinehart & Winston.

Lickona, T. (1983). *Raising good children: Helping your children through the stages of moral development.* New York: Bantam.

Lifton, R. J. (1976). *The life of the self.* New York: Simon & Schuster.

Lind, E. A., Conley, J., Erickson, B., & O'Barr, W. M. (1978). Social attributions and conversation style in trial testimony. *Journal of Personality and Social Psychology, 36,* 1558–1567.

Livson, N., & Peskin, H. (1981). Psychological health at age 40: Predictions from adolescent personality. In D. Eichorn, J. A. Clausen, N. Hahn, M. P. Honzik, & P. H. Mussen (Eds.), *Present and past in mid-life* (pp. 183–194). New York: Academic Press.

Loevinger, J. (1962). Measuring personality patterns of women. *Genetic Psychology Monographs, 65,* 53–136.

Loevinger, J. (1976). *Ego development.* San Francisco: Jossey-Bass.

Lowenthal, M. F., Thurnher, M., & Chiriboga, D. (1975). *The four stages of life.* San Francisco: Jossey-Bass.

Luria, A. R. (1961). *The role of speech in the regulation of normal and abnormal behavior.* New York: Boni & Liveright.

Luria, A. R. (1979). *The making of mind.* Cambridge, MA: Harvard University Press.

Luria, A. R. (1981). *Language and cognition.* New York: Wiley & Sons.

Lyons, N. (1983). Two perspectives on self, relationships and morality. *Harvard Educational Review, 53,* 125–145.

Maccoby, E., & Jacklin, C. (1974). *The psychology of sex differences.* Stanford, CA: Stanford University Press.

Martin, J. R. (1984). Bringing women into educational thought. *Educational theory, 34,* 341–353.

Martin, J. R. (1985). *Reclaiming a conversation: The ideal of the educated woman.* New Haven, CT: Yale University Press.

Maslow, A. J. (1962). *Toward a psychology of being.* Princeton, NJ: Van Nostrand.

McConnell-Ginet, S., Borker, R., & Furman, N. (1980). *Women and language in literature and society.* New York: Praeger.

McIntosh, P. (1985). Feeling like a fraud. Wellesley, MA: Stone Center *Work in Progress,* paper no. 18.

McLaughlin, F. J., Sandler, H. M., Sherrod, K., Vietze, P. M., & O'Connor, S. (1979). Social-psychological characteristics of adolescent mothers and behavioral characteristics of their first-born infants. *Journal of Population, 2,* 69–73.

McMillan, C. (1982). *Women, reason, and nature.* Princeton, NJ: Princeton University Press.

Mill, J. S. (1962). Coleridge. In G. Himmelfarb (Ed.), *Essays on politics and culture.* New York: Doubleday. (Originally published 1840.)

Miller, J. B. (1976). *Towards a new psychology of women.* Boston: Beacon Press.

Minuchin, S., Montalvo, B., Gurney, B. G., Rosman, B. L., & Schumer, F. (1967). *Families of the slums: An exploration of their structure and treatment.* New York: Basic Books.

Moessinger, P. (1978). Piaget on equilibration. *Human Development, 21,* 255–267.

Moulton, J. (1983). A paradigm of philosophy: The adversary method. In S. Harding & M. B. Hintikka (Eds.), *Discovering reality* (pp. 149–164). Dordrecht, Holland: Reidel.

Murray, F. B. (1983a). Equilibration as cognitive conflict. *Developmental Review, 3,* 54–61.

Murray, F. B. (1983b). Learning and development through social interaction and conflict: A challenge to social learning theory. In Liben, L. (Ed.), *Piaget and the foundations of knowledge.* Hillsdale, NJ: Lawrence Erlbaum.

Neugarten, B. L. (1969). Continuities and discontinuities of psychological issues into adult life. *Human Development, 12,* 121–130.
Nicholson, L. (1980). Women and schooling. *Educational Theory, 30,* 225–233.
Noddings, N. (1984). *Caring.* Berkeley, CA: University of California Press.

Olsen, T. (1978). *Silences.* New York: Delacorte Press/Seymour Lawrence.
Osofsky, H. J., & Osofsky, J. D. (1971). Adolescents as mothers. In S. Chess & A. Thomas (Eds.), *Annual progress in child psychiatry and child development* (pp. 556–568). New York: Brunner/Mazel.

Palmieri, P. (1979). Paths and pitfalls: Illuminating women's educational history. [Review of *Collegiate women: Domesticity and career in turn of the century America*]. *Harvard Educational Review, 79,* 534–541.
Parikh, B. (1975). *Moral judgment development and its relation to family environment factors in India and in the United States.* Unpublished doctoral dissertation, Boston University.
Parker, C. A. (Ed.). (1978). *Encouraging development in college students.* Minneapolis: University of Minnesota Press.
Perry, W. G. (1970). *Forms of intellectual and ethical development in the college years.* New York: Holt, Rinehart & Winston.
Perry, W. G. (1981). Cognitive and ethical growth: The making of meaning. In A. Chickering (Ed.), *The modern American college* (pp. 76–116). San Francisco: Jossey-Bass.
Piaget, J. (1951). *Plays, dreams, and imitation in children.* New York: Norton.
Piaget, J. (1952). *The language and thought of the child.* London: Routledge & Kegan Paul. (Originally published 1932.)
Piaget, J. (1965). *The moral judgment of the child.* New York: Free Press. (Originally published 1932.)
Piaget, J. (1973). *To understand is to invent.* New York: Grossman.
Piercy, M. (1973). Unlearning to not speak. In M. Piercy, *To be of use* (p. 38). New York: Doubleday.
Piliavin, J. A. (1976). On feminine self-presentation in groups. In J. I. Roberts (Ed.), *Beyond intellectual sexism* (pp. 138–159). New York: McKay.
Polanyi, M. (1958). *Personal knowledge.* Chicago: University of Chicago Press.
Pollak, S., & Gilligan, C. (1982). Images of violence in Thematic Apperception Test stories. *Journal of Personality and Social Psychology, 42,* 159–167.

Rappaport, A. (1960). *Fights, games and debates.* Ann Arbor: University of Michigan Press.
Reinharz, S. (1984). *On becoming a social scientist.* New Brunswick, NJ: Transaction.
Rest, J. (1983). Morality. In J. H. Flavell and E. M. Markman (Eds.), *Cognitive development:* Vol. 3. of P. H. Mussen (Ed.), *Handbook of child psychology* (4th ed.). New York: John Wiley & Sons.
Rich, A. (1977). Conditions for work: The common world of women. In S. Ruddick & P. Daniels (Eds.), *Working it out* (pp. xiv–xxiv). New York: Pantheon.
Rich, A. (1979). *On lies, secrets, and silence: Selected prose—1966-78.* New York: Norton.
Richardson, L. W., Cook, J. A., & Macke, A. S. (1981). Classroom management strategies. In L. W. Richardson & V. Taylor (Eds.), *Issues in sex, gender and society: A feminist perspective* (pp. 11–14). Lexington, MA: D. C. Heath.
Riesman, D., Denny, R., & Glazer, N. (1961). *The lonely crowd* (2nd ed.). New Haven, CT: Yale University Press. (Originally published 1950.)
Rosenberg, M. (1979). *Conceiving the self.* New York: Basic Books.
Rosenberg, R. (1982). *Beyond separate spheres: Intellectual roots of modern feminism.* New Haven, CT: Yale University Press.
Rossi, A. (1980). Aging and parenting in the middle years. In P. Baltes & O. G. Brim (Eds.), *Life-span development and behavior* (Vol. 3). New York: Academic Press.
Rubin, L. (1976). *Worlds of pain: Life in the working-class family.* New York: Basic Books.

Ruddick, S. (1977). A work of one's own. In S. Ruddick & P. Daniels (Eds.), *Working it out* (pp. 128–143). New York: Pantheon.

Ruddick, S. (1980). Maternal thinking. *Feminist Studies, 6,* 70–96. Reprinted in A. Cafagna, R. Peterson, & C. Staudenbaur (Eds.). (1982). *Child nurturance: Volume 1, philosophy, children, and the family.* New York: Plenum Press.

Ruddick, S. (1984). New combinations: Learning from Virginia Woolf. In C. Asher, L. DeSalvor, & S. Ruddick, *Between women* (pp. 137–159). Boston: Beacon Press.

Ruddick, S., & Daniels, P. (Eds.). (1977). *Working it out.* New York: Pantheon Books.

Russell, D. E. H. (1986). *The secret trauma: Incest in the lives of girls and women.* New York: Basic Books.

Sadker, M. P., & Sadker, D. M. (1982). *Sex equity handbook for schools.* New York: Longman.

Sadker, M. P., & Sadker, D. M. (1985, March). Sexism in the schoolroom of the 80's. *Psychology Today,* pp. 54–57.

Saltzstein, H. D., Diamond, R. M., & Belenky, M. F. (1972). Moral judgment level and conformity behavior. *Developmental Psychology, 7,* 327–336.

Sampson, E. E. (1978). Scientific paradigm and social value: Wanted—a scientific revolution. *Journal of Personality and Social Psychology, 36,* 1332–1343.

Sanford, N. (1956). Personality development during the college years. *Journal of Social Issues, 12,* 4.

Sanford, N. (1962). Developmental status of the entering freshman. In N. Sanford (Ed.), *The American college* (pp. 253–289). New York: Wiley.

Sanford, N. (1982). Social psychology: Its place in personality. *American Psychologist, 37,* 896–903.

Sarton, M. (1951). *The small room.* New York: Norton.

Sassen, G. (1980). Success anxiety in women: A constructivist interpretation of its source and its significance. *Harvard Education Review, 50,* 13–24.

Scribner, S., & Cole, M. (1973). The cognitive consequences of formal and informal education. *Science, 182,* 553–559.

Scribner, S., & Cole, M. (1981). *The psychology of literacy.* Cambridge, MA: Harvard University Press.

Serbin, L. A., O'Leary, K. D., Kent, R. N., & Tonick, I. J. (1973). A comparison of teacher response to pre-academic and problem behavior of boys and girls. *Child Development, 44,* 796–804.

Sherman, J., & Beck, E. (Eds.). (1979). *The prism of sex.* Madison, WI: University of Wisconsin Press.

Shure, M., & Spivack, G. (1978). *Problem solving techniques in childrearing.* San Francisco: Jossey-Bass.

Sigel, I. E., & Cocking, R. R. (1977). *Cognitive development from childhood to adolescence: A constructivist perspective.* New York: Holt, Rinehart & Winston.

Sirotnik, K. A. (1983). What you see is what you get: Consistency, persistency and mediocrity in classrooms. *Harvard Education Review, 53,* 16–31.

Smith, D. (1974). Women's perspective as a radical critique of sociology. *Sociological Inquiry, 44,* 7–13.

Spacks, P. (1981). The difference it makes. In E. Langland and W. Gove (Eds.), *A feminist perspective in the academy* (pp. 7–24). Chicago: University of Chicago Press.

Spacks, P. (1982). In praise of gossip. *Hudson Review, 35,* 19–38.

Spanier, B., Bloom, A., & Boroviak, D. (1984). *Toward a balanced curriculum: A source book for initiating gender integration projects.* Cambridge, MA: Schenkman.

Speizer, J. J. (1981). Role models, mentors and sponsors: The elusive concepts. *Signs, 6,* 692–712.

Steinem, G. (1981, May). The politics of talking in groups. *Ms., 9,* pp. 43, 45, 84, 86–89.

Stimpson, C. (1978, May). Women's studies: An overview. *Ann Arbor Papers in Women's Studies* (Special Issue), pp. 14–26.

Stipek, D. J., & Hoffman, J. M. (1980). Children's achievement-related expectancies as a function of academic performance, histories, and sex. *Journal of Educational Psychology, 72,* 861–865.

Swacker, M. (1976). Women's verbal behavior at learned and professional conferences. In B. L. Dubois & I. Crouch (Eds.), *The sociology of the languages of American women* (pp. 155–160). San Antonio, TX: Trinity University.

Tarule, J. M. (1980). The process of transformation: Steps toward change. In E. Greenberg, K. M. O'Donnell, W. Berquist (Eds.), *Educating learners of all ages*. San Francisco: New Directions for Higher Educations *29*, 23–36.

Thorne, B. (1979, September). *Claiming verbal space: Women, speech, and language in college classrooms*. Paper presented at the Research Conference on Educational Environments and the Undergraduate Woman, Wellesley College, Wellesley, MA.

Thorne, B., & Henley, N. (Eds.). (1975). *Language and sex: Difference and dominance*. Rowley, MA: Newbury House.

Thorne, B., Kramarae, C., & Henley, N. (Eds.). (1983). *Language, gender, and society*. Rowley, MA: Newbury House.

Tolstoy, L. (1981). *Anna Karenina*. (J. Carmichael, Trans.). New York: Bantam. (Originally published 1876.)

Treichler, P., & Kramarae, C. (1983). Women's talk in the ivory tower. *Communication Quarterly, 31*, 118–132.

Vaillant, G. (1977). *Adaptation to life*. Boston: Little Brown.

Veroff, J., Douvan, E., & Kulka, R. A. (1981). *The inner American: A self-portrait from 1957–1976*. New York: Basic Books.

Vygotsky, L. S. (1962). *Thought and language*. Cambridge, MA: MIT Press.

Vygotsky, L. S. (1978). *Mind in society*. Cambridge, MA: Harvard University Press.

Wallace, P. A. (Ed.). (1982). *Women in the work place*. Boston: Auburn House.

Ward, M. C. (1971). *Them children: A study in language learning*. New York: Holt, Rinehart & Winston.

Weil, S. (1951). Reflections on the right use of school studies with a view to the love of God. In S. Weil, *Waiting for God* (pp. 105–116). New York: Harper Colophon Books.

Weil, S. (1972). *Gravity and grace*. London: Routledge & Kegan Paul.

Weissman, M., & Paykel, E. (1974). *The depressed woman*. Chicago: University of Chicago Press.

West, C., & Zimmerman, D. H. (1977). Women's place in everyday talk: Reflections on parent-child interaction. *Social Problems, 24*, 521–529.

West, C., & Zimmerman, D. H. (1983). Small insults: A study of interruptions in cross-sex conversations between unacquainted persons. In B. Thorne, C. Kramarae, & N. Henley, (Eds.), *Language, gender, and society* (pp. 103–118). Rowley, MA: Newbury House.

Wilson, S. (1977). The use of ethnographic techniques in educational research. *Review of Educational Research, 47*, 245–265.

Wolfe, T. (1976). The me-decade and the third great awakening. *New York Magazine, 9*, 34, 26–33.

Woolf, V. (1957). *A room of one's own*. New York: Harcourt Brace. (Originally published 1929.)

Woolf, V. (1980). In A. O. Bell (Ed.), *The diaries of Virginia Woolf* (Vol. 3). New York: Harcourt Brace Jovanovich.

Wright, G. von. (1971). *Explanation and understanding*. London: Routledge & Kegan Paul.

Youniss, J., & Smoller, J. (1985). *Adolescent relations with mothers, fathers and friends*. Chicago: University of Chicago Press.

Zimmerman, B. J., & Blom, D. E. (1983a). On resolving conflicting views of cognitive conflict. *Developmental Review, 3*, 62–72.

Zimmerman, B. J., & Blom, D. E. (1983b). Toward an empirical test of the role of cognitive conflict in learning. *Developmental Review, 3*, 18–38.

Zimmerman, D. H., & West, C. (1975). Sex roles, interruptions, and silences in conversation. In B. Thorne & N. Henley (Eds.), *Language and sex: Difference and dominance* (pp. 105–130). Rowley, MA: Newbury House.

Index